Keith Turner is at present Headteacher at Cullompton Comprehensive School, Devon. He has had many years teaching experience and also held the post of Assistant Examiner for Geography O level.

John Lawson is at present Head of Humanities and Head of Geography at Shelley High School in Yorkshire. He has had many years teaching experience and has been a geography examiner with the JMB for the past ten years.

Pan Study Aids for GCSE include:

Accounting

Biology

Chemistry

Commerce

Computer Studies

Economics

English Language

French

Geography 1

Geography 2

German

History 1: World History since 1914

History 2: Britain and Europe since 1700

Human Biology

Mathematics

Physics

Sociology

Study Skills

PAN STUDY AIDS

GEOGRAPHY 2

John Lawson and Keith Turner

A Pan Original
Pan Books   London, Sydney and Auckland

First published 1988 by Pan Books Ltd,
Cavaye Place, London SW10 9PG

9 8 7 6 5 4 3 2 1

© John Lawson and Keith Turner 1988

ISBN 0 330 29419 9

Text design by Peter Ward
Text illustration by M L Design
Photoset by Parker Typesetting Service, Leicester
Printed and bound in Spain by
Mateu Cromo SA, Madrid

CONTENTS

INTRODUCTION TO GCSE

From 1988, there will be a single system of examining at 16 plus in England and Wales and Northern Ireland. The General Certificate of Secondary Education (GCSE) will replace the General Certificate of Education (GCE) and the Certificate of Secondary Education (CSE). In Scotland candidates will be entering for the O grade and Standard Grade examinations leading to the award of the Scottish Certificate of Education (SCE).

The Pan Study Aids GCSE series has been specially written by practising teachers and examiners to enable you to prepare successfully for this new examination.

GCSE introduces several important changes in the way in which you are tested. First, the examinations will be structured so that you can show *what* you know rather than what you do *not* know. Of critical importance here is the work you produce during the course of the examination year, which will be given much greater emphasis than before. Second, courses are set and marked by six examining groups instead of the previous twenty GCE/CSE boards. The groups are:

> Northern Examining Association (NEA)
> Midland Examining Group(MEG)
> London and East Anglian Group (LEAG)
> Southern Examining Group (SEG)
> Welsh Joint Examinations Council (WJEC)
> Northern Ireland Schools Examination Council (NISEC)

One of the most useful changes introduced by GCSE is the single award system of grades A–G. This should permit you and future employers more accurately to assess your qualifications.

GCSE	GCE O Level	CSE
A	A	–
B	B	–
C	C	1
D	D	2
E	E	3
F	F	4
G		5

Remember that, whatever examinations you take, the grades you are awarded will be based on how well you have done.

Pan Study Aids are geared for use throughout the duration of your courses. The text layout has been carefully designed to provide all the information and skills you need for GCSE and SCE examinations – please feel free to use the margins for additional notes.

N.B. Where questions are drawn from former O level examination papers, the following abbreviations are used to identify the boards:

UCLES (University of Cambridge Local Examinations Syndicate)
AEB (Associated Examining Board)
ULSEB (University of London Schools Examination Board)
SUJB (Southern Universities Joint Board)
O&C (Oxford & Cambridge)
SCE (Scottish Certificate of Education Examination Board)
JMB (Joint Matriculation Board)
SEB (Scottish Examining Board)
ODLE (Oxford Delegacy of Local Examinations)
WJEC (Welsh Joint Examinations Council)

SKILLS

GCSE syllabuses require candidates to have competence in most of the following:

1 FIELDWORK SKILLS	Observation; collection, representation, analysis, interpretation and use of data; recording; classifying; measurement; field sketching.

2 GRAPHICAL REPRESENTATION

Construction and interpretation and knowing the limitations of a number of techniques:

(a)   pie graphs, bat graphs, radial graphs, triangular graphs; scatter graphs; line graphs;

(b)   flowcharts;

(c)   distribution maps;

(d)   systems diagrams.

3 PHOTOGRAPHS

Describe the main features, explain relationships of:

(a)   aerial photographs;

(b)   oblique photographs;

(c)   satellite photographs.

4 ATLAS MAPS

Describe and explain distribution, both human and physical.

5 WEATHER MAPS

Describe weather conditions; identify frontal and anticyclonic systems; predict the weather.

6 TOPOLOGICAL MAPS

Read and understand simplified maps, including cost–distance and time–distance maps.

7 ORDNANCE SURVEY MAPWORK	(*a*) Read maps at a number of scales 1:2500, 1:10,000, 1:25,000, 1:50,000.

(*a*)   Read maps at a number of scales 1:2500, 1:10,000, 1:25,000, 1:50,000.

(*b*)   Symbol recognition.

(*c*)   The use of four- and six-figure grid references.

(*d*)   The measurement of distance.

(*e*)   The construction and annotation of sketch and cross-sections.

(*f*)   The recognition of landforms from contour patterns.

(*g*)   The recognition and description of fluvial, glacial and coastal landscapes.

(*h*)   The identification and description of drainage patterns.

(*i*)   The description and explanation of settlement and communication patterns.

(*j*)   The comparison with aerial photographs.

(*k*)   Deduction of human activity from map evidence.

8 GENERAL SKILLS

(*a*)   Problem solving.

(*b*)   To reason soundly, draw conclusions, suggest solutions, predict outcomes from given data.

(*c*)   To detect bias.

(*d*)   To be aware of, and develop an understanding of, different values and attitudes.

(*e*)   Group collaboration.

(*f*)   To have an awareness and a concern for the environment.

(*g*)   To be able to interpret and/or apply geographical models.

SYLLABUS SUMMARY

	Method of assessment	Differentiation method	Type of coursework/fieldwork	General subject content
SOUTHERN 'A' SYLLABUS	Paper 1 – 25% compulsory questions, includes OS mapwork Paper 2 – 50% choice of questions from 4 units Geog enquiry – 25%	Common papers with questions containing inclines of difficulty	1 individual fieldwork investigation of a problem, question or hypothesis	4 units: a Population and settlement b Agriculture and industry c Physical environment and human activities d Development
SOUTHERN 'B' SYLLABUS	Paper 1 – 33% compulsory questions Paper 2 – 27% compulsory questions Coursework – 40%	Common papers with questions containing inclines of difficulty. Differentiation by outcome	2 coursework assessments – 20% 1 enquiry-based practical unit – 20%	4 modules: a Employment and economic influence b Leisure, recreation and tourism c The divided world d Environmental management
LONDON AND EAST ANGLIAN SYLLABUS A	Paper 1 – 25% compulsory questions Paper 2 – 45% choice of questions from 4 modules Coursework – 30%	Common papers mainly with questions containing inclines of difficulty. Differentiation by outcome	2 geog enquiries, 1 fieldwork based, 1 based on option module	4 modules 3 core modules: a Agriculture/industry b Population/settlement c Landscape/water 1 optional module from Atmosphere & people, Energy, Transport, Leisure, Human welfare
LONDON AND EAST ANGLIAN SYLLABUS B	Paper 1 – 24% compulsory questions Paper 2 – 36% choice of questions from 3 themes Coursework – 40%	Common papers with questions allowing for different levels of response. Differentiation by outcome	3 items: a Fieldwork. 20% based on 1 theme b 2 items based on other 2 themes – can be fieldwork or secondary data 2×10%	3 themes: a Issues in urban geog b Issues in economic geog c Issues in physical geog
LONDON AND EAST ANGLIAN SYLLABUS C	Paper 1 – 50% choice of questions Paper 2 – 30% including compulsory OS mapwork Coursework – 20%	Questions containing inclines of difficulty. Differentiation by outcome	1 long field-based individual study or 2 short studies, 1 on fieldwork. The other may be based on secondary sources	A *systematic* study of physical and human geog of British Isles and 1 tropical area

	Method of assessment	Differentiation method	Type of coursework/fieldwork	General subject content
LONDON AND EAST ANGLIAN SYLLABUS D	Paper 1 – 30% multiple choice Papers 2/3 – 45% choice of questions based on the 5 themes Coursework – 25%	Differentiated papers. Common Paper 1 Papers 2 and 3 aimed at different levels of ability. Questions containing gradients of difficulty	1 fieldwork investigation of a problem, question or investigation	A regional study of 5 themes in the UK and West Africa: a Population and settlement b Agriculture c Transport d Industry e Physical geog
MIDLAND SYLLABUS A	Paper 1, 2 or 3 – 75% Choice of questions in Paper 3 Coursework – 25%	Differentiated papers. Each paper aimed at different levels of ability, Paper 3 being the highest	1 major or 2 or 3 shorter pieces of geog enquiry. At least 1 must be based on fieldwork	3 sections: a People and the physical environment b People and places to live c People and their needs
MIDLAND SYLLABUS B	Paper 1 or 2 – 72% Coursework – 28%	Differentiated papers. Each paper aimed at different levels of ability (but with some overlap). Paper 2 aimed at higher levels	1 longer or 2 or 3 shorter pieces of first-hand investigation in the field	Investigation of 5 themes based on Great Britain and West Africa: a Physical environment b Population and settlement c Agriculture d Transport e Industry
MIDLAND SYLLABUS C	Paper 1 or 2 – 50% compulsory questions 2 geog enquiries – 30% 2 decision-making exercises – 20%	Differentiated papers. Paper 2 aimed at more able pupils, but there is some overlap in abilities each paper is aimed at	2 geog enquiries – some of the data for at least 1 to be drawn from fieldwork 2 decision-making exercises involving an analysis and evaluation of data on a specific issue	5 modules: a Resources b Environmental interactions c Residential environments d Economic development e Movement
MIDLAND SYLLABUS D	Paper 1 or 2 – 50% some choice of questions 3 coursework units – 30% Geog enquiry – 20%	Differentiated papers. paper 2 aimed at more able pupils, but there is some overlap in abilities each paper is aimed at	3 common coursework units with inclines of difficulty 2 teacher-planned enquiries or 1 individual pupil-planned enquiry	Individual schools plan own curriculum satisfying certain conditions
NORTHERN SYLLABUS A	Paper 1 – 30% objective test Paper 2 – 45% compulsory questions Geog enquiry – 25%	Common papers. Different levels of difficulty within question	A personal folder of a number of separate or a single extended study. It must include some first-hand fieldwork but some secondary resource material allowed. Work in the field may be on a group or individual basis	Study of 5 basic concepts in the context of 7 topics: a Population geog b Food and water supplies c Energy resources d Geog of industry e Urban geog f Recreation, leisure, tourism g Hostile physical environments and human response

Syllabus summary

	Method of assessment	Differentiation method	Type of coursework/fieldwork	General subject content
NORTHERN SYLLABUS B	2 schemes: Scheme 1 – Paper 1 40% compulsory questions Coursework 35% 4 class tests Geog enquiry – 25% Scheme 2 – Paper 1 40% compulsory questions Paper 2 35% compulsory questions Geog enquiry – 25%	Common papers. Questions with different levels of difficulty within them	Coursework – 4 timed tests (1 on EEC, 1 on wider world, 1 on inter-relationships between EEC and wider world, 1 teacher-planned). Geog enquiry – same as for Syllabus A	Study of 6 topics in 3 regions (British Isles, EEC, Wider World): a Population and settlement b Agricultural systems c Energy and natural resources d Secondary industry e Tertiary industry f Transport and trade
NORTHERN SYLLABUS C	Paper 1 – 30% compulsory questions Paper 2 – 40% compulsory questions Geog enquiries – 30%	Common papers. Questions contain different levels of difficulty	2 geog enquiries – personal records each worth 15%. Each enquiry drawn from a different theme. First-hand data essential for 1 enquiry, but secondary data permissible for the other	Study of 3 themes: a Urban geog b Economic geog c People and the environment Examples equally drawn from local area, British Isles, other developed areas, less developed areas
NORTHERN SYLLABUS D	Paper 1 – 20% compulsory questions Paper 2 – 30% choice of questions Coursework assessment – 50%	Common papers. Questions with inclines of difficulty	3 coursework units, 1 on each of: a Study of physical environment b Planned problems c Area studies 1 student-planned or 2 teacher-planned enquiries – must include first-hand collection of data in the field	7 subject areas: a Weather and climate b Land forms and processes c Agriculture d Industry and energy e Economic development and trade f Population and migration g Settlement
NORTHERN IRELAND			Geog enquiry – extended, personal-based on first-hand enquiry	4 themes: a People and natural resources b Settlement and society c Economic activity and development d People and environment
WELSH	Paper 1 or 3 – 40% differentiated Paper 2 – 40% common Individual study – 20%	Differentiated Papers 1 and 3. Paper 3 taken by more able students. Papers 1, 2 and 3 stepped questions	Individual study	3 sections: a Physical environment b Economic activity c Population, settlement, urbanism

SPECIFIED TOPICS

	NORTHERN A	NORTHERN B	NORTHERN C	NORTHERN D	MIDLAND A	MIDLAND B	MIDLAND C	MIDLAND D (write your own)	SOUTHERN A	SOUTHERN B	LEAG A	LEAG B
PHYSICAL ENVIRONMENT AND HUMAN INFLUENCE												
Structure of the earth				✓	✓	✓			✓			
Tectonics	✓		✓	✓	✓	✓			✓			
Rock types				✓	✓	✓			✓			
LANDFORMS AND PROCESSES												
Weathering				✓		✓			✓			
Rivers			✓	✓	✓	✓			✓			✓
Ice				✓		✓			✓			
Sea				✓		✓			✓	✓		✓
Hydrological cycle		✓	✓		✓	✓	✓					✓
Water supply		✓	✓	✓	✓		✓					✓
Pollution			✓									✓
WEATHER AND CLIMATE												
Meteorology				✓	✓				✓			
Synoptic maps				✓	✓				✓			
Factors affecting climate				✓		✓			✓			
World climates				✓		✓			✓			
Ecosystems		✓	✓		✓							
Equatorial forest environment		✓										
Temperate continental interior climate		✓										

	NORTHERN A	NORTHERN B	NORTHERN C	NORTHERN D	MIDLAND A	MIDLAND B	MIDLAND C	MIDLAND D (write your own)	SOUTHERN A	SOUTHERN B	LEAG A	LEAG B
PROBLEMS, HOSTILE ENVIRONMENTS, HAZARDS	✔		✔				✔			✔		✔
Conflict/over-use of environments			✔	✔			✔					
POPULATION AND SETTLEMENT												
World distribution	✔	✔		✔	✔	✔			✔	✔	✔	
Population movement (permanent/daily)	✔	✔	✔	✔	✔	✔	✔			✔		
Causes of world growth	✔	✔		✔		✔						
Effects of world growth	✔			✔					✔			
Demographic transition model		✔				✔						
Overpopulation		✔										
TYPES OF SETTLEMENT	✔	✔		✔		✔						
SETTLEMENT PATTERNS	✔		✔	✔	✔	✔						
URBAN ENVIRONMENTS												
Urbanization	✔		✔	✔		✔	✔			✔		
Urban land use		✔	✔	✔	✔	✔	✔		✔		✔	
Urban problems	✔		✔		✔		✔		✔		✔	
Planning/new towns		✔	✔		✔				✔		✔	
Millionaire cities	✔											
Urban models		✔										
Conurbations		✔		✔								
DEVELOPMENT												
Contrasts in development	✔		✔	✔	✔	✔	✔		✔	✔		✔
Interdependence – world trade, multinationals	✔	✔	✔	✔	✔		✔		✔	✔		✔
Ways of reducing world inequalities			✔	✔					✔			
AGRICULTURE												
Factors affecting agricultural location	✔	✔	✔		✔	✔						✔
Agricultural systems/types	✔	✔		✔	✔	✔	✔		✔			

	NORTHERN A	NORTHERN B	NORTHERN C	NORTHERN D	MIDLAND A	MIDLAND B	MIDLAND C	MIDLAND D (write your own)	SOUTHERN A	SOUTHERN B	LEAG A	LEAG B
The farm as a system	✔			✔					✔			✔
Conservation/conflict of land use	✔	✔	✔	✔		✔	✔		✔	✔		
New agricultural techniques		✔							✔			
World food trading patterns	✔											
Food shortages, nutrition	✔									✔		
INDUSTRY												
Factors affecting industrial location	✔	✔	✔	✔	✔	✔	✔		✔			✔
Distribution of industries	✔		✔	✔	✔	✔				✔		✔
Foot-loose industries		✔	✔									✔
Multinationals	✔		✔									✔
Industry as a system	✔			✔			✔		✔			
Service industries		✔	✔						✔			✔
Industrialization	✔	✔		✔					✔			✔
Environmental problems	✔	✔		✔								✔
UK principal contrasts	✔		✔			✔						
Third World industries	✔					✔						
ENERGY												
Types of energy production		✔		✔	✔	✔	✔		✔			
Conservation and alternatives				✔			✔		✔			
UK energy sources	✔				✔		✔					
Environmental problems	✔	✔		✔			✔			✔		
Movement of energy/fuels	✔											
Third World energy	✔											
World resources	✔	✔			✔		✔					
Politics and energy		✔			✔		✔					
Declining/new power schemes			✔		✔		✔					

	NORTHERN A	NORTHERN B	NORTHERN C	NORTHERN D	MIDLAND A	MIDLAND B	MIDLAND C	MIDLAND D (write your own)	SOUTHERN A	SOUTHERN B	LEAG A	LEAG B
COMMUNICATIONS												
Networks		✔				✔						
Modern transport methods		✔				✔						
Transport developments and industrial location			✔				✔					
Urban transport systems			✔									
Time distance/cost distance						✔						
ORDNANCE SURVEY MAPWORK												
Compulsory		✔			✔				✔			
Choice	✔			✔		✔				✔		

ENERGY

CONTENTS

Contents

There are two basic types of energy providers: fossil fuels which will eventually be used up, and non-fossil fuels which are inexhaustible.

In order to generate energy, fossil fuels are burned and are therefore exhaustible; they include solids such as coal, lignite and peat; liquids such as mineral oil; gases such as natural gas and coal gas; and more recently developed solid sources, e.g. uranium. Non-fossil fuels do not involve the burning of raw materials in order to produce energy and hence they are virtually inexhaustible. At the moment they do not contribute significantly to the world's energy resources.

Until the mid-eighteenth century, man used inexhaustible methods – human power, animal power, wind and water – to provide energy. After that time he began to use fossil fuels, particularly coal, and as his knowledge increased, oil and natural gas became progressively more important. Increasingly, either as fossil resources become scarcer, or pollution from them becomes a problem, man is looking again at inexhaustible sources of energy which he can control and use more efficiently with his grasp of technology.

WOOD

This accounts for approximately eight per cent of the world's energy consumption. The Developing World relies heavily on wood as a source of fuel as oil and electricity generation are often beyond the economic means of the country. Firewood is the most important means of fuel because at the moment it is cheap, accessible and relatively plentiful. This situation is likely to change as consumption increases, and it is probable that these areas of the world must look towards reafforestation projects at some time in the future because the use of wood has unfortunate consequences. Trees hold the top soil in place and when cut down, rain can wash this top soil away resulting in poorer crops, and in certain parts of the world allowing the deserts to spread.

A World Bank team have been working on this problem in Ethiopia. They have rejected the idea of immediate reafforestation as a solution and instead have indentified two possible alternatives to the use of wood as a source of energy:

1 Using the stalks of grain crops grown locally.
2 Using the residues from the harvesting and processing of Ethiopia's main export crop, coffee.

Fig 1.1 Problems caused by using wood for fuel

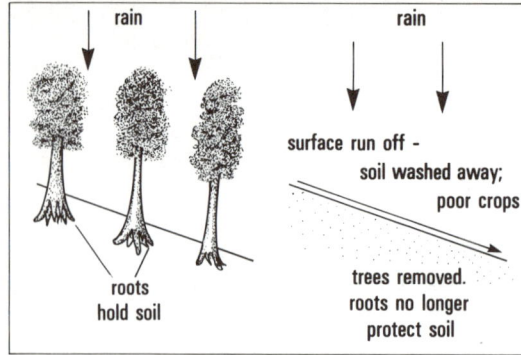

They have recommended that these waste products are shredded, ground and pressed into bricks which will burn. A $5m pilot project introduced as a result of this study will produce 25,000 tonnes of fuel each year between 1986 and 1988. If successful, this scheme will be expanded in Ethiopia and extended to other energy-starved areas where continued deforestation will create additional food production problems.

In the Developed World, wood remains a minor but significant source of fuel. In Australia, for example, it provides two per cent of total energy consumption identical to its HEP provision, while in the USA the same percentage conceals large regional variations, e.g. Vermont ten per cent. Scientists believe that wood may eventually provide between ten and twenty per cent of the USA's energy consumption and have identified certain areas where policy decisions will have to be made:

(*a*)   Better management of resources.

(*b*)   Intensive cultivation of agricultural land which is at present economically marginal.

(*c*)   Use of quick growing species, such as eucalyptus.

(*d*)   Scientific research to minimize air pollution.

COAL

Coal formed during the carboniferous period of the Earth's history some 280 million years ago, has been important in developing the industrial capacity of nations throughout the world. During the nineteenth century, as the realization of coal's importance as a source of energy developed, areas which had abundant supplies became important manufacturing areas, attracting established industries from locations adjacent to water power and helping to create new industries.

RANKING

Coal is ranked as follows: peat, lignite, bituminous, anthracite. Anthracite, the highest ranking, is the best quality coal as it has been subjected to the most intensive compression, expelling oxygen and leaving a higher carbon content.

EXPLOITATION

The first fields to be exploited were those where access was easy. Coal was found at or near the surface, where seams were exposed on valley sides for example.

Fig 1.2 Coal: drift and shaft mines

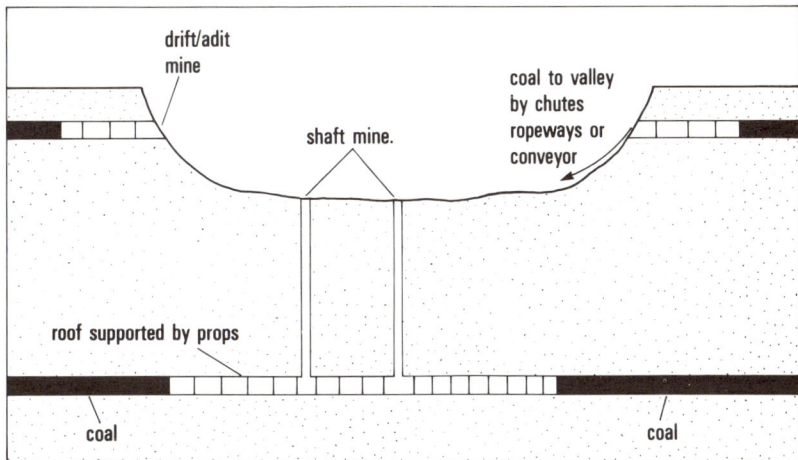

As these reserves were worked out, shafts had to be sunk to reach concealed coal. Mining technology was improving and the additional construction expense was justified because the market for coal was expanding as the Industrial Revolution gained momentum. During this century, investment in mechanization continued to increase both output and productivity. Gradually, because of industrial and domestic consumer preference for other energy products (coupled with an increasing awareness of pollution problems) the demand for coal declined and many producers found that they were overproducing. Some attempted to solve this problem by aggressive marketing to other countries, which helped alleviate their problem but created additional difficulties elsewhere. Australia, Poland and the USA all export coal to the UK where production is currently in excess of demand. The consequence of overproduction has been a cut back in output, the closure of uneconomic capacity and the loss of jobs in the industry. The statistics opposite illustrate the industry's decline in the UK.

Pit closures have resulted in the industry having labour relations problems. In North America, the United Mineworkers of America have had a dispute with the Amax Corporation about their contract of employment. Amax did not renew their contract, the miners went on

	Collieries	Miners
1972	289	281,500
1974	259	252,000
1978	222	240,000
1984	174	183,000
1987	106	108,000

strike, and the consequence is that sixty per cent of the coal mined in Mid-West fields is now mined by non-union labour.

In the UK the year-long miners' dispute with the National Coal Board has had a number of consequences:

1   The National Union of Mineworkers has split – the Nottingham area left the National Union on 6 July 1986 and formed the Union of Democratic Mineworkers. An effective national strike in future is therefore less likely.
2   The National Coal Board reported a massive operating loss of £2,225m – £1,800m as a direct result of the dispute.
3   One-sixth of the coal faces were lost.
4   Many miners accepted the premature retirement offer of the Board.
5   It is likely that pits will be more mechanized in future and less labour intensive.
6   Other industries suffered. Costs to the steel industry in the UK are calculated at £180m; the Central Electricity Generating Board who purchase seventy per cent of UK production, had to use more oil to maintain electricity supplies; British Rail lost £240m in revenue – before the dispute they had 12,000 wagons delivering sixty million tons per year from pit heads to power stations.

The political and social consequences of pit closures, which may destroy the economy of a community or an area, are great. Governments are aware of this problem and have taken steps to attempt to minimize the impact of the decline of mining; in Germany, for example, the Federal Government and individual state governments have set aside funds to attract new industry into these areas. Miners leaving the industry can retrain for other employment using funds provided by the European Economic Community.

The pattern of a declining dependence on coal from the early 1950s to the early 1980s has one major exception – the Republic of South Africa. Coal provides over eighty per cent of its primary energy needs. It has no gas or crude oil fields on shore, limited access to offshore production through the Kudu gas field off Namibia, and difficulty in obtaining oil supplies from overseas because of its policy of apartheid. (This embargo is not totally effective.) Its coal use is equivalent to that of the UK although its population is only half that of the UK. Ninety-seven per cent of its electricity is generated from coal and the probability is that this will increase during the next few years. Because of problems in obtaining oil supplies, three plants (using over thirty million tonnes of coal per year) convert coal to oil. South Africa obtains a large amount of revenue by exporting a substantial volume of coal each year. After gold, coal is its most important foreign revenue earner.

Coal reserves throughout the world are substantially greater than those of oil and natural gas. At the present rate of production and with known reserves they will last 300 years. Their exploitation has been reassessed as a result of the substantial rise in oil and gas prices experienced in the mid and late 1970s; the inevitable future decline in oil and gas production; and a wish to avoid overdependence on supplies of these products from areas which are currently, or may in future be, politically unstable. The result has been that in some areas, e.g. the USA, production has already increased; in others, new investment is planned which will result in either an increasing or a more cost efficient output. Coal has a long-term future, not only in electricity generation, but some scientists suggest that its prime use eventually may well be in gaseous or liquefied forms as a source of energy in those transportation uses in which electricity cannot be employed.

NORTH AMERICA

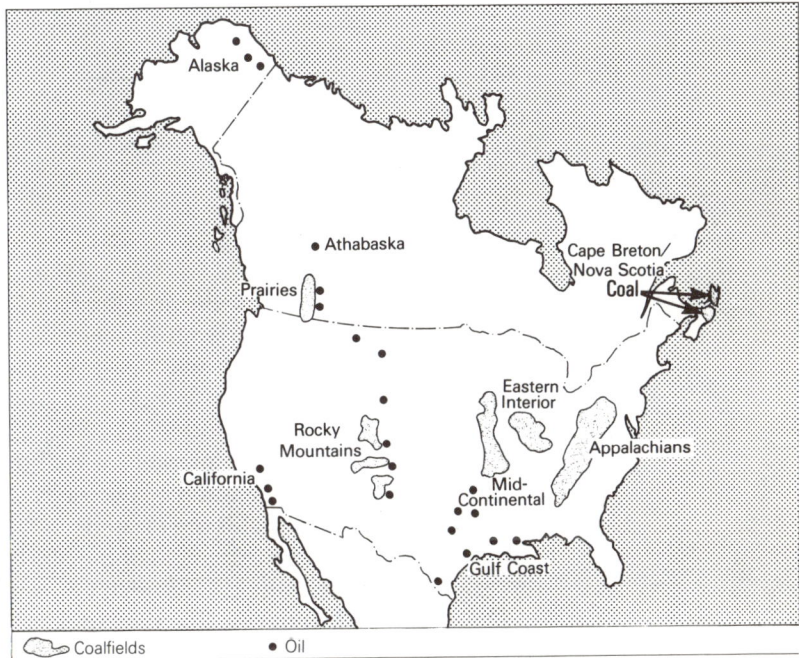

Fig 1.3 North America: coal and oil fields

The map shows the three principal coal mining areas of the USA:
(a)   The Appalachians.
(b)   The interior fields of Indiana and Illinois.
(c)   The western fields of the Rocky Mountains and adjacent plains.

The Appalachian fields have the longest history of exploitation and are suffering from many of the problems typical of the older mining areas of Britain and Western Europe. As demand for coal decreased, the Appalachian area was hardest hit. Mechanization and rationalization aimed at reducing costs created unemployment in communities where there were few, if any, alternative sources of employment. The Clean Air Act of 1970 caused particular problems for this region which produces coal containing a high sulphur content. The consequent loss in sales exacerbated the industry's unemployment problems, as did the decline in some of this area's traditional industrial markets, particularly steel.

Although the Appalachians and interior fields are still important, it is possible to see a distinct shift in emphasis towards the western fields. The Clean Air Act of 1970 while damaging the eastern fields, has encouraged exploitation in the west which contains coal with a low sulphur content. The coal in western fields can be mined by open cast methods which are less labour intensive and therefore less costly (on average fifty per cent cheaper than in the east). The future development of mining in the west is assured if the Federal Government wishes to continue with its present policy of expanding coal production as rapidly as possible, thereby continuing to reduce dependence on oil (see the table below):

% Energy production	1970	1980	1990
Coal	18	21	25
Oil	44	45	40
Natural gas	33	27	22
Nuclear power	1	3	8
Others	4	4	5

The principal problems for the area are likely to be the costs involved in transporting the coal eastwards to its main markets, and the strong environmental lobby which will insist on operators adhering strictly to legislation requiring them to reinstate land subjected to open cast mining to its original condition.

As in the UK, the major market for coal (over seventy per cent of production) is in the generation of electricity.

The main Canadian fields are located:

(a)   In the Maritime Provinces of the North-East.

(b)   In the western fields of British Columbia and the prairies.

The Maritime Provinces, like the Appalachian region of the USA, have a long history of exploitation. Because of the availability of sites for producing HEP and their small reserves, they have never assumed the importance of the Appalachian region.

As in the USA, investment in and exploitation of the western fields is becoming increasingly more important despite the enormous distances to the industrial areas of Eastern Canada. Transport links eastwards, both by rail and water, are being improved and a thriving export trade has developed with the Japanese through west coast ports.

UNITED KINGDOM

The UK coal mining industry has had to face competition from other sources of energy, cheap coal imports from abroad, and over-production from domestic sources. The consequence has been a rationalization of production, the closure of uneconomic pits, and a damaging period in industrial relations and a cut back in capacity. Despite these problems, the industry can look forward to a significant role in the future energy and strategy of the country.

Fig 1.4 UK coalfields

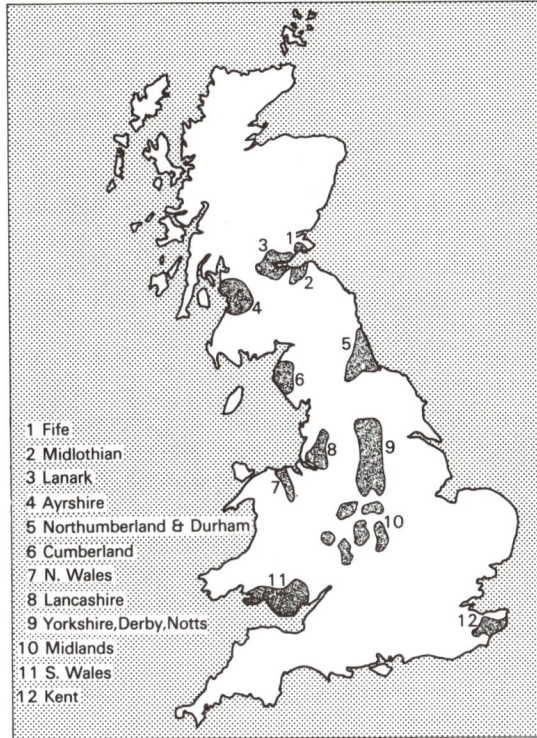

1 Fife
2 Midlothian
3 Lanark
4 Ayrshire
5 Northumberland & Durham
6 Cumberland
7 N. Wales
8 Lancashire
9 Yorkshire, Derby, Notts
10 Midlands
11 S. Wales
12 Kent

Coal is likely to play an increasingly important role in supplying the energy requirements of Northern Ireland. The Kilroot power station outside Belfast is converting from oil to coal and some one million tonnes of coal a year will be required from open cast mines in western Scotland. The port of Ayr is to be upgraded to provide extra coal shipping facilities and Troon may also have to be used.

£7m is to be invested to develop an open-cast lignite mine at Crumlin on the eastern shores of Lough Neagh. This area has reserves calculated to be in the region of 400m tonnes and an on-site power station will burn these to provide one-third of the electricity needs of the province from the mid-1990s.

In Britain there are three important new developments.

£1bn is being spent developing the Selby coalfield in Yorkshire which will produce ten million tonnes per year.

£400m is to be spent on a new project at Asfordby in the Vale of Belvoir, Leicestershire. This will be one of the largest coalfields in Europe with reserves in excess of 150 million tonnes.

The third major proposed project is in a 14-sq-km area between Berkswell and Kenilworth in the West Midlands where high quality coal can be mined which is suitable for the power stations clustered along the Trent.

Fig 1.5 New coalfield – Midlands

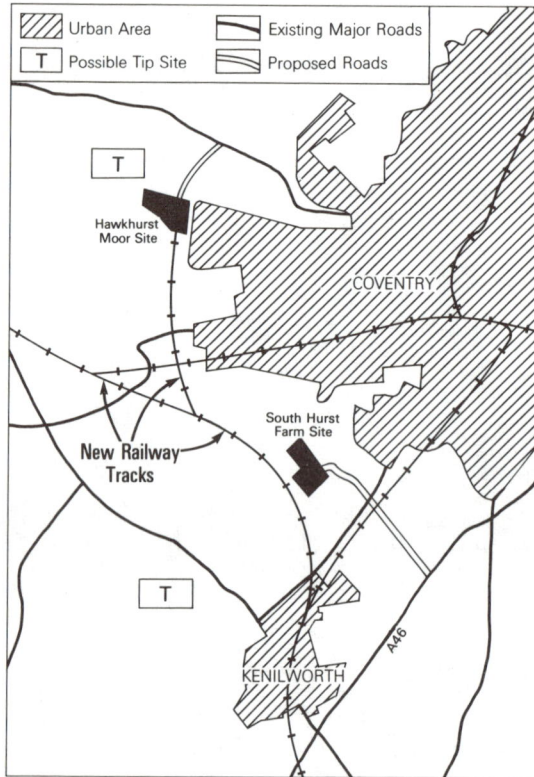

This last project illustrates the problems which developments of this type bring to any area. Industry needs to have access to energy, but the development of these energy sources often conflicts with the views of local people who are concerned about their environment.

1   The Coal Board wishes to invest £400m in developing a superpit which would produce three million tonnes of coal per year, making it by far the most productive single pit in the country. This development would give the Board access to 165 million tonnes of easily mined coal and would eventually provide employment for 1,800 people.

2   Local communities have formed a Colliery Opposition Group. They fear that the quality of their lives would be adversely affected by the siting of a colliery in this area; that there will be environmental problems; and that they will have a long period of disruption stretching over eleven years while the colliery is built. They are also concerned about the possibility of additional transport links and the disposal of waste.

3   The Coal Board subsequently announced that it would consider two possible sites within the area, Hawkhurst Moor in the north, and

South Hurst Farm in the south, on the grounds that a more detailed analysis of the two alternatives was warranted by the potential impact and importance of the proposed development. Consultants will draw up detailed assessments of the environmental impact of both sites before submitting a detailed plan for one.

4   They will have to take into account the fact that South Hurst Farm is in a rural setting and the new pit buildings would cover a medieval site but would be shielded by woodland. Hawkhurst Moor, on the other hand, is adjacent to an already industrialized area but stands on high ground.

MARKETS

The main market for UK coal production is the Central Electricity Generating Board. Contractually, ninety-five per cent of the coal it burns must be obtained from the NCB but it is likely that the CEGB will wish to reduce this dependence on British supplies. Their coal burning power stations (68 out of 102) are located mainly along the valley of the Trent which has the advantages of proximity to the Yorkshire, Derby and Nottinghamshire coalfields and access to large amounts of water, and along the lower Thames which can obtain coal from coastal fields or abroad.

British Coal aims to quadruple industrial sales to twenty-eight million tonnes a year by 2000, but to achieve this it will have to persuade industrialists to convert the oil-fired boilers installed in the 1970s back to coal burning. It has already started a major campaign and is placing adverts in the national press.

Since 1979, British Coal – the former National Coal Board – has cut its work force by over 90,000. In 1985, it set up British Coal Enterprise in an effort to promote job creation in areas which have experienced large-scale redundancies. British Coal Enterprise has had the problem that the size of its local pit communities makes it difficult to create sufficient jobs once a mine has been closed, and in addition, many mines are not in areas which have the transport and communication network necessary to attract expanding companies. The agency's funding is in the region of £40m and it aims to create some 10,000 new jobs in 1986.

British Coal have, in fact, rejected the views of an independent review body, in November 1986, that in the case of Cadeby Colliery, near Doncaster, it had a moral obligation to the wider community to keep the pit open (unemployment in the Doncaster area is over twenty-four per cent). The Board's position is that reduction in revenue caused by lower coal prices and the government requirement that it does not lose money after 1988–89, means that it must stick to its strategy of closing uneconomic pits.

EUROPE

As in the United Kingdom, coal was the basis of industrialization in many parts of Europe and for more than a century, mining employed hundreds of thousands of people. Gradually, competition from other sources of energy (especially oil), a decline in those heavy industries providing its market (e.g. iron and steel production), along with increasing competition from cheaper imported coal, meant that production was concentrated upon more economic pits, and jobs were lost.

FRANCE

Fig 1.6 France: energy

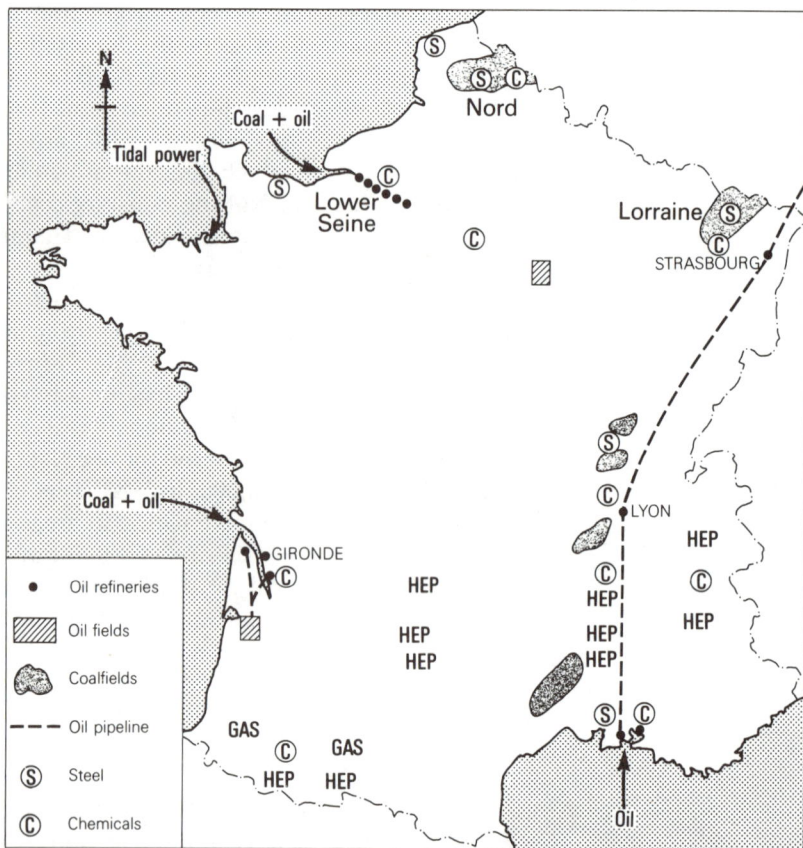

The three main coalfields in France are the Nord/Pas de Calais, the Lorraine, and the Massif Central which contains a number of small fields. The Nord/Pas de Calais field was for many years the most important, but now Lorraine has become the major producer. Its seams are thick. There has been a massive amount of mechanization but the coal is often of poor quality. The main markets for coal from the Nord/Pas de Calais coalfield are coke ovens and thermal power stations. The fact that seams are thin and often contorted, coupled with competition from other sources of power, has meant the rationalization of production and the closure of large numbers of mines. State planning has encouraged new industries to locate in this region in an effort to offset the decline in mining and other traditional industries. The motor car industry, for example, is located here. (Compare with Germany and the UK.) In addition to central initiatives, local government and business groups are encouraging industrial relocation and there are high hopes that the proposed Channel Tunnel will give new impetus to light industrial growth.

GERMANY

The main West German fields are the Saarland, Aachen (particularly the Aachen and Eschweiler basins) and the Ruhr. Lignite which is used principally to generate electricity, is mined in the Cologne/Düsseldorf area.

THE RUHR

Fig 1.7 The Ruhr coalfield
– West Germany

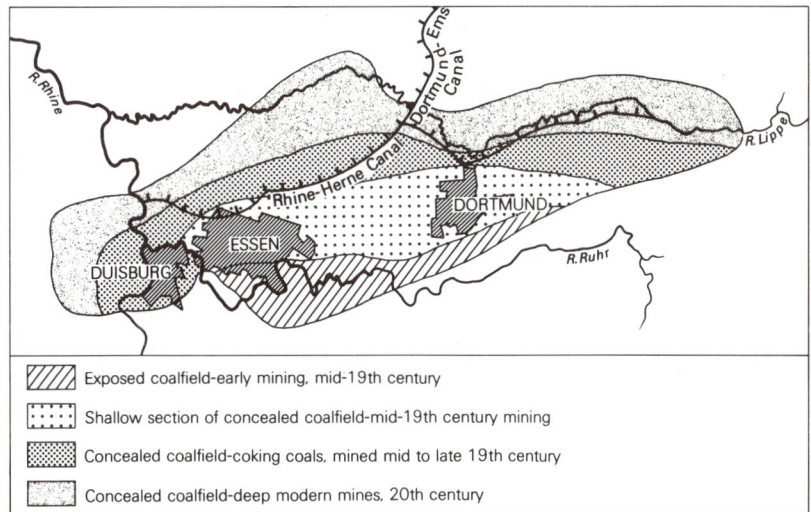

Exposed coalfield-early mining, mid-19th century

Shallow section of concealed coalfield-mid-19th century mining

Concealed coalfield-coking coals, mined mid to late 19th century

Concealed coalfield-deep modern mines, 20th century

This coalfield produces approximately eighty per cent of West Germany's coal output. Initially, open cast or adit methods were used to mine the coal in the Ruhr Valley itself, but as these easier seams were exhausted, the mining effort moved progressively northwards into the concealed coalfield. The scale of demand from local industry meant, however, that more difficult seams in the Ruhr continued to be worked until the early 1960s. The move northwards into, and now beyond, the Lippe valley, has meant an increase in production costs as mines become deeper and deeper; more modern mining methods have, even with increased productivity, only partly offset these increases. The possibility of cheap water transport via the Rhine and the extensive canal network was a tremendous advantage for Ruhr coal.

Despite the Federal Government guaranteeing the industry a market in steel and electricity generation, competition from imported coal and other energy sources for other markets has meant that the industry has had to cut back output, close mines and concentrate production in the north of the coalfield.

As in the UK, the coal industry will continue to be an important factor in the West German economy. The Ruhr possesses reserves of many varieties of coal which will last several hundred years, and the use of nuclear power is under increasing scrutiny from both politicians and the public. Recent EEC proposals for a further cut back in production and the removal of all state subsidies to the mining industry are unlikely to be favourably received, and indeed, it is probable that they will be rejected.

SOUTH AFRICA

South Africa is one of the richest mineral areas in the world. Diamonds were once its principal mineral export but coal is now more important. The mining industry – in Natal Province, for example – uses both shaft and open-cast mines to obtain coal. Many of the seams are horizontal and thick and thus production is mechanized and the deposits cheaper to exploit. Wage rates are lower than in many other countries – many black workers from neighbouring states find employment in mining.

Initially, South African coal was used to meet its own domestic and industrial requirements but exports became important in the early 1970s following rises in oil prices. (See section on oil in this chapter.) Japan, Europe and North America began to import large quantities of cheap South African coal – particularly from the port of Richard's Bay, the world's largest coal port. These markets may be under threat because of calls for economic sanctions against South Africa's policy of apartheid; the American Congress and the EEC, for example, are likely to ban coal imports. For many years, South Africa has processed coal to obtain oil: this process, which is very expensive, is worthwhile because coal reserves are enormous and it is an investment in their future use. In addition, it reduces dependence on unreliable oil imports.

WORLD PRODUCTION OF COAL AND LIGNITE

In 1980, the world output of coal was 2,740 million tonnes while that of lignite was 966 million tonnes.

Country	% of total world coal production	% of total world lignite production
USSR	18	16.5
USA	26	4.5
Poland	7	4
UK	4.5	–
S. Africa	4	–
India	4	–
Australia	3	3.5
W. Germany	3	13.5
Canada	1	–
E. Germany	–	27
Others	29.5	31

China is also a major producer, producing a combined total of 600 million tonnes of coal and lignite.

1 Most of the world's producers of coal and lignite are in the northern hemisphere.

2 Coal is mined in many countries of the world, not just a few countries.

3 USA is the major producer of coal and East Germany is the major producer of lignite, each of which produce approximately one-quarter of the world production of each energy source.

4 The three major producers of coal produce approximately half of total world production.

5 Countries from all parts of the world are coal producers, including communist and non-communist, developed and developing nations.

6 East and West Germany together produce over forty per cent of the world's lignite, but only three per cent of total world coal.

7 South Africa, Australia and Poland are the major exporters of coal, particularly to Europe and the USA, which consume enormous quantities.

CHECKLIST ▶   **WOOD AND COAL**

1 Wood continues to be an important source of energy, particularly in the Developing World.

2 The use of wood creates problems of soil erosion.

3 Wood may increase in importance provided that resource management is more scientific.

4 Coal, after dominating energy supply for many years, suffered from competition from other sources of energy in the 1970s and 1980s.

5 Cut backs in demand meant that production concentrated on more economic pits and many jobs were lost.

6 New pits create conflicts between producers, local residents and environmental groups.

7 Coal appears to have a long-term future because reserves are much greater than those of oil; new technology will find additional uses for the mineral.

OIL AND NATURAL GAS

These are often, although not always, found in the same area. Initially, the gas was burned but developing technology allowed it to be tapped off and used in many industrial and energy projects.

OIL

During the late nineteenth century, the use of oil in the transport industry began and has continued until the present. The twentieth century saw an expansion in its use as a source of domestic heating, in providing energy for industry and as a raw material in many industrial processes.

It is possible to distinguish several phases in its world impact:

1 From 1910–1973, oil production was controlled by western multinational companies who exploited oil fields throughout the world. Their influence guaranteed a steady supply of oil at relatively cheap prices to the industrialized nations of the world.

2 During the period 1973–84, the Organization of Petroleum Exporting Countries (OPEC) dominated the world market place. This organization, with thirteen member states, was formed to safeguard the interests of the major producers. Difficulties arose because of the different political and economic needs of the members; high production was needed to finance modernization within their countries, e.g. housing, desalinization plants and an industrial infrastructure, yet overproduction could mean a fall in prices with a large loss of income. Price rises began to become significant as OPEC exerted its influence and its 1979 decision to raise the price of crude oil to $34 per barrel was a mistake because it lost oil some of its markets. Energy conservation was encouraged by governments, alternative sources were explored vigorously, and in consequence, demand for oil fell.

3 From 1984–present, term contracts and spot deals have become important. Under the term contract, a company makes an agreement with a producer to take an amount of oil at the official price for a period of years. Spot deals are made on a single cargo at a negotiated price. Many Third World producers place some of their oil on the spot market because it allows them to sell to any customer. Approximately forty per cent of all oil is traded in this way and many regard the spot market price as the most accurate reflection of oil's worth.

As already indicated, the rise in prices of the OPEC era lost markets for oil and heightened awareness of energy conservation. The result has been a general decline in production and OPEC's market share has dropped significantly from 52 per cent in 1976 to 30 per cent in 1985.

Owing to its continuing importance to man, oil has become an important political and economic commodity:

1 Oil is South Africa's most vulnerable point of dependence on the outside world, and therefore all OPEC members officially embargo South Africa to show their disapproval of its policy of apartheid.

Fig 1.8 The rise and fall of oil prices

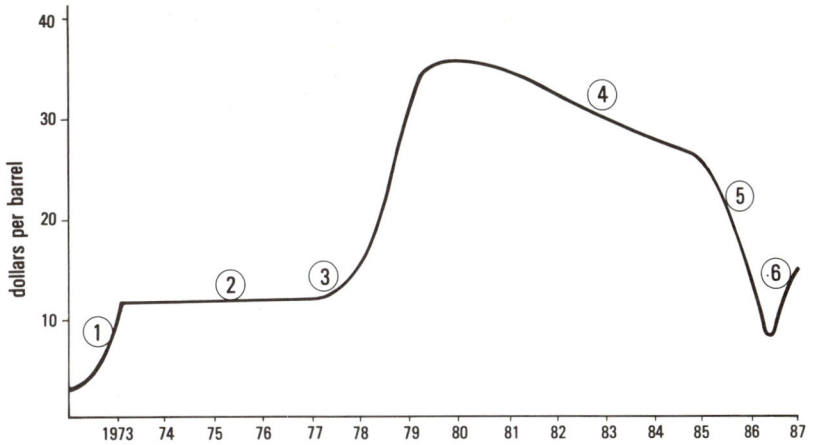

1 OPEC raises prices 3–12 dollars in one year.
2 Period of stability.
3 Demand increases and Iran unstable – prices rise.
4 OPEC under pressure; non OPEC production increases; demand falls; prices fall.
5 Price decrease gathers momentum; 10 dollars per barrel in April 1986.
6 Production ceiling agreement by OPEC moves price up to 15 dollars September 1986.

Despite this embargo, South Africa continues to import about 200,000 barrels per day through clandestine channels.

2 The Gulf War is another illustration of its political importance. Both Iran and Iraq need oil revenues to purchase arms in order to sustain their war effort. Both countries have attacked tankers in the Gulf to disrupt their opponent's sales and Iraq has attacked Iran's principal oil terminal at Kharg Island which handles almost all of its 1.5 million barrels per day exports. As a result, Iran is to construct a new 42-in pipeline to the port of Asoluyeh, via the coastal city of Bushehr, to transport oil out of the range of Iraqi war planes. Kuwait and Saudi Arabia both support Iraq but Kuwait wants to keep production steady to maintain prices while Saudi Arabia wants to increase production to boost its own imports, which may in turn reduce oil prices and Iraq's revenue from them.

3 Shell has closed its Curaçao Refinery which has been operating since 1919. This refinery provided forty per cent of Curaçao's income and its closure will double the island's unemployment rate to more than forty per cent.

4 Loss of revenue can have political consequences in terms of tax cuts. The estimated revenue from Britain's North Sea Oil was estimated at £15.5bn for 1985/86; £11.5bn for 1986/87. On that basis, the Treasury assumed that it could make cuts in income tax. The fall in oil prices meant that the 1985/86 revenue was only £11.5bn and the 1986/87 projection became £7.2bn. Income tax cuts of the type supposed could therefore not be implemented.

5 Pollution from oil spills has activated political pressure on governments. In Britain, for example, the Royal Society for the Protection of

Birds, concerned about the death of 5,000 sea birds as a result of one accident off Wales, is campaigning for a coastal exclusion zone to protect rare nesting grounds. Because of accidental spillage and deliberate tank washing at sea off Britain's coast, the Department of Trade has set up a Marine Pollution Control Unit (which includes aircraft with sophisticated sensors) to locate oil slicks which can then be dispersed by chemical sprays. BP has set up an oil spill response service at Southampton which has dealt with over forty major incidents – almost all of non-BP origin – stretching from the Shetlands to the Gulf of Mexico.

6   The fall in oil prices means that some producers with enormous debts to the international community may be unable or unwilling to repay them. Mexico, for example, has debts of over $97m; every 15 per cent fall in the price of crude oil costs it $2bn each year.

7   A fall in the oil price can assist the economy of non-producers, e.g. Japan and Germany gain economically as oil prices fall, as do Third World non-producing countries like Brazil which has to import more than half its energy requirements.

8   A fall in oil prices can also cause job losses and other problems for the oil industry. Contracts may be lost to companies who provide a wide variety of services to the industry. Aberdeen is a good illustration of what is currently happening. The fishing industry, the basis of its wealth, declined but fortunately it developed as a servicing port for North Sea exploration and twelve years of prosperity followed. Falling prices have meant that diving companies have less work, too many service vessels are chasing too few contracts, and in consequence, jobs have been lost.

Fig 1.9 Scottish workforce – North Sea

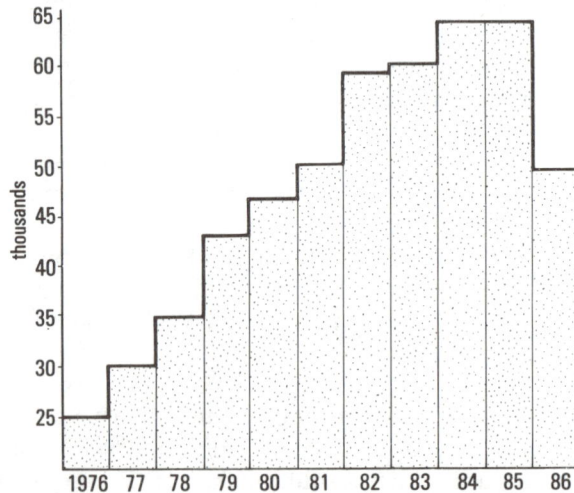

Scotland generally has benefited enormously from North Sea exploration as the illustration (Fig 1.9) shows but the immediate prospects are for job losses in the region, totalling perhaps 15,000.

CONTINUING EXPLORATION

Despite falling revenues and the difficulties that brings, exploration for oil and its associated gas continues throughout the world as illustrated by the following examples:

The Falklands

Basins off Argentina, e.g. the Malvinas and the Megallanos, have yielded oil. In the 1970s, Western Geophysical, a US company employed by the British government, identified areas to the south and east of the Falklands which were similar and of excellent geological potential. Many experts believe that this region may contain as much oil and gas as the North Sea, although there are potential problems because of the water depth. Permits have already been granted for on-shore drilling on the East Falklands.

East Indies

The Kangean area of Bali has encouraging potential, as has Southern Sumatra which is part of Indonesia. Indonesia, a country three times the size of Texas, has explored only twenty of the forty identified sedimentary basins. The state oil company, Pertamina, estimates that between thirty and forty billion barrels of oil await exploitation and the terms offered by the government to the oil companies are very generous. Its current production is its OPEC quota but with oil prices falling, Indonesia is keen to expand output to maintain the seventy per cent of its foreign exchange that oil provides. Recent discoveries by a consortium of BP and Lasmo Hundbay, amounting to some 150 million barrels, have increased interest among the large multi-nationals who now want permission to explore the frontier areas.

Venezuela

Oil exports account for more than ninety per cent of its foreign exchange earnings and although Venezuela has enormous proven reserves, virtually identical to those of the USA, it is developing a dual strategy of more exploration and better recovery from existing fields. A recent substantial find in the state of Apure, near Guafita, has encouraged this trend, as have estimates that twenty billion extra barrels can be obtained from existing fields by using more intensive recovery methods. The heavy crude oils of the Orinoco basin await development (some 1.18 trillion barrels) and trials run by the state oil company indicate that by using steam injection methods, forty to fifty per cent of these resources are recoverable. The country's two-pronged strategy is likely to mean that Venezuela remains a most important source of production for western states for many years.

Venezuela also has large deposits of gas, both on and off shore (south of Trinidad) and there are plans for exploiting these and seeking further supplies.

China

China needs to discover offshore oil if it is to achieve some of the ambitious economic targets it has set. If possible, it intends to double its oil output by the year 2000 and at present its production, which is equivalent to that of the UK, is from hundreds of onshore fields. Offshore potential depends upon western technology and in 1983, exploration began following the government's decision to designate exploration areas and grant licences.

Total, a multinational company, is developing a small field in the Gulf of Beibu, near the North Vietnam border; others are the result of Chinese/Japanese co-operation. The Chinese have organized their efforts in a similar way to the UK by creating the Chinese National Offshore Oil Corporation which takes some of the oil profits. The area which may prove most interesting to the oil companies, the East China Sea, has not yet been opened to the West.

USA

The USA is the world's third largest producer behind the USSR and Saudi Arabia. The OPEC price rises and the crisis in American-Iranian relationships following the fall of the Shah, saw the USA attempt to decrease its dependence upon Middle Eastern oil.

Strategy 1 Energy conservation, e.g. smaller cars, fewer 'gas guzzlers'.

Strategy 2 research into alternative forms of energy and a reassessment of the place of coal in future energy policy.

Strategy 3 The creation of the Synthetic Fuel Corporation which has four projects under active consideration – two for oil shales, one each for coal gasification and heavy oil.

Strategy 4 Develop to the full known oil reserves, continue exploration for new fields, and investigate the possibilities of enhanced oil recovery (EOR).

Oil fields

The principal oil fields are:
1 California. This has three main areas: the Central Valley; the coastal area of South California; and the Los Angeles Basin.
2 The mid-continental fields of Texas, Oklahoma and Kansas.
3 The Gulf Coast fields of Texas and Louisiana.
4 Alaska.

California, Texas and Louisiana continue to dominate US production but the Alaskan field, centred on Prudhoe Bay, will become increasingly important as they begin to decline – indeed, Alaska contains one-third of all proven US reserves. As the output from these three important fields declines, it is likely that marginal areas, such as the Williston Basin under Montana and North and South Dakota, will increase their production.

Exploration is gathering momentum in the Beaufort Sea and Mackenzie Delta area of the far north-west. Exploration here has included the construction of man-made islands. BP's subsidiary, Sohio, built an island in the Beaufort Sea in 1983 at a cost of £100m. 1,250,000 cubic yards of gravel were extracted from the river delta during the brief Arctic summer and shipped by barge to the site to form an island 350 ft across.

Cook Inlet and the Gulf of Alaska in the north-west are also being explored and offshore exploration is underway in the Gulf of Mexico and along the Continental Shelf of the eastern coast.

The impact of oil on a community can be judged by reference to Houston in Texas. (See also Chapter 2 below.) In 1982, the city's oil boom burst. 150,000 jobs in oil and oil-related business disappeared. The situation was such that the Houston Chamber of Commerce donated £7m to set up the Houston Economic Development Council. Its reports identify commercial space research as the key to the city's economic future and Lockheed and IBM have, in fact, taken office accommodation near the space centre.

Refining capacity

The USA still needs to import considerable quantities of oil from foreign producers and refinery location reflects this need. Both the north-west and the north-east industrial regions, e.g. along the Delaware River, have extensive refining capacity for imported oil. About sixty per cent of all refining capacity is located on the coast, over half of it along the Gulf, to service the Gulf fields. The other major refining capacity is located in inland industrial centres, e.g. along the St Lawrence Valley and the Great Lakes.

The USA is both the largest producer and consumer of natural gas. Texas, Louisiana and Alaska are the most important areas of production and high demand is met by imports from Mexico and Canada. Exploration, except for the possibility of using the shale beds of the Appalachians, mirrors that of oil – the Mackenzie Delta, Beaufort Sea and Arctic areas.

CANADA

The two principal production areas are in the Prairie Provinces of Alberta/Saskatchewan and the Arctic coast of the north-west. There are large oil reserves in the Edmonton, Calgary and Lethbridge areas and the Arctic fields are increasing their production.

Alberta has the world's largest deposits of tar sands, the best known of which are the Athabaska deposits. The sands must be expensively processed to yield oil and comparative costs of extraction illustrate just how expensive it is to exploit them (Saudi Arabia 50 cents per barrel; North Sea $12 per barrel; Athabaska $20 per barrel). The need to aim for self-sufficiency has meant since 1984 a revival of interest in these deposits, and more detailed consideration of the possibility of exploiting similar deposits in the Peace River area.

Canada, like the USA, is continuing to explore the Arctic area and the eastern Continental Shelf.

Refinery location

This mirrors that found in the USA, namely on the oil fields, on the coast, or in industrial centres such as Montreal and Winnipeg with access to piped oil.

Natural gas

Canada's production – centred on Alberta and north-eastern British Columbia – is much more than its demand. Gas is piped to the Montreal and Quebec areas and excess capacity is exported to meet demand in the USA.

UNITED KINGDOM

From 1960 onwards Britain began to use increasing quantities of imported oil, particularly from the Middle East. Although costs were reasonable it made sound economic sense to seek, and if possible, develop, its own resources. These resources are found both on shore and under the sea.

On shore

The first onshore field was at Eakring in Nottinghamshire which opened in 1939 but the most important now is at Wytch Farm in Dorset which has been operating since 1979. There are four wells on the site which together produce 5,500 barrels of crude oil per day: Europe's largest onshore production. Nearby, at Kimmeridge, some 200 barrels a day have been produced since 1960.

The exploitation of these onshore reserves has gained momentum and development is likely to take place on Furzey Island, Dorset, which has a reservoir of oil stretching under the sea. Production here could reach 40,000 barrels per day.

Onshore exploration is particularly attractive to oil companies as under present legislation, fields that yield less than 10,000 b.p.d. are exempt from Petroleum Revenue Tax which would take about seventy-five per cent of profits.

Many areas of the Midlands and southern England are covered by drilling permits but oil companies must seek planning permission and face opposition from environmental organizations, both in terms of sites and associated pipeline/transport links.

North Sea oil

The major development in oil exploration and exploitation has been in the North Sea. During the mid-1960s there was much exploration in the area, culminating in the first oil production from the Argyll field in 1975. By 1980, Britain had become self-sufficient and development was so rapid that by 1983 it was the fifth largest producer in the world and a major oil exporter. Record production was achieved in 1984 with an output of over two and a half million barrels from fields such as Brent, Forties, Cormorant, Fulmer and Magnus.

New fields are to be developed during the next few years, e.g. the

Fig 1.10 North Sea: oil and gas

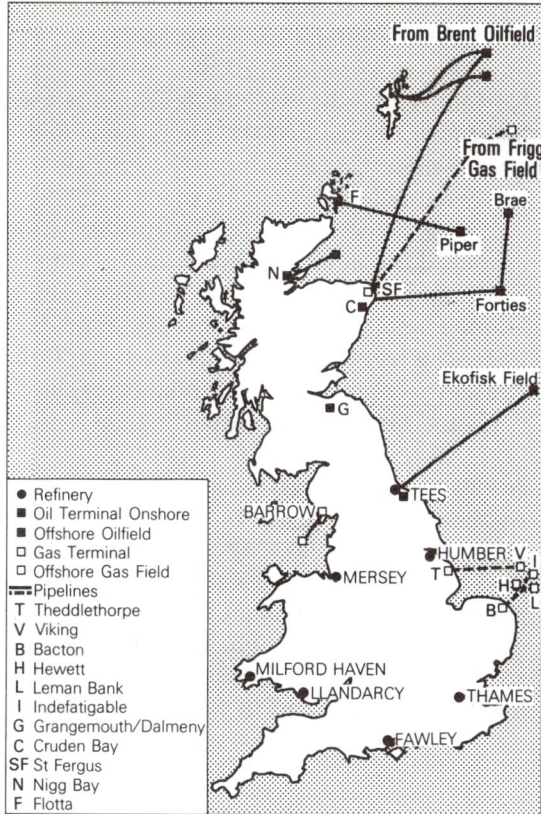

Tern field, 95 miles north-east of Scotland, will begin production in 1989 with an estimated life of twenty years. Peak production of some 66,000 b.p.d. will be achieved in the early 1990s.

The British government in its 1984 round of offshore licensing aimed to open up the 'frontier areas' of the North Sea which are more difficult and expensive to work. The Faeroes and Rockall Troughs, for example, are in waters up to 200 m deep, although the technology exists to explore them. Other areas were also licensed, including parts of the Western Shetlands Basin and the Humber estuary.

Refining capacity

This is located principally in coastal areas such as the Thames estuary, Southampton Water (Fawley), the Mersey estuary, Teesside and South Humberside.

Natural gas

Britain's demand for gas, prior to the discovery and exploitation of the North Sea sources, was met by coal gas or by natural gas imported in a liquefied state to Canvey Island from Libya. The discovery of natural gas at Slochteren in Groningen (Netherlands) encouraged seismic surveys which in 1961 proved positive. The signing of the

Continental Shelf Act 1964 was quickly followed by the first strike in 1965 in the West Sole field off the Humber. Other fields off Norfolk and Suffolk (Indefatigable, Lemon Bank, Hewitt) were subsequently brought into production, the gas being piped ashore at Bacton in Norfolk. The third stage of development was off Scotland when the Brent field, served by a 450 km pipeline to St Fergus in Aberdeenshire, was opened. Gas is fed into the grid system and natural gas liquids will eventually be moved by pipeline to Mossmorran for processing.

Rising demand has led to further exploration and in 1984, BP proposed the development of four new fields (Cleeton, Ravenspurn, Hyde and Hoton) adjacent to West Sole with a pipeline link to Humberside. It is hoped that these fields will be in production by 1990. The level of demand is such that British Gas imports gas from Norway's Frigg Field, is negotiating to purchase gas from its Sleipner field, and may consider importing gas from the Netherlands.

Benefits from North Sea gas and oil

About ten per cent of total UK tax revenue is provided by the oil companies who have also created new or saved existing jobs by placing orders in the UK for equipment ranging from rigs and support vessels to small maintenance items. Our use of domestic oil and gas saves large sums which would have been spent buying foreign supplies, and oil exports bring in additional funds. Expertise developed in the North Sea by UK companies is now in demand elsewhere, in the Far East for example.

NORWAY

Norway's industrial development was limited by its lack of fossil fuel, its domestic supplies being only small reserves of coal from Spitzbergen. Agreements on drilling rights in the North Sea gave Norway access to oilfields and production began in 1971 and had reached ten million tonnes by 1975. Oil from the Ekofisk field is moved by pipeline to Teesside.

Norway is probably the European country most prone to fluctuations in the energy market. The current (1986) fall in oil prices will, it is estimated, cut its 1985 income of 46 billion kroner by fifty per cent. Revenue from oil is important and the government is therefore reluctant to cut output and is keen to explore and exploit new fields. Exploration for oil has moved gradually northwards and the Staffjord field, north of Bergen, began production in 1979. In 1985, the Draugen and Haltenbanken fields were discovered, and currently, the Tromso and Spitzbergen regions are under investigation. The Spitzbergen area is particularly difficult in terms of terrain and glacial movements, and this, along with the Barents Sea, is a likely source of dispute over drilling rights between Norway and the USSR.

The vast majority of Norway's natural gas is exported by pipeline to the UK or through Denmark to other European consumers.

WEST GERMANY, FRANCE AND THE NETHERLANDS

All these countries are important markets for oil but have minimal domestic supplies: West Germany – two small fields in the Ems and Hanover area; France – two small fields in the Paris Basin and south-western France; the Netherlands – a small field at Schoonebek. All rely upon huge imported quantities of oil brought by tanker and distributed through an extensive pipeline network. Refineries tend to be:

(*a*)   coastally located, e.g. in Bremen, Emden, Hamburg or Rotterdam, Marseilles;

(*b*)   along rivers, e.g. the Seine or the Rhine;

(*c*)   inland along pipeline developments, e.g. the Ruhr, Bavaria, Strasbourg, Lyon.

The port of Rotterdam, in addition to importing vast quantities of oil for redistribution throughout Europe, is an important spot market centre for world oil, including imported Russian oil.

Natural gas

Small supplies of natural gas are found in Hanover (Germany) and in the Lacq and Toulouse areas of France but both countries need to supplement their small domestic supply with imports from Algeria and the Netherlands.

The Netherlands is one of the world's largest producers of natural gas, principally from the Groningen area of the north-east. This region produces huge amounts of gas, some of which is used locally by industry attracted to this remote part of the Netherlands by government grants and cheap energy, the bulk however is moved by an extensive pipeline network to Belgium, north Germany, south Germany, Paris and south-east France. Extensive offshore deposits have also been discovered which when exploited will provide valuable foreign exchange for the Netherlands.

USSR

Russia is the world's largest producer of crude oil and relies upon this product for about sixty per cent of its foreign exchange. Overall, production is falling (four per cent in each of the last two years) because of the steady decline in production from the Ural area, e.g. the Tyumen region which accounts for some sixty per cent of total production. Since the late 1970s, the focus of development has switched to newer fields in Western Siberia where capital costs are much higher, the climate harsher, yields lower, fields deeper and work morale lower.

The USSR is reluctant to drop its prices to current market levels and this has led to a sharp decline in export sales. Only India and Finland appear to be buying Soviet oil in the usual quantities and its sales of some 80 million tons a year to non-Comecon countries would appear to be under threat. This will affect its ability to purchase western technology and to buy grain if there are any shortfalls in Soviet harvests.

The Soviet Union has, however, a unique cushion. Its Eastern European allies, who form the economic grouping known as Comecon, are charged the average price of the last five years. This means that it would be cheaper at present for them to buy on the world market but tight agreements prevent them from doing so.

KUWAIT

Fig 1.11 Kuwait – oil

Kuwait produces about four per cent of the world's oil and illustrates the impact of that mineral on the economy of a producing country in the Middle East. It has the second largest proven oil reserves, some of which lie off shore in the Gulf and these may prove a source of contention with Kuwait's neighbour across the Gulf – Iran.

The major areas of production are in the north-east and south-east of the country, the Burgan area being particularly important. An extensive pipeline network connects the fields to the oil terminal at Mina al Almadi where some oil is refined and the majority pumped to the offshore loading facility in the Gulf for export.

The revenues from oil have been used to transform Kuwait. As a desert area it has always had a problem obtaining fresh water, but the construction of three huge desalinization plants which allow seawater to be processed into drinking water, has solved this problem. Al Kuwait, the capital, has been the site of an extensive modern building programme, including well-equipped hospitals, hotels and shopping complexes. Many of these have been built by foreign companies who have used labour from neighbouring states and these migrants, along with others attracted by Kuwait's expanding economy, make up a significant percentage of the population. The transport system of the country has been completely modernized during the last twenty years with a system of well-built major roads connecting the outlying areas to the coast, and an urban motorway network in Al Kuwait itself. As Kuwait has one of the highest rates of car ownership in the world, the network is subject to continual improvement.

This area, the Gulf, is important to Western Europe and Japan for oil supplies. The Iran/Iraq War has placed the whole region in danger of becoming involved directly or indirectly in that conflict. Oil and politics again are intertwined and Kuwait must tread a careful path between its warring neighbours. Any threat to close the Straits of Hormuz, thereby depriving the West of a significant percentage of its oil imports, is likely to create additional tension as moves are likely to be taken to guarantee international access through the Straits.

WORLD PRODUCTION

Country	% of world production
USSR	18
USA	15
Saudi Arabia	13
Iran	10
Venezuela	5
Iraq	4
Kuwait	4
Nigeria	3
Others	28

1 Oil is found mainly in the northern hemisphere.
2 The importance of the Middle East and other developing countries.
3 The dominance of the superpowers – America and the USSR.

CHECKLIST ▶

OIL AND NATURAL GAS

1 Stages in the world trade in oil.
2 The economic and political importance of oil and the influence of OPEC.
3 The effect of price fluctuations on producers and consumers.
4 The exploration and development of new resources.
5 North Sea oil and gas – Britain and Norway have both become important producers.
6 Regional examples.
7 The impact of oil revenues on a Middle Eastern country.

Although hydroelectric power is increasing in importance its contribution to the world's energy supplies, it remains small. Certain natural conditions encourage its production:

1   Heavy reliable rainfall with a fairly even distribution throughout the year.
2   A low evaporation rate.
3   Rock structures which increase the percentage of surface run off are easy to tunnel through if necessary, and form a natural catchment area.
4   Gorges or valleys which enable dams to be built easily and cheaply.
5   Natural falls of water.
6   Large rivers with reasonable water flow – these can be dammed to provide power.

Some countries, such as Norway and Sweden, had little or no fossil fuels when they wished to develop their industrial base. Norway's fossil fuel was limited to supplies of coal found at Spitzbergen, an island within the Arctic Circle and only 650 miles from the North Pole. (About 400,000 tonnes of coal a year are currently obtained from this source by 1,200 miners based at Longyearbyen.) In these circumstances, both countries – which possessed many of the natural advantages listed above – decided to develop hydro production in preference to the more expensive option of importing coal from other European countries.

Although the initial outlay to develop plants and reservoirs is great, continuing costs are low. This is perhaps one of the reasons why many areas of the world with great potential have not been developed. In addition, suitable regions may be far away from areas where the electricity is needed, and although the technology exists to move electricity efficiently over large distances, the construction of a grid network would be expensive.

Many schemes have been developed which principally provide electricity for a particular industrial complex, with any excess capacity being moved and used elsewhere: the Kemano scheme in British Columbia which was built to provide power for the aluminium plant at Kitimat; the Rjukan plant in Norway which supplied power for the nearby fertilizer plant. Others have been constructed with the intention of meeting a multiplicity of needs: those on the Columbia, Colorado and Tennessee rivers of the USA plus schemes in California, along with schemes on the Rhône and Durance in Europe, have been constructed to provide HEP; regulate water flow; provide water for local irrigation schemes; improve navigation; and create a tourist potential. These schemes, known as integrated schemes, have been very successful in meeting their many objectives.

Governments have sometimes encouraged the construction of hydroelectric plants in more remote areas to act as a focus for further industrial development (growth poles). Some sites in the Pyrenees of France are on a fairly small scale but natural falls of water have meant fairly cheap production. These schemes have succeeded in attracting industrial developments, e.g. south of Lourdes. Kemano, in British Columbia, is also intended to act as a growth pole in an area which needs industrial development.

It is likely that HEP will continue to be important in providing a significant contribution towards the energy requirements of both Norway and Sweden. Although Norway has discovered significant reserves of oil, it is probably the country most prone to fluctuations in the energy market and cannot rely on using money from this source to import. Sweden's decision to phase out nuclear power stations means that it too will also continue to rely on HEP for energy.

Fig 1.12 La Grande River: hydroelectric power in Northern Quebec

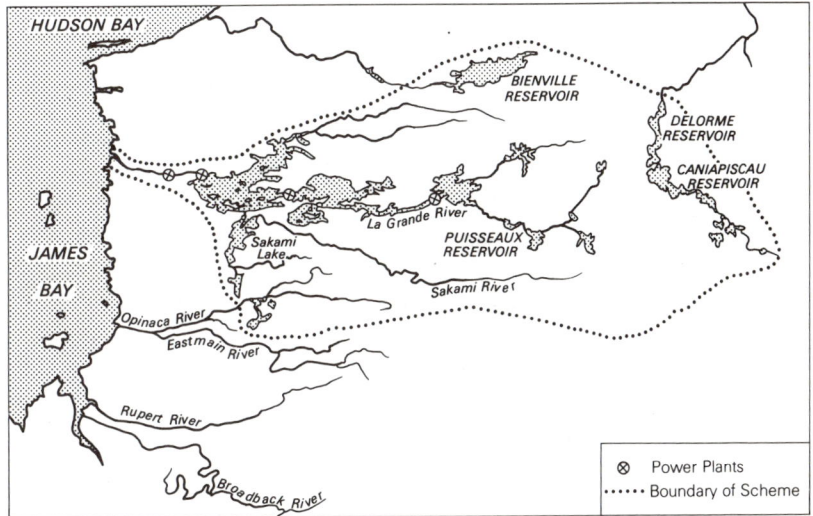

1 The scheme began in 1972.
2 Dams were built along with four separate power plants to generate 8,500–9,000 megawatts.
3 Part of the flow of other rivers e.g. the Opinaca were diverted into the Grand River system.
4 Original intention to use the Rupert and Broadback rivers abandoned because of sacrifice of valuable timber, mineral potential, and livelihood of 5,000 Cree Indians who live there.
5 Scheme opened up this area of Quebec for further development because of access required for transport.
6 Provides low cost electricity for Quebec area.

Country	% of total world generation
USA	22
Canada	16
USSR	11
Norway	6
Japan	5
Sweden	5
France	4
Brazil	4
Italy	3
Others	24

1   Over one-third of world generation is found in North America.
2   The developed nations dominate production.
3   Temperate latitudes with mountainous areas are important.
4   Three-quarters of the world's HEP generation is concentrated in nine countries.

CHECKLIST ▶   HYDROELECTRICITY

1   The conditions necessary to develop HEP.
2   Lack of fossil fuels encouraged HEP in areas such as Norway and Sweden.
3   Many schemes are multi-purpose, involving HEP, irrigation and flood control.
4   The use of HEP as a growth pole to attract industrial development.
      Candidates are advised to make detailed notes on an integrated scheme, e.g. Tennessee Valley Authority, the Rhône Scheme.

NUCLEAR POWER

The mid-1950s marked the beginning of the use of nuclear power for peaceful purposes with the opening of the Calder Hall complex in England. These early stations of the Magnox type were located away from centres of population, on or near large sources of water which was used for cooling, and were on geologically sound areas because of their enormous weight. Developing technology in electricity transmission meant that remoteness from the main areas of electricity demand ceased to be a problem. These locational factors continue to determine siting in many areas of the world.

Many countries saw nuclear power as an important means of solving their future energy problems but nuclear plants, in addition to generating electricity, also seem to generate strong feelings among both proponents and opponents of the use of nuclear technology. Because of these conflicting pressures, the future development of nuclear power is likely to vary tremendously from country to country; some, such as France, have pushed ahead and intend to continue with enormous developments; others, like Sweden, have made a decision to phase it out completely in the near future.

Fig 1.13 Britain – nuclear
power stations

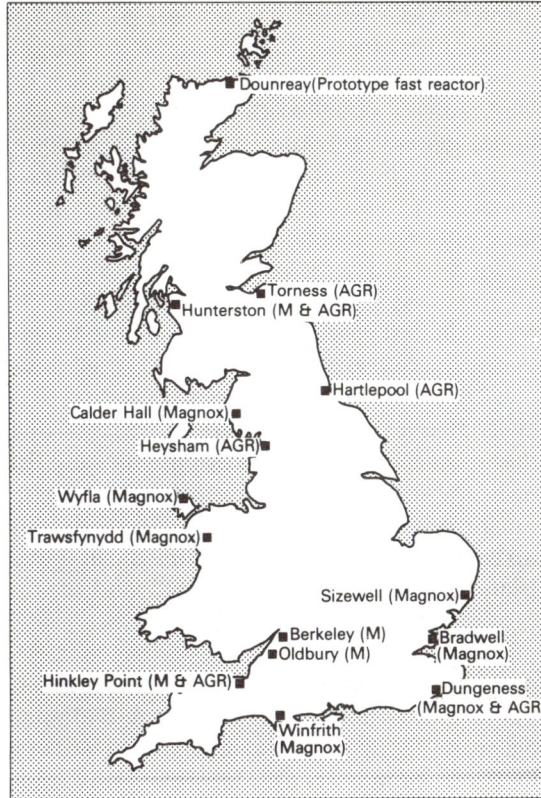

UNITED KINGDOM

Eleven nuclear power stations in Britain produce about seventeen per cent of our total electricity supply and the projection is that this will reach twenty-five per cent by the year 2000. The Central Electricity Generating Board has drawn up plans to build twelve new nuclear power stations by that date at a cost of some £15 billion. The Board's projections are that electricity demand – at present stagnant – is unlikely to increase in the immediate future and the effect therefore of increasing output from nuclear stations must inevitably be to reduce the Board's dependence upon coal. Additional plants are planned for some of the existing stations, Hinkley Point, Dungeness, Wylfa, Winfrith, Dunidge Bay and Trawsfynydd, with a possible third plant at Sizewell. (A public enquiry is considering its findings and recommendations on the Board's request to build a pressurized water reactor (PWR) at Sizewell – plant 2.) The CEGB commitment to the use of nuclear power is illustrated by the fact that it has invested in the next generation of fast breeding reactors being built in France and will take electricity (initially some 1,000 megawatts per year) across the Channel to Britain by power line.

USA

The USA developed few nuclear plants at the time of Britain's first involvement in the 1950s and early 1960s. Over a five-year period, however, between 1966 and 1970, nuclear generating capacity in the USA quickly equalled that in Britain. Between 1970 and 1979, additional generating capacity was built despite the objections of those opposed to nuclear power. Some states, including California with its abundance of oil and gas, were slow to opt for nuclear power generation; others, lacking in energy resources, such as New England, pushed ahead with constructions. By 1979 there were 115 nuclear stations operating, generating fifteen per cent of the country's electricity. In that year, however, the Three Mile Island plant at Middleton, Pennsylvania, experienced a partial melt down in its Number 2 reactor – with the result that approximately 150,000 residents had to be evacuated from the surrounding area. The outcome of the accident was that projected nuclear developments were the target of much detailed scrutiny and public debate, and in consequence, there has been a drastic revision of projected future nuclear generation. Although clean up costs at the plant are thought to be in the region of $1bn, Three Mile Island reopened in October 1985 and was generating at its 800 mw capacity by January 1986.

The recent Chernobyl disaster has made the industry's future even more insecure as it has brought the Three Mile Island problem to the public's attention yet again. Some stations nearing completion are overrunning on costs and are likely to face objections when they apply for production licences. Many may prove to be commercially unviable for the private companies who have invested huge amounts of money to build them.

CANADA

Quebec and Ontario provinces are the main centres of nuclear power generation in Canada, reflecting their industrial importance and their shortage of other sources of energy.

FRANCE

France's first nuclear plant was built at Marcoule on the lower Rhône, near Avignon, coming on stream in 1956; others followed in Brittany and the Loire valley. The take-off point for development came in 1973 with the government's decision to reduce dependence on imported oil by expanding its nuclear programme. Thirty-two nuclear plants are currently operating and twenty-eight more under construction. Over sixty per cent of France's electricity is produced by nuclear stations and French industrialists have the cheapest electricity in the EEC.

The World's first full-sized fast breeder reactor, Superphenix, has been built at Creys-Malville (a French/Italian/German project). It will produce 1,200 mw of electricity, enough for a city of one million people. Fast breeders burn plutonium, made as a by-product in normal

Fig 1.14 Nuclear power
station – Europe

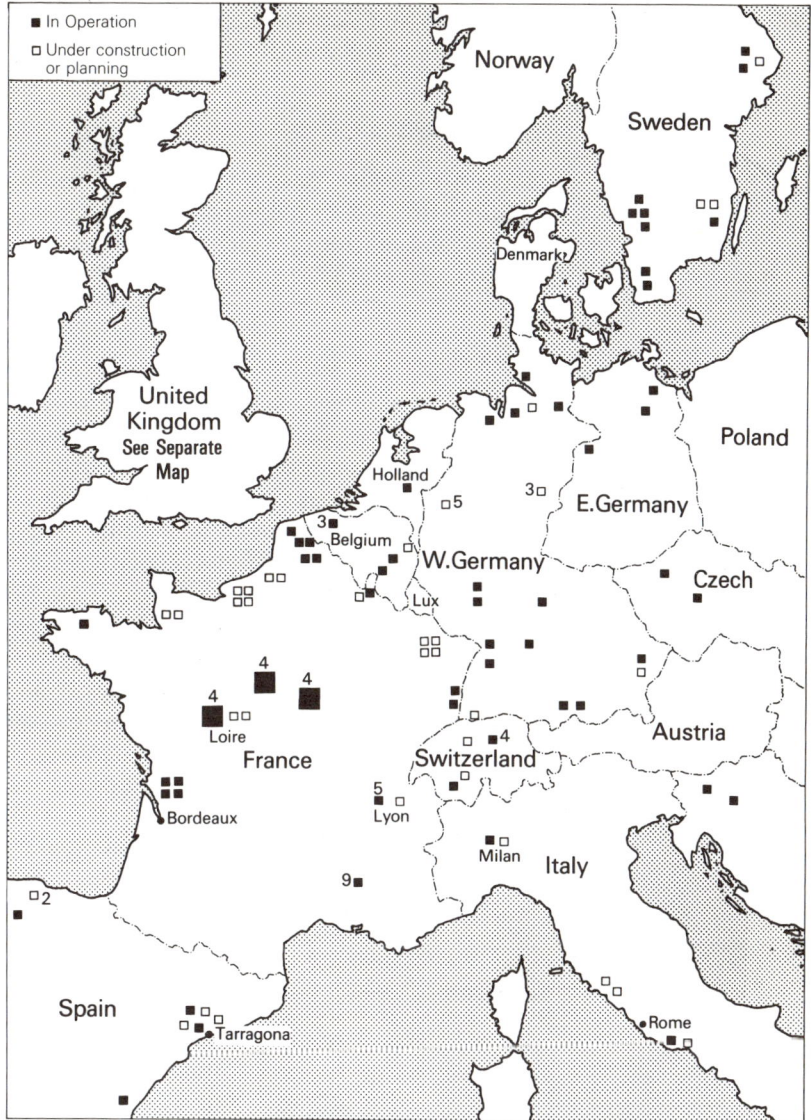

uranium burning nuclear reactors. More importantly, breeders also
make their own plutonium. A blanket of uranium arranged around
the breeder's core is transformed slowly into plutonium. For the first
time, scientists can build a generator that creates or breeds more fuel
than it burns. Designing a way to keep the core cool was a problem –
the solution was to place it in a pond of sodium metal. The reactor's
heat melts the sodium which is pumped away from the core to drive
steam turbines that generate electricity. As molten sodium reacts
explosively with water and steam, Superphenix has been fitted with
emergency cooling systems that do not use water. Construction costs
mean more expensive electricity but the lessons learned will mean
cheaper production in future.

PROLIFERATION

European and American expertise is in demand to develop capacity elsewhere in the world.

1 SOUTH AFRICA

French expertise has, for example, resulted in their assistance to South Africa – they helped build its nuclear power station at Koeberg, the second reactor of which came on stream in July 1985. (Reprocessing at La Hague.)

2 CHINA

China is due to complete a nuclear power station at Daya Bay in the economic development region of Guandong in 1992. It is a joint venture between the Chinese government and the Hong Kong Nuclear Investment Company using British (GEC) generating units. It will supply three per cent of China's generated power, although initially, eighty per cent of its capacity will be fed to Hong Kong.

3 PORTUGAL

Portugal is examining the possibilities of a joint venture with British and Canadian firms to build nuclear reactors to meet its developing energy needs. The final decision may well depend on costs as it is calculated that some forty per cent of the technology and equipment necessary will have to be imported. It has the advantage of domestic uranium from mines in the Urgeirica area which is at present converted into 'yellowcake' (uranium oxide) and shipped out to other nuclear-generating countries through the port of Leixoes (Oporto).

4 JAPAN

After its experience in the Second World War, Japan was reluctant to be involved in the use of nuclear power. The rise in oil prices in the 1970s changed attitudes and some thirty-two plants are now operating, providing twenty-five per cent of the nation's electricity. Japan's energy strategy envisages an expansion in capacity so that by the year 2000, nuclear generation will provide most of its electricity.

CUT BACK IN CAPACITY

Sweden has twelve reactors producing fifty-eight terawatts of electricity – over half of its energy requirements. In 1980, a referendum was held and it was decided to halt any new developments and phase out existing capacity by 2010. This decision has not been welcomed by industrialists who have the lowest electricity costs in the world. The pulp and paper industry, for example (see Chapter 2 below), requires enormous amounts of energy. It was, however, welcomed by the Danes who have no nuclear capacity and want the reactors closed as quickly as possible. To cut down consumption, the Swedes are developing district heating systems in urban areas. Water is heated up at one or two power stations and pumped through a mains system to provide hot water and central heating.

Having no coal, gas, and only meagre traces of offshore oil, Sweden must look towards:

(a)   more HEP production;

(b)   develop renewable resources or indigenous fuels such as peat, wood, household refuse or waste liquids from one of its main industries: pulp and paper-making. Already, the government is encouraging the planting of willows which grow quickly, and experimenting with windmills at Malmo.

THE NUCLEAR ENERGY DEBATE

Those in favour of nuclear energy, for example the CEGB writing in November 1986, cite:

1   It is vital: without nuclear power the world would run out of fossil fuel supplies far too quickly, and the first to suffer would be the 'have-not' countries of the third world which are trying to develop their economies and so eradicate poverty.

2   It is even more vital to the UK in the short term: without nuclear stations the CEGB could not maintain secure supplies of electricity from 1990–91 even if it took all the steps proposed by the conservationist lobbies.

3   It is safe: since commercial nuclear power started a quarter of a century ago there has been no dangerous release of radioactivity from any nuclear station – in this country or the rest of the world – of a design used or proposed for use in Britain. As the Russians themselves have acknowledged, the Chernobyl accident could not have happened in any other type of reactor in the world.

4   It has notable environmental advantages: properly designed, built and operated – as in the UK – nuclear stations have less impact on the environment than any other form of power generation of similar capacity. They take up less space, burn less fuel and produce less waste than coal-fired stations, and they do not contribute to acid rain pollution. Radiation from nuclear power stations is minuscule – about one thousandth of that which is already there from natural sources.

5   It is economic: even if there were practically no recovery in fossil fuel prices from their present low level (which is much lower than the latest Friends of the Earth forecast) Sizewell B would be economically superior to a new coal-fired station – and later PWRs, with no launching costs to bear, would be considerably more economic. As regards existing nuclear stations, replacing their output by electricity from fossil-fuelled stations in 1985–86 would have added £500 million to the CEGB's costs.

6   It increases fuel diversity: a larger nuclear component on the CEGB system would lessen the risk to consumers of a severe disruption in the supply of any one power station fuel. (Last year coal generated 80 per cent of electricity supplies, compared with nuclear's 16.7 per cent.)

7   It is available and fully developed *now*: none of the renewable energy technologies is at present a viable alternative to nuclear or coal-fired plants and each presents its own environmental problems.

8   Its wastes – which are small in volume – can be safely disposed of: the technology has been developed; what is lacking at the moment is public acceptance.

9   It does not pose a security threat: terrorists could not make a nuclear bomb with the spent fuel from nuclear power stations – even if they had their own Sellafield where the plutonium could be extracted.

10   It is essential to Britain's economic strength and employment prospects: without the cheaper electricity offered by nuclear power, British industry would be less able to compete with electricity-intensive industry overseas. Indeed, the Secretary of State for Energy, Peter Walker, has estimated that 250,000 jobs hinge on nuclear power.

Those against:

1   The stagnant demand for electricity reported, for example, by the Central Electricity Generating Board.

2   The chances of a major nuclear accident.

3   Sabotage or theft by terrorists.

4   Proliferation of nuclear weapons.

5   The disposal of nuclear waste from power stations.

6   The developing nuclear reprocessing industry.

In the UK leaks from Sellafield and the accident at Three Mile Island, Pennsylvania, in 1979 have given those opposed to developments additional ammunition. In two weeks in February 1986, two leaks occurred. First, plutonium gas was released into the atmosphere in the main chemical separation building and one worker was exposed to the equivalent of one year's radiation. Secondly, on 18 February, radio-active material escaped from a contaminated water storage plant – 'a low hazard potential incident'. A leak of fifteen tons of milder radio-active carbon dioxide from Trawsfynydd in Wales occurred shortly afterwards. Following the second leak at Sellafield, the Irish govern-

Fig 1.15 Nuclear waste disposal

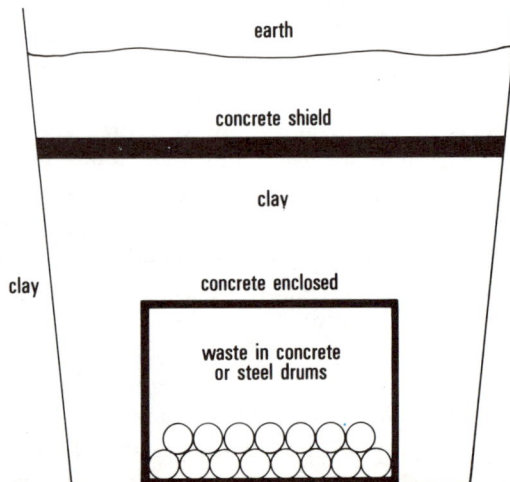

ment expressed its concern and called for the setting up of a European Inspectorate supervised by the EEC.

The activities of organizations such as Greenpeace have kept this issue in the public eye. They have campaigned against the dumping of nuclear waste into the sea, half-way between Land's End and the north coast of Spain, by harassing ships involved and in 1983/84, succeeded in getting the dumping stopped; they have also campaigned against the pipeline disposal of material from Sellafield into the Irish Sea.

The British government's intention to dump more nuclear waste on land has created additional controversy. The drawing up of a short list, including Bradwell, Filbeck, Elstow (Bedfordshire) and South Killing-holme (Humberside) has mobilized public opposition – Humberside County Council collected 50,000 signatures against dumping in four months. (The industry needs to convince the public that radioactive waste can be disposed of without hazard, and the public inquiry into the preferred site will no doubt take evidence on this matter.) The dumping of nuclear waste has been going on for some twenty-seven years at Drigg, near Sellafield, but by the year 2000, this dump will be filled.

On the new site, the original proposal was that low level wastes (some 25,000 cu m each year) would be dumped in drums some 30 ft down and covered with earth; higher level wastes (about 1,000 cu m a year) would be dumped in concrete or steel drums and enclosed in concrete and covered by earth. These trenches will be constructed in clay which is largely impermeable and would act as a filter if radio-active particles ever did leak. Public pressure meant that plans to dump high level waste, which will take at least 300 years to lose most of its radioactivity, have been suspended.

THE CHERNOBYL FACTOR   Chernobyl (population 50,000), the site of the major accident in 1986, is located 50 miles due north of Kiev (population 1.5m). It is one of thirty reactors in the USSR (providing some fifteen per cent of its electricity), most of which are located in the western more densely populated half of the country.

It appears that there were five main stages in the accident to the reactor:

1   Cooling water leaks into graphite core.
2   A chemical reaction took place between the water and graphite, producing hydrogen gas.
3   The gas pressure buckled the fuel rods and the core heated up.
4   The top of the core was blown off.
5   The hydrogen mixed with the air and exploded, scattering radioactive debris and creating a radioactive cloud.

Radiation levels around the area have been calculated at 200 Rems per hour. (0.5 Rems per year are the maximum permitted exposure in the UK.) Settlements were evacuated, some unfortunately nine days after the accident (49,000 people in all were moved), and over 200 were affected by radiation illnesses, some forty seriously. Water sources and the surrounding croplands were also seriously affected. The long-term effects on both people and agricultural land are likely to be serious: some people will almost certainly die of cancer in the future; and crops and soil could be contaminated for at least ten years, and perhaps as many as 300. Lead and borum which cut off the nuclear reactions, and sand which cuts off the supply of oxygen, were dropped on to the reactor by helicopter.

Radioactive material drifted away from the disaster site and eventually covered a huge area. The first signs in the West of a nuclear problem came in Sweden where sophisticated monitoring equipment at a nuclear plant noted the increasing radioactivity, as did similar equipment in Norway, Denmark and Finland. East Germany subsequently reported radiation levels 100 times above normal; Yugoslavia, ten times. In Britain, rainwater was more radioactive, up twenty per cent at Wylfa in Wales, and background radiation increased. Checks were made on milk, vegetables and animals slaughtered for meat throughout Europe.

This accident brought sharply into focus the fact that radiation is no respecter of national boundaries and that a nuclear accident in one country is very likely to have an effect in others. Chernobyl has acted as a catalyst for debate throughout the world on the issue of nuclear energy. The CEGB's strategy to reduce its dependence on coal and increase its nuclear capacity is likely to lead to this debate in the UK continuing for a considerable time.

	1983	% power station capacity
Coal	64	20
Nuclear	12	73
Oil	21	1
Hydro wind	3	7

CHECKLIST ▶ **NUCLEAR POWER**

1 Nuclear capacity first developed in UK.
2 Examples of the development and spread of the use of nuclear energy.
3 The implication of Sweden's decision to phase out nuclear power stations.
4 The nuclear debate – arguments for and against nuclear power.
5 Accidents (Three Mile Island, Sellafield and Chernobyl) and the problems of waste disposal.

ALTERNATIVE SOURCES OF ENERGY

Euphorbia

This is known in America as the 'gasoline plant' as its latex is similar to that of crude oil. This is a wild plant growing in Northern California and can provide between two and ten barrels of crude oil per acre, but with genetic developments, it is thought that the yield could rise to fifty barrels per acre.

Crambe
When crushed, this produced an oil similar to rapeseed which could replace oil as a high temperature lubricant.

Sugar cane
Brazil powers large numbers of vehicles using alcohol (ethanol) made from the juice of sugar cane. The fall in the sugar market led to excess sugar cane production and the government decided to convert the sugar into alcohol.

The production of biomass (energy derived from plant and animal matter) is important in Brazil and Zimbabwe. Brazil, for example, is considering developing its chemical industry by using ethanol to generate ethylene, the basis for plastics, polyesters and fibres.

Bagasse (the fibrous waste of sugar cane) could become a substitute for gas, coal and oil in the petrochemical industry as supplies dwindle or become more expensive to obtain.

Geothermal power
This is already a reality in some parts of the world, e.g. Iceland, USA and Japan. In Britain there is extensive research into its possibilities. £14m has been spent in Cornwall, two wells have been sunk one and a half miles into hot granite; water is pumped down one and hot water rises in the other.

Wind power
Experiments are going ahead in Devon and the Orkneys into the use of wind power to produce electricity. At Ilfracombe, in Devon, a huge windmill is being used in a £1m programme funded by the Wind Energy Group. It is thought that there is enormous export potential for an efficient system in North America, the Spanish Islands and in parts of the Pacific for this technology. As part of its strategy to disengage from nuclear power, Sweden (see section on Nuclear Power) is experimenting with wind power at Malmo.

Wave power
Norway has developed a pilot wave power project near Bergen. Present analysis suggests that costs will be no more than 4p per kwh and the government see it as not only the basis for cheap power generation, but also as the basis of an enormous export drive.

In Britain, there is much discussion and debate about whether wave power, given equal financial support, could produce electricity more cheaply than either coal or nuclear power. One pilot project is going ahead on South Uist with costs being met by a commercial company, James Howden Engineering, the Departments of Trade and Environment and the EEC.

Tidal power

The French developed the first tidal power station on the Rance in northern Brittany in 1966. The Canadians, after this French success, began investigations but delayed construction. Following the enormous rise in the cost of energy in the 1970s, they opened a tidal barrage in 1983 in the Bay of Fundy (Newfoundland).

In the UK, between 1983 and 1985, a feasibility study took place on the possibility of constructing a barrage across the River Severn. Two possible sites were identified:

(a)   between Cardiff and Weston-super-Mare;

(b)   at English Stones near the Severn Bridge.

Power generation would be possible by 2000 and the scheme would have the advantage of providing an additional transport link across the estuary.

Solar power

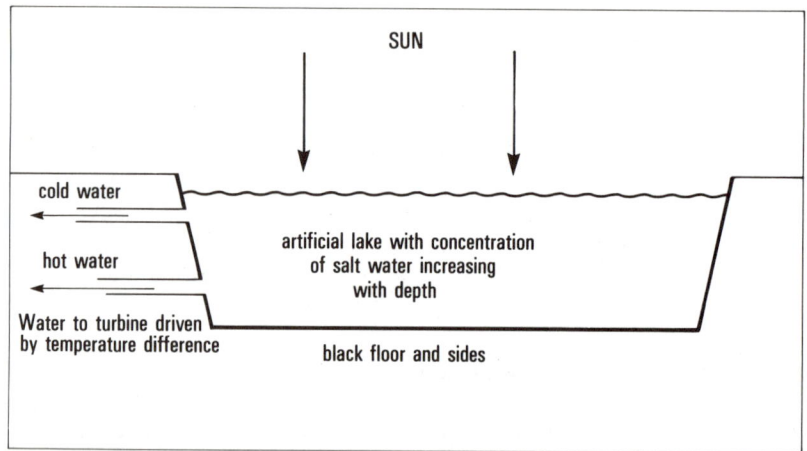

Fig 1.16   Solar energy

Its use stretches back to the middle of the last century when the French used solar energy to power a small steam engine. The energy crisis of the 1970s renewed considerable interest in this form of energy production by both governments and individuals. Many dwellings now have their own solar heating systems and solar power stations have been built. The largest system in the world is at Barstow in California which has a peak output of 12,100 kw. Computer controlled mirrors follow the sun and focus its energy on a collecting tower. The French have developed a similar facility at Targassone in the Pyrenees which is Europe's largest power station – capable of supplying up to 2,500 kw to the National Grid. This station has a field of 200 mirrors, each with an area of 54 sq m – they focus on a receiver at the top of an 80-m tower. Heat is carried off to a generator in molten salt.

Solar ponds are an alternative method of producing solar energy. Israel developed the first solar pond in 1979 and its output is some 5,000 kw. A Californian facility has an output of 12,000 kw.

The ponds contain dissolved salts, the concentration gradually increasing with depth. Solar energy passes through the salty water and raises the temperature at lower levels to about 90°C. A combination of the dark floor and sides of the pond, coupled with the presence of salts, prevent convection currents setting up to distribute the heat throughout the pond and the conditions are thus ideal to drive a turbine to generate electricity.

CHECKLIST ▶

ALTERNATIVE SOURCES OF ENERGY

1 The search for alternatives to coal, oil, natural gas and nuclear power.
2 They contribute very little at present but may become increasingly significant.

ENVIRONMENTAL OBJECTIONS TO PRESENT ENERGY SOURCES

The environmental objections to nuclear power are outlined in the section on Nuclear Power. Environmental groups in Sweden are opposed to the further development of hydroelectric power stations to offset the increased demand for electricity, caused by the decision to cease production from nuclear stations. They argue that additional stations with the attendant transmission lines, will destroy or have an adverse effect on areas of great beauty, wildness and remoteness. They favour the development of other alternative sources of energy with a smaller environmental impact.

Environmental objections to coal are that: strip or open-cast techniques cause great damage to the countryside which becomes unsightly; shaft mining creates the need for large storage dumps; new rail and road links must be created, causing additional environmental damage and inconvenience to local people; and subsidence may affect nearby property.

Coal is also a dirty fuel which, when burned, is a pollutant. Domestic and industrial use created problems and resulted in the UK in the Clean Air Act. This had a dramatic effect in industrial areas such as Sheffield and Halifax – they became visible from surrounding high ground.

Coal used in power stations and other large combustion plants contributes to the release of sulphur dioxide into the atmosphere. This has the effect of turning rain 'acid'. It is thought that acid rain weakens trees, particularly conifers which do not shed their leaves and therefore accumulate toxins, which are then attacked by a virus responsible for carrying on a process leading to their defoliation and eventual death. The campaign mounted by organizations such as Greenpeace and Friends of the Earth to reduce this type of pollution will ultimately reduce the number of new forest areas affected, but will not save those which have already been damaged by acid rain and virus infection.

Costs to industry to combat this problem would be large: to fit flue gas scrubbers to the twelve largest coal burning stations in the UK would cost around £2m. EEC proposals concerning sulphur dioxide

Fig 1.17 Acid rain

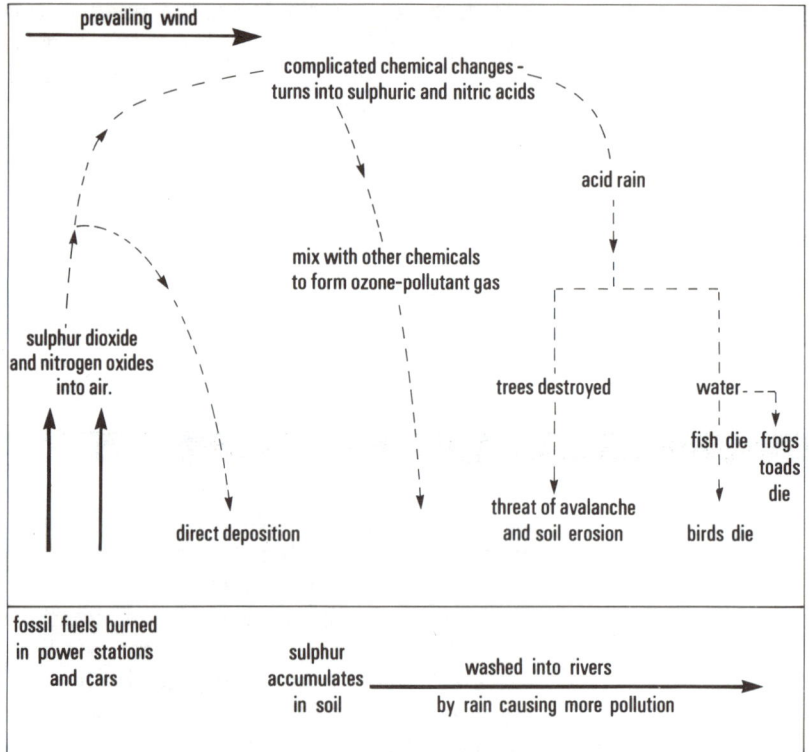

prevailing wind →

complicated chemical changes –
turns into sulphuric and nitric acids

acid rain

mix with other chemicals
to form ozone-pollutant gas

sulphur dioxide
and nitrogen oxides
into air.

trees destroyed   water

fish die frogs
toads
die

direct deposition   threat of avalanche
and soil erosion   birds die

fossil fuels burned
in power stations
and cars

sulphur
accumulates
in soil

washed into rivers

by rain causing more pollution

emissions would have a great effect on the UK which, it is calculated, produces over four million tons per annum. Conversely, they would have little effect on Germany or Holland which have much tighter domestic controls, or on France and Belgium because of their switch to nuclear power.

The scale of this world problem is illustrated by the fact that 20,000 Scandinavian lakes are affected (1,800 lakes in Norway contain no fish), forty per cent of West Germany's forests, increasingly large areas of Sweden and Finland, parts of Japan, parts of the Canadian Shield, and Lakes Erie and Ontario.

In the UK, one of the greatest increases in acidity is in the Lake District. In the Peak District, the Brecon Beacons and the North Yorkshire Moors, acid levels have been measured at a concentration high enough to irritate the skin.

One-third of Swiss forest is dead or dying. Traditionally in that country, trees have formed a natural barrier to hold back the avalanches of winter. Since a quarter of the land is forested and a further quarter comprises mountains where snow builds up, the threat to towns and villages in those areas is serious and contingency plans are being made to evacuate people at risk. Officials are quoted as saying that throughout the country, as many as 150,000 people may be forced to flee their homes in winters to come.

One recent report by the German Alpine Society confirms fears and suggests that the Alps could become an area of scree and rock, devoid of trees within fifteen to twenty years. Its survey shows that attempts to replace diseased trees with young ones are unsuccessful because mountain goats and other animals, deprived of their feeding grounds by forests disappearing, are eating the young trees.

In Britain, trees, rivers and lakes are being affected in the same way. Water problems tend to be worse where lakes or rivers are in coniferous areas because these trees tend to concentrate acids and afforestation techniques release harmful chemicals from the soil. Birds, toads, frogs and otters are also affected, as are wildflowers.

In 1986, the British government finally decided to address the problem. Pressure from our neighbours, who receive seventy per cent of our sulphur dioxide, and the EEC led to an agreement to fit three power stations with anti-sulphur equipment. Work will begin in 1988 but will not be completed until 1997 and even then, Britain will not have achieved its EEC target.

The debate on oil's impact on the environment is often not about the sites of extraction but about the movement of oil. Reference has already been made to the effect on bird life of accidental spillage from or deliberate washing of tanks in oil tankers. Marine life is also devastated by such incidents, as are tourist areas such as the south coast of Britain where local authorities must clean up polluted beaches.

The trans-Alaska pipeline caused environmental concern. Oil was found in the north of the State but because of freezing in the Beaufort Sea, had to be transported to the ice-free south coast, over 1,200 km away. Environmentalists were insistent that great care was taken that: minimal damage was caused to plant communities which in turn could affect the habitat for local animals; the pipeline did not impede the traditional migration pattern of the caribou; and due regard was given to avoiding accidental spillage.

Proposed onshore developments in Dorset have caused similar concerns, centred on transporting the oil. BP have proposed four options: expanding the existing rail link from Furzebrook to Poole; pipelines underwater to Poole Harbour; across the New Forest to Southampton Water; or west to Portland Harbour. Dorset heathland is disappearing rapidly and environmentalists fear that a rail terminal expansion or the construction of pipelines could exacerbate this situation, losing an important insect, reptile and bird habitat.

Oil and coal combustion have helped create the problem of smog. (See section on Climate.) The fraction of oil (petrol) used to power the internal combustion engine has an additive, lead, which is causing concern as a pollutant. Since 1982, the British government has been campaigning against its use and has been trying to persuade other EEC countries to agree to a deadline for such a ban. Greece and Denmark have vetoed any attempt to change policy. Car-makers in Britain may, however, agree voluntarily to introduce models which can run on lead-free petrol. The government has, however, been slow to act because in April 1983 it accepted the recommendation of the

Ninth Report of the Royal Commission on Environmental Pollution which stated 'The Government should begin urgent discussions with the UK oil and motor industry in order to agree a timetable for the introduction of unleaded petrol'.

There appears to be no intention at present of making lead-free petrol mandatory in Europe while in the USA it has been mandatory in new cars since 1975, reducing the health risks significantly.

ENERGY – GLOSSARY

acid rain rain containing pollution, particularly industrial wastes, which may affect natural vegetation.

adit mine shafts excavated at a shallow angle to a mineral seam.

American Congress two elected houses of the American Parliament – the Senate and the House of Representatives.

apartheid policy of separate development in South Africa.

bagasse the fibrous waste of sugar cane.

biomass the energy derived from plant and animal matter.

CEGB Central Electricity Generating Board – responsible for producing UK electricity.

Chernobyl site of nuclear accident in USSR.

Comecon economic union of Communist States in Eastern Europe.

crambe plant which produces material similar to oil when crushed.

deforestation removal of trees from an area.

desalinization plant removes salt from sea-water to make drinking water.

drift mine shafts excavated at a shallow angle to a mineral seam.

EEC European Economic Community.

euphorbia wild plant which produces material similar to oil.

exports goods moved to another country.

fast breeding reactor part of a nuclear plant which burns and makes its own plutonium.

fossil fuels solids, liquids and gases burned to produce energy. These are exhaustible.

geothermal power use of heat locked inside the Earth to produce energy.

Greenpeace an organization which attempts to protect the environment.

growth pole place which attracts other industries.

hemisphere name given to the whole area found either north or south of the Equator.

hydroelectric power production of electricity by use of the force of water.

infrastructure the provision of roads, housing, sewers and water.

integrated water scheme these schemes provide hydroelectricity, flood control and irrigation water for growing crops.

multinational company a company which operates in many countries of the world.

NCB National Coal Board (from 1987, British Coal), nationalized organization responsible for operating the vast majority of UK collieries.

nuclear power production of electricity by the process of nuclear fission (the splitting of the nuclei of atoms of uranium or plutonium).

OPEC organization of petroleum exporting countries formed to protect the economic interests of major oil producers.

open cast mine mineral seams near the surface are exposed by removing the top layers of soil.

overproduction more of a product is produced than is needed.

plutonium this is a radioactive metallic element which is burned to produce nuclear energy.

pressurized water reactor (PWR) type of nuclear power plant.

reactor part of a nuclear power station that contains the core filled with nuclear fuel.

reafforestation planting of trees to replce those removed from an area.

refinery where oil is processed and broken down into a number of fractions, e.g. petrol.

Straits of Hormuz narrow sea-lane at the entrance to the Persian Gulf.

Three Mile Island site of nuclear accident in Pennsylvania.

uranium a radioactive metal used as a fuel in nuclear reactors.

INDUSTRY

CONTENTS

Contents

CLASSIFICATION OF INDUSTRY

Primary industries These are concerned with extraction of minerals, the utilization of forests, fishing and agriculture.

Secondary industries These process raw materials into manufactured goods.

Tertiary industries These include the so-called non-productive or service sectors of the economy, e.g. tourism, insurance and banking.

PRIMARY INDUSTRIES

MINERALS These may be found in the sea, in the atmosphere, e.g. nitrogen, in association with solidified magma, e.g. tin, lead, copper or zinc, or in beds within the earth, e.g. coal, iron ore and bauxite. These resources are finite in the sense that once man removes or extracts these minerals from the earth they are not replaced. As minerals in demand become scarcer, their value increases and some countries actually stockpile strategically important minerals to ensure continuity of future supply, e.g. uranium. Prices, and therefore the profitability of mineral extraction, fluctuate according to supply and demand. Over-production may mean a mineral becomes unprofitable and mining in a particular area may cease, either permanently or temporarily, e.g. tin mining in Cornwall in 1986. Technological advances, for example, the development of plastics, may mean a drop in demand for a particular mineral and a price fall in consequence.

If there are a number of potential sites containing a mineral in great demand, several factors may help to determine in what order a company may exploit them:

1 The quality of the ore Some iron ores, for example, are much richer than others. The haematite and magnetite of northern Sweden are approximately 70 per cent rich; the Jurassic ores of Lorraine only 30 per cent rich.

2 The quantity of ore contained within an area Those areas which possess enormous reserves are more likely to be mined first as the life expectancy of the project is likely to be greater, and the high capital investment in machinery and extraction likely to be more easily recouped.

3 The depth at which the ore deposit is found Surface deposits may be quarried or exploited by open cast methods. Shaft mines are more expensive to operate.

4 Geological problems Folding and faulting contort seams, make mining more difficult and therefore more costly. Thin seams, as opposed to thick deposits, also create cost problems.

5 Labour costs People who work in adverse conditions, e.g. extremes of temperature, command higher wages.

6 Transport costs If the mineral has to be moved huge distances and a transport network provided, the company must consider the economic return likely.

7 Political stability Those deposits in a country where political unrest is not a factor are likely to be preferred to those where it is a strong possibility.

8 Government demands The deal negotiated with a particular government in terms of mining rights, profit sharing, tax demands.

MINING METHODS

1 Open cast/pit
This is the cheapest form of mining and is used wherever the mineral is on or near the ground surface. As part of an increasing effort to avoid landscape despoliation, soil removed is stored nearby so that when the mineral is extracted the area can be re-landscaped. A dragline removes the overburden (rock which lies on top of the ore to be excavated) and after using dynamite, the ore is removed by huge mechanical diggers. Usually, the ore is then taken to a benefication plant where it is washed, sorted and crushed to remove any waste.

2 Adit/drift mining
This occurs where seams of the required deposit outcrop at the surface. If the angle of dip is not too great, tunnels are excavated and the material is brought to the surface by conveyor belt.

3 Shaft mining
Deeper deposits which are economically viable are reached by sinking vertical shafts and then constructing horizontal galleries.

4 Settlement tanks
In some areas, high pressure hoses are trained on hillsides containing

soft minerals such as kaolin, e.g. the St Austell area of Cornwall. The liquid is then collected into settlement tanks.

Fig 2.1 Shaft and adit mines

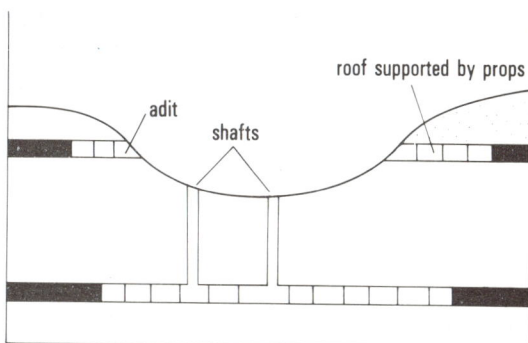

MINING OF BAUXITE

This mineral is the result of a breakdown, usually under tropical conditions, of certain types of igneous material. Material is leached out and deposited near the surface which means that it is possible to extract the ore using cheaper open cast methods. After extraction, the bauxite ore is separated from clay water and other impurities and this aluminium oxide is then purified by mixing with caustic soda to form alumina.

Fig 2.2 Bauxite mining in Jamaica

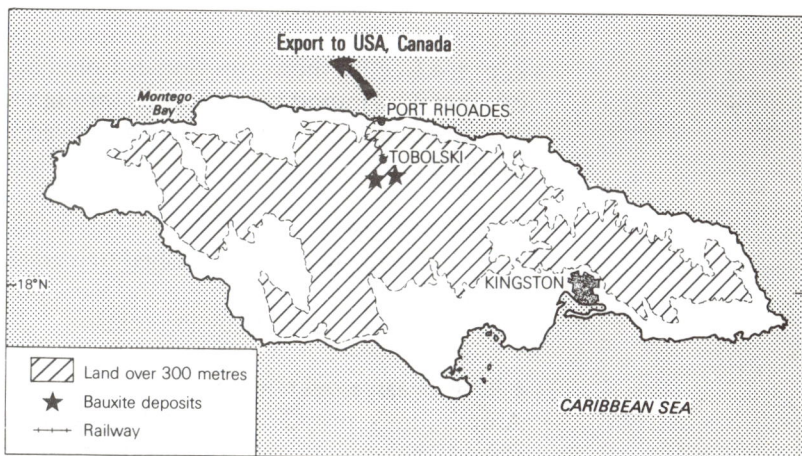

Australia is the world's major producer but three Latin American countries, Guyana, Jamaica and Surinam are very important. In Jamaica, ore is found in three areas of the island's interior. The main mining centres using open cast techniques and American capital are around Tobolski where there are extensive deposits of rich ore. Some of the bauxite is partly refined into alumina using coking coal from the USA. Most, however, is exported from Port Rhoades as bauxite to ports such as Baton Rouge in USA. Huge bulk ore carriers are used which reduce transport costs significantly.

The alumina is smelted by electrolysis to form aluminium. This process involves mixing the alumina with cryolite which is only found in commercial quantities at Ivigtut in south-east Greenland from where it is shipped to Copenhagen and sold on the world market. Smelting usually occurs in temperate areas rather than at the point where the bauxite is mined because the process requires huge amounts of electricity – usually, but not always, generated on site. The two superpowers, USA and USSR, dominate aluminium production.

ALUMINIUM SMELTING AT KITIMAT (W CANADA)

This site has a number of advantages:

1 Supplies of electricity from the power station at Kemano
This area of British Columbia has a number of advantages for producing electricity – a high annual rainfall (more than 1,000 mm per year) well distributed throughout the year, valleys for collecting water (by damming the Nechako river with the Kenney dam, an enormous reservoir collecting water from a large catchment area was created), few problems with winter freeze up, and the possibility of creating a good head of water by drilling a tunnel through the Coast Range from the reservoir to the Kemano power station.

2 Port facilities
Kitimat stands on the sheltered Douglas Channel – a deep water fjord kept ice free by the warm British Columbian Current. Bulk carriers can therefore import raw materials through the year.

Processed aluminium can also be moved by sea to Washington and California.

3 Government grants
The Canadian government wished to increase employment prospects in this area of British Columbia and were prepared to make a substantial contribution to construction costs.

4 Relatively easy access to markets
Aluminium's properties, including its strength, resistance to corrosion, malleability and conduction, mean that it is used extensively in aircraft production. California and Washington (Seattle) are important nearby west coast centres.

COPPER

The properties of refined copper, including its conducting ability, malleability and its ability in creating alloys mean that it has a large

Fig 2.3 Aluminium
smelting at Kitimat,
Canada

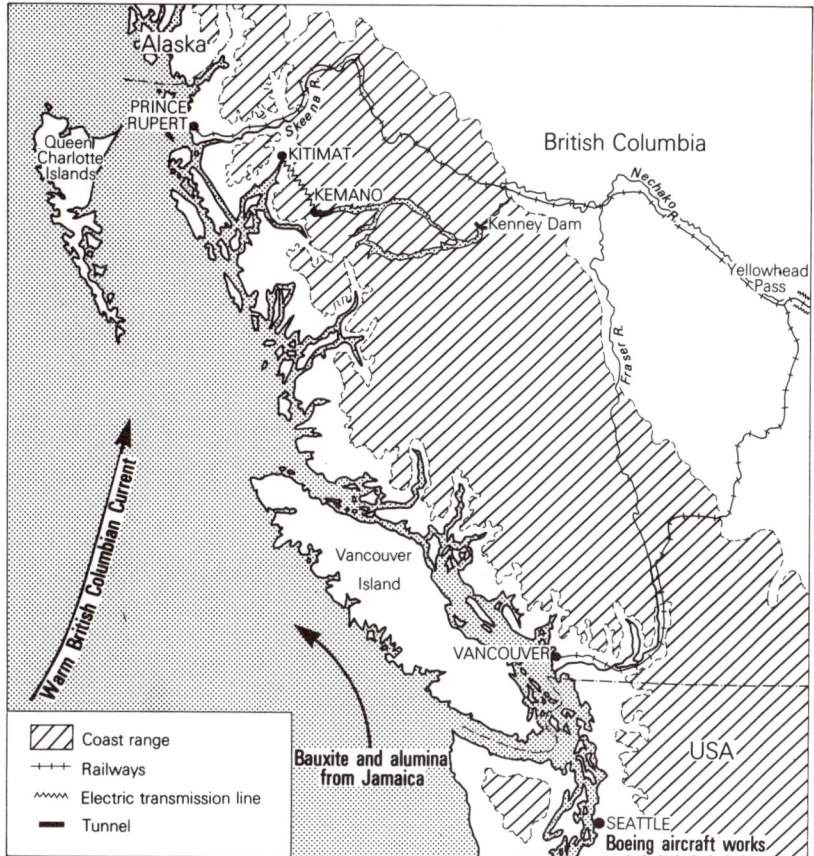

potential market. In consequence, it is often exploited in areas of difficulty as illustrated by the following examples:

1 Northern Chile

The mines at Chuquicanata and El Salvador are in the Atacama Desert on the fringe of the Andes (3,000 m). Large reserves which can be exploited by open cast methods compensate for the poor quality of the ore. Because of its remote location, materials, machinery, housing, labour and food must be brought to the area, thus adding to costs. Water supplies have to be pumped from high in the Andes or from the oasis town of Calama. Most of the mines have no processing plant and sell the ore to the state-owned mineral coroptation; two large American corporations (Anaconda and Kennecott) finance the larger-scale activities at Chuquicanata and El Salvador and the smelting facility at Portrerillos.

The ore that is smelted uses coal brought from Mediterranean (central) Chile. Smelting allows casting to blister copper which is ninety-eight per cent pure. Blister copper, and the small amount of

Fig 2.4 Copper mining in Chile

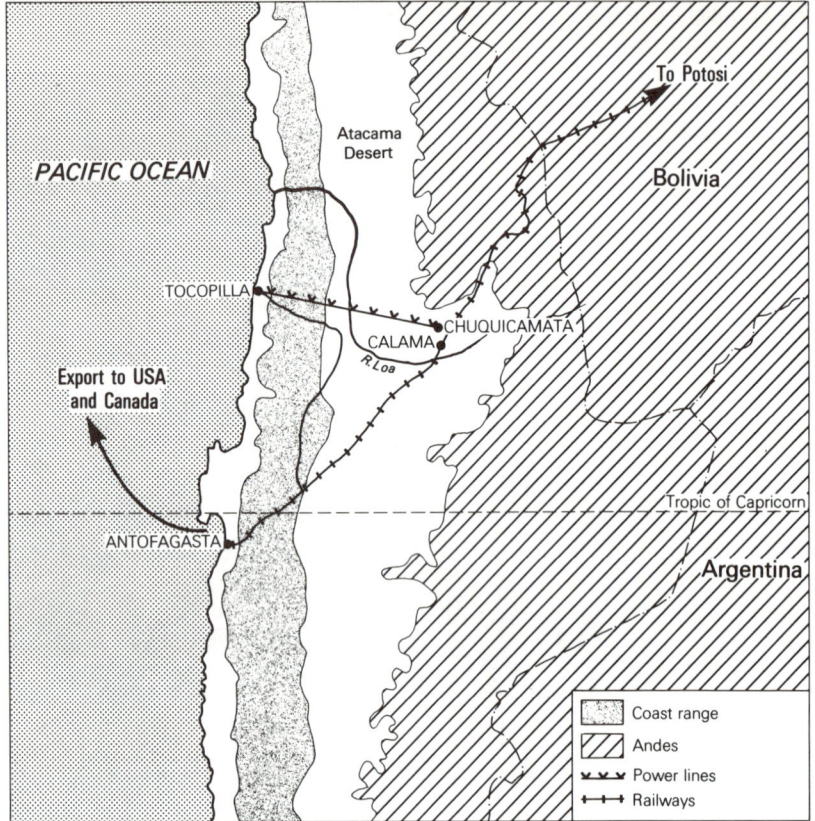

pure copper obtained by electrolytically refining blister copper (electricity is brought by cable from Tocopilla to Chuquicanata) is exported through the port of Antofagasta.

2 Zambia

The copper, of low grade, is obtained by shaft mines – some in excess of 3,000 ft deep. The demand for copper, along with the availability of large amounts of coal from the Zimbabwe coalfields, meant that these deposits were worth exploiting. In addition, the construction of the Kariba Dam (started in 1956) made available huge supplies of electricity. This dam, constructed where the Zambezi flows through a narrow gorge, created a lake 175 miles long and 20 miles wide, and supplies power not only to the copper belt but also to the cities of Harare and Bulawayo. As a landlocked state, Zambia relies upon rail access through other countries to export copper which accounts for in excess of eighty per cent of its export earnings. Western Europe and Japan are important customers.

Fig 2.5 Zambia – copper belt

TIN

Although output is dominated by South East Asian countries, particularly Malaysia, Indonesia and Thailand, Bolivia in South America is an important producer, a large proportion of its output coming from the area between Oruru and Uncia. The richer veins (ten per cent tin content) have been exhausted, leaving lean veins (less than one per cent tin content) to be exploited by shaft mines.

Because of the low tin content, much of the tin ore is concentrated to reduce its bulk before transportation and only a very small percentage of tin ore is smelted at Oruru, using power supplied from the HEP station at Corani.

Being landlocked, Bolivia must export tin through other states, particularly Chile and its ports of Arica and Antofagasta. This again increases costs as tariffs must be paid. These tariffs, along with transport and high mining costs (low ore grades, low productivity and little investment) make it extremely difficult for Bolivia to compete with the alluvial tin mined and exported more easily by Malaysia. In 1986, the Bolivian government decided to restructure Comibol, the state-owned mining company which resulted in a loss of 18,000 of the 28,000 jobs in the tin industry. Wage cuts were made – some workers receiving only one dollar per day.

Fig 2.6 Tin mining in Bolivia

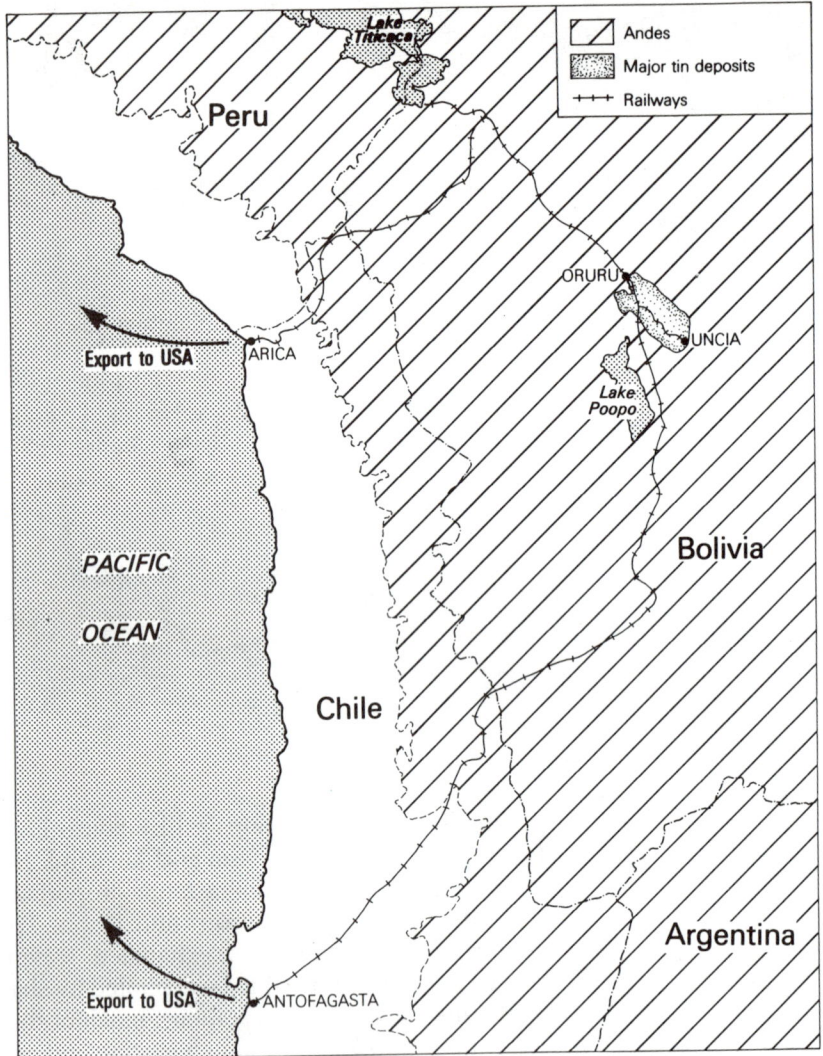

Cornwall

Cornwall has been an important producer of tin since the Roman era. The main mines at Geevor, near Land's End and Wheel Jane and South Crofty near Redruth, reflect the fact that this metal is found in mineral veins near the edges of granite bosses. Mining fortunes in this century have fluctuated because of competition from overseas – a decline in demand for example when cheap tin became available from Malaysia – the difficulty of mining some of the veins, and the fluctuation in prices paid to producers. Although output increased from 3.2 million tonnes per year to 5.2 million tonnes between 1975 and 1985, there were underlying difficulties as the world demand for tin plate was falling and Cornish production costs were in the region of

£7,500–£7,800 per tonne. World prices began to fall dramatically, and by October 1985, had reached £8,140 per tonne. At this point, with much tin stockpiled, formal trading on the London Metal Exchange was suspended with the result that prices on the unofficial market fell to £6,000 per tonne. The effect on Cornwall has been mine closures, a large number of redundancies, and additional problems for a county which has a high unemployment rate. The local economy will suffer significantly as it is calculated that the industry is responsible for providing the locality with some £27m annually.

IRON ORE

The iron ore content of ore bodies may vary enormously from the magnetite ore of Sweden with a 68 per cent metal content to the Jurassic deposits of Northamptonshire with a 35 per cent metal content.

As demand for ore grew, deposits of whatever grade began to be exploited, particularly when it became possible to increase metal content without necessarily smelting first. Transport costs in this case became more economical and steel centres could therefore use supplies from distant sources.

1 Kiruna – Gallivare

Fig 2.7 Iron ore mining in north Sweden

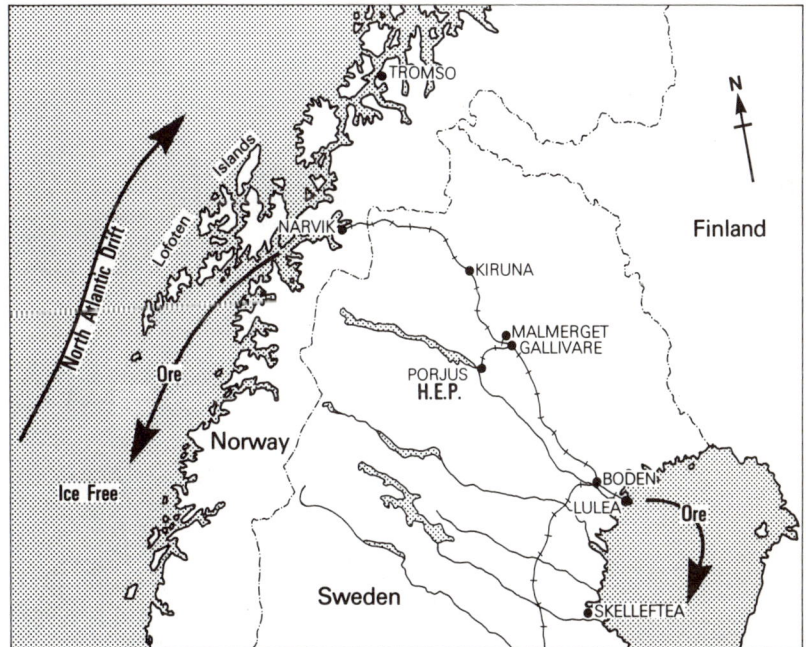

This area of northern Sweden was exploited initially in the latter part of last century. The ore is located at or near the surface, and in consequence, open cast techniques can be used, although shaft mining is increasing. This area has long cold winters and working conditions are hard; labour costs are high, reflecting both the working conditions and the difficulty of attracting suitable workers.

As the industry developed, a more efficient transport system was required to move the ore. A railway network was developed, linking the ore fields with both Lulea on the Gulf of Bothnia and Narvik in northern Norway. Lulea is only open to ships for seven months of the year as the Gulf freezes up; Narvik in contrast is open all year round because of the influence of the North Atlantic Drift, and therefore sixty per cent of the ore is exported from this port. A small proportion of the ore mined is used locally in the steel works at Lulea but most is transported by bulk carrier to steel centres in West Germany, the Netherlands and the United Kingdom.

2 Lorraine (France)
The ore is low grade (30–40 per cent) but mining is worthwhile because the deposits are large, at or near the surface and are not affected by folding or faulting – excavation is therefore relatively inexpensive. The area also has the advantage of excellent water transport to the Ruhr, Belgium and Luxemburg; the Moselle for example has been canalized to allow large barges to move the ore.

3 Schefferville (Canada)
The Schefferville deposits are large and of high quality. Their nearness to the surface means that open cast mining is possible, although excavation has to stop during severe winters. High grade ores at the western end of Lake Superior were worked out at the same time as

Fig 2.8 Iron ore mining at Schefferville

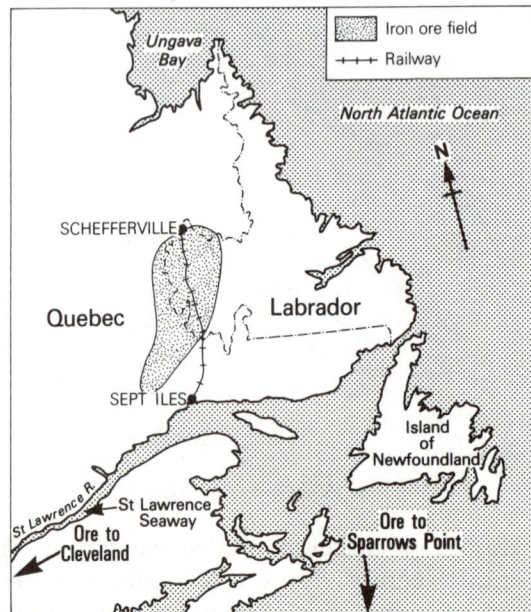

demand was increasing; in consequence, Schefferville has become increasingly important and large amounts of US capital have been invested.

The geographical location of the field (adjacent to the coast and the entrance to the St Lawrence) has been an enormous advantage. Ore is transported by rail from Schefferville to Sept Iles on the St Lawrence and from there by bulk carrier to West Europe, via the St Lawrence seaway and the Great Lakes, to lakeside steel plants such as Cleveland or to large east coast works such as Sparrows Point.

URANIUM

There are four principal uranium deposits:
(*a*)   on the Canadian Shield (west of Hudson Bay);
(*b*)   in South Africa, near Johannesburg;
(*c*)   on the Colorado Plateau of the USA;
(*d*)   in the Northern Territory of Australia.
Its importance is in weapon development, and increasingly, as a source of power because 1 lb of uranium will give as much energy as 1,300 tons of coal. Because of its high value, transportation costs are not significant but processing is very expensive.

Australia

The Northern territory of Australia has a number of uranium mining centres including Rum Jungle, Coronation Hill and the Edith River area. At Rum Jungle some of the ores can be mined by using open cast techniques thus reducing costs, although the climatic conditions mean that some of this saving is offset by increased labour costs. A local refinery reduces the ores to uranium oxide.

Output is mainly exported to Europe and Japan after moving by rail to the port of Darwin.

THE EFFECT OF MINING ON THE ENVIRONMENT

Mining can create problems by spoiling the natural landscape with waste heaps (the Cornish Alps around St Austell), buildings and communication networks. (See also p. 26 above.)

It can also have a tremendous effect on the lives of people living in an area as the following example shows.

The Amazon Basin in South America has recently been the site for extensive exploration for minerals by both Brazilian and multinational companies. A huge mineral field was discovered at Carajas and this is now producing iron ore using European and Japanese capital. Similar rock formations have been found in other parts of the Basin and companies have been granted prospecting rights in a number of these areas. The result is that one-third of the area occupied by seventy-seven Indian reserves (17 out of 52 million hectares) has been requisitioned by mineral companies. Many of these native people have had no contact with advanced societies and the fear is that their way of life

may be totally destroyed, that they will experience the social problems of others (e.g. the Eskimos and Aborigines) who have come into
contact with more advanced societies, and that their natural environment will be destroyed, leaving them unable to cope when mineral
exploitation ends.

FORESTRY

The commercial exploitation of the Earth's forests is mainly confined
to the boreal or temperate coniferous forest (softwood) and the
tropical broadleafed forests (hardwood).

TROPICAL BROADLEAF AREAS

Demand for these hardwoods has been increasing in the developed
world but there are a number of difficulties associated with their
exploitation, particularly the fact that the timber required does not
grow in stands (the same type of trees together) but tends to be
scattered throughout the forest. In consequence, to remove valuable
timber (e.g. mahogany or teak), large areas of other timber have to be
cleared and the forest cover is therefore removed, contributing to
problems of soil erosion.

Inaccessibility to roads, rivers and export ports is also a problem, as
is reliable labour. All these difficulties combined tend to increase
production costs.

Commercial exploitation, combined with shifting agriculture (see
Book 1, Chapter 2) means that tropical areas are quickly losing their
forest cover.

CONIFEROUS FORESTS

The conifer is found in broad bands across the northern areas of
North America and Eurasia. These trees, such as fir, spruce and pine,
are adapted to survive in a harsher climate: they have needle-shaped
leaves which reduce loss through transpiration, they have thick bark,
a tap root, their triangular shape is such that snow cannot accumulate
in sufficient quantities to cause damage, and wind damage is
minimized.

The timber industry is highly mechanized: felling is done by chain-
saw; logs removed by winch and large-tracked vehicles. 'Tote' roads
have been constructed to allow easy access to and removal of timber.
Where possible, rivers or lakes are used as a cheap form of transport –
large amounts of timber can be either towed or floated easily and
cheaply. Initially, exploitation was similar to that of tropical hardwoods at present: little attention was given to a scientific approach.
Now the coniferous areas are 'farmed': cleared land is replanted using
the strongest trees from nurseries; weaker trees removed and quick
growing species used where possible. In addition, many forests are

used as an important leisure resource, bringing additional financial benefits to local communities.

Most softwoods are used in the country of origin; only ten per cent of production enters world trade, the major exporters being Canada, USSR and Sweden.

The USSR has the largest forest resources of any country in the world and three-quarters of these are coniferous woodlands. There has been a major effort over many years to exploit timber resources commercially to meet increasing demand domestically and from overseas.

The major export ports for sawn timber are on the northern coasts of the Soviet Union: Archangel on the White Sea, Pechora on the Barents Sea, and Leningrad and Riga on the Baltic Sea. Pacific coast ports and those on the Black Sea handle exports to Japan and the Middle East.

In addition to farming forest resources scientifically the state, which controls both the forests and the organizations processing the timber, has invested heavily in modernizing saw mills.

The major use of timber is in the production of paper. The timber is either processed mechanically or chemically into pulp. Mechanical pulp is usually used for newsprint; chemical pulp in the production of better quality paper or cardboard.

Fig 2.9 Paper and newsprint production: Shawinigan

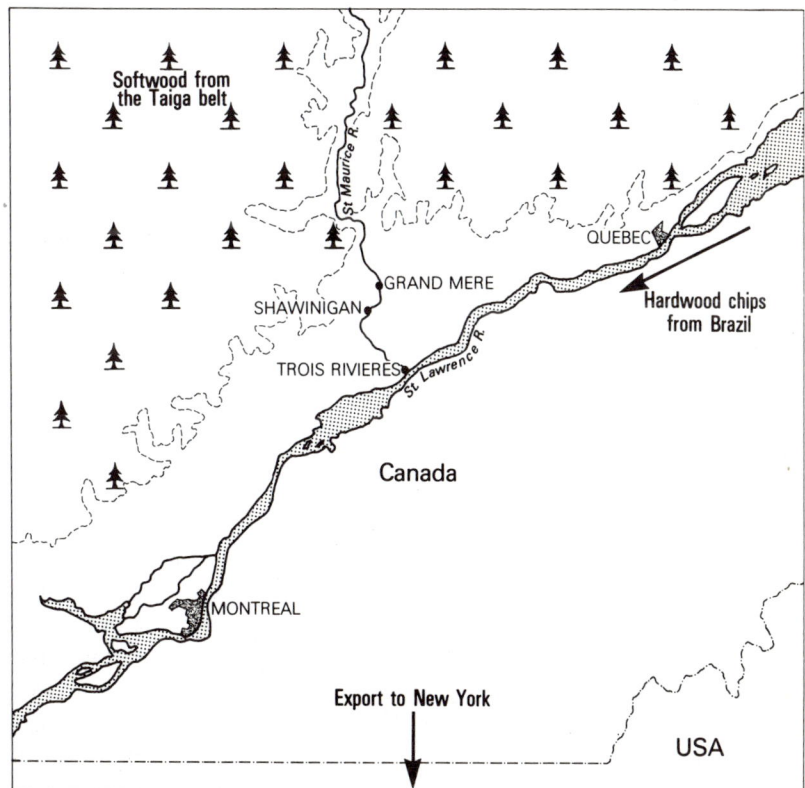

PAPER AND NEWSPRINT PRODUCTION AT SHAWINIGAN, EASTERN CANADA

The raw materials for this industrial complex are obtained from both local and overseas sources.

The wood is obtained from the coniferous forests to the north and is moved to the factory by using the St Maurice River. China clay is supplied by the UK (from Cornwall) and hardwood chips are brought from Brazil and Western Canada. The St Lawrence enables these materials to be transported by large ocean-going vessels.

The paper industry requires large amounts of water for processing the timber into pulp and Shawinigan is located alongside the river St Maurice; it also requires large amounts of power generated in this case by an HEP station at Grand Mere, further upstream on the same river.

New York is one of the centres of the USA publishing industry and provides a ready market for Shawinigan's products – as do the nearby Canadian cities of Montreal and Quebec.

SWEDEN

Sweden can be divided into four regions (see Fig 2.10 above). The timber industry is mainly confined to Norrland which has important stands of spruce and pine. Many of the forests are state owned and are exploited carefully. Because of its situation, this region is affected by acid rain (see Chapter 1 above) and there is growing concern at the potential damage this may cause. Although exploitation covers much of Norrland, the principal lumbering region is found south of the river Angerman. As in North America, the rivers which flow mainly in a north-west to south-east direction, are used to provide transport for cut timber. The coastal plain of Norrland is the site for a large number of saw and pulp mills, powered by electricity generated by stations sited along the fall line where there is a natural fall of water.

FISHING

Fishing is one of the oldest human activities. In many parts of the developing world it is used to supplement products of subsistence agriculture – in West Africa, South America, East Indies and China for example; in parts of the developed world it is an important commercial enterprise, particularly in North America, Europe and Japan.

Fish feed on microscopic organisms called plankton. These are found in large quantities, particularly where the sea is shallow (sunlight can percolate through this sea area), such as on the continental shelf, and where there is a mixture of warm and cold water currents. A sandy sea bed is advantageous as it provides a good spawning ground for fish.

Where these conditions exist, fish are plentiful and man 'harvests' them – particularly if he has been encouraged to do so by favourable

Fig 2.10 Four regions of
Sweden

geographical conditions – good natural harbours, proximity of
grounds to densely populated areas, inhospitable and unproductive
agricultural land nearby.

Commercial fishermen have harvested more efficiently during this
century without any thought for conserving stocks. Nets have
become larger in size and smaller in texture thereby catching larger
numbers of fish in total, including many young species. The result
has been a loss of breeding stock and many sea areas are thus
'overfished'. States have been quick to protect their waters by
extending fishing limits (some to 200 miles) but this has caused
problems with those countries who have fished an area which they
regard as 'traditional', e.g. the dispute between Iceland and UK over
waters off Iceland and the dispute between UK and Denmark over
waters off the UK.

In addition to overfishing some areas, 'inland' seas such as the

Mediterranean and Baltic have been badly affected by industrial pollutants which kill the fish.

Both individual nations and the EEC have attempted to regulate catches and thus conserve stocks. Herring fishing, for example, was forbidden for a four-year period. All of these measures mean that some fishermen have had their livelihood threatened. The large northern fishing ports of the UK (Hull, Grimsby and Fleetwood) have lost most, if not all, of their distant trawler fleets which used to fish off Iceland and northern Norway; inshore fisherman in south-west England have seen their industry decline despite their willingness to form co-operatives in order to market their catches more effectively. The entry of Spain into the EEC is further complicating the European industry as that country, which has an enormous fishing fleet, will be given phased access to all Community water.

NORWAY

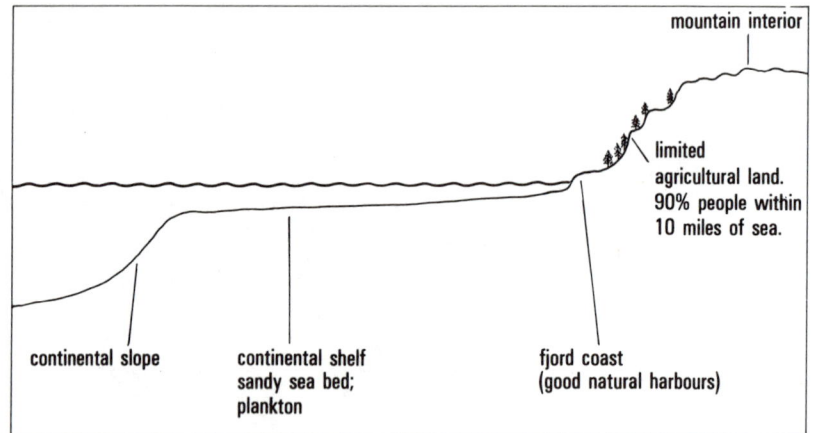

Fig 2.11 Fishing in Norway

The importance of the fishing industry in Norway is a result of ideal conditions for plankton (see page 78) and good spawning grounds for fish. In addition, Norway has a fjord coastline which provides good natural harbours. Other factors peculiar to the country are also significant: agricultural land is scarce; despite considerable state subsidies, only about three per cent of the land is cultivated and more than half of the country is over 600 m above sea level with steep slopes, bare rock, scree, low temperatures and heavy rainfall. Fishing has therefore traditionally been a supplement to agricultural activity.

Herring fishing was important off southern Norway but as stocks have been depleted, mackerel has taken its place. Cod is the important species caught off northern Norway, particularly in the area around the Lofoten Islands. Important fishing centres are at Tromso, Bergen, Hammerfest, Stavanger and Larvik. As in other parts of the developed world, the labour force directly involved in fishing is declining but the processing industry associated with it (canning, freezing and fertilizer manufacture) retains its importance.

Traditional activities such as whaling and sealing are no longer important because of the pressure to converse whales and the outcry against the culling of baby seals. Although Norway, along with the USSR and Japan, opposed the ending of whaling at the International Whaling Commission meeting in July 1985, the decision to classify the minke whale as a protected species hit the Norwegian industry hard. Japan will face similar problems from 1987 because of the decision to classify North Pacific sperm whales as a protected species.

HIGHLANDS AND ISLANDS OF SCOTLAND

Fishermen here have recently developed their industry rather differently than elsewhere in the UK. They tend to market their catches to Eastern European factory ships – 'Klondykers' – which anchor off major ports in the Western Isles. These foreign boats are thus able to 'use' waters which in normal circumstances they would have no access to. Local vessels benefit by having a reliable 'market'. The area has also begun to develop commercial fish farming with assistance from the EEC. Eight salmon farms (five on Lewis, one in Harris and two in South Uist) have opened since 1983.

NORTH AMERICA

Five areas are particularly important: Alaska, Washington, California (all west coast), Louisiana (Gulf Coast) and Newfoundland/Atlantic Provinces (north-east coast). Alaska's catch is small but of high value while Louisiana's is large in volume but of low value.

NEWFOUNDLAND/ATLANTIC PROVINCES

Fig 2.12 Bay of Fundy – fishing

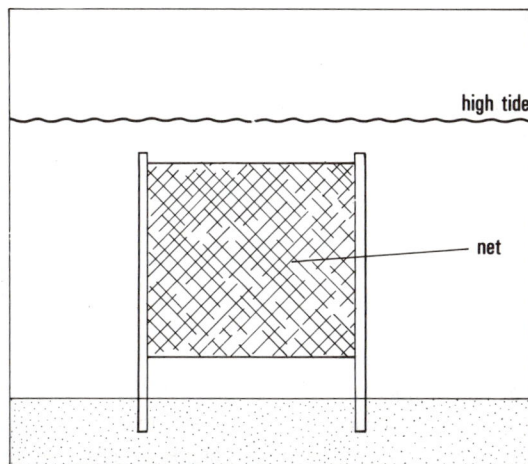

The Bay of Fundy has a large tidal range and local fishermen use this to advantage by constructing large fixed nets in the Bay. These are covered at high tide when fish swim into the nets; at low tide the fishermen can collect their catch.

Many small inshore fishing communities experience very low incomes and from the mid 1960s, the provincial government has encouraged as many of these communities as possible to migrate to larger settlements where there may be more diverse employment opportunities.

Offshore areas of importance include the Grand Banks. At one time commercial fishermen left mother boats in small craft and fished using lines. This was gradually replaced by more conventional methods but some of the natural dangers still remain, particularly fog, larger vessels heading towards the St Lawrence and the possibility of icebergs.

FALKLAND ISLANDS

In the search for fish, many large trawlers and factory ships utilize the waters off the Falkland Islands in the South Atlantic. Eastern Europe, Japan, Argentina and Taiwan all have large numbers of vessels in the area (650 in total) and the result is that fish stocks are badly depleted and the wild life of the Islands which depends upon fish for survival is now threatened. There is a distinct possibility that Britain will limit access to foreign trawlers by extending its fishing limit to 150 miles and granting a small number of licences. At present the waters are unrestricted and in 1985 some 381,000 tonnes of squid, blue whiting and other fish to the value of £250 million were taken. Fish caught are transferred to freezer vessels anchored in Berkeley Sound, a huge, natural deepwater harbour.

Any fishing limits of the type many advocate might create international problems, as Argentina, who claims sovereignty over the Falklands, has recently signed a fishing agreement with Russia and Bulgaria giving them access to waters Britain may well claim.

CHECKLIST ▶

PRIMARY INDUSTRIES

1   Factors determining mineral exploitation:
   (a)   Quality.
   (b)   Quantity.
   (c)   Geology.
   (d)   Costs.
   (e)   Political factors.
2   Methods of mining: open cast, adit, shaft and settlement tanks.
3   Examples of mining which illustrate how companies are prepared to spend huge amounts of money to overcome natural obstacles in order to obtain minerals.
4   The problem experienced when an area depends upon mineral exploitation: Bolivia and Zambia are finding that dependence upon one or two minerals can create economic and

social problems if prices fluctuate or costs increase. Political instability then becomes a distinct possibility.

5 Forestry – divided into the exploitation of hardwoods and softwoods.
6 'Farming' of the forests in softwood areas to provide sawn timber and the raw materials for the paper industry.
7 Fishing as a supplement for subsistence agriculture and as a commercial enterprise.
8 Different ways in which the industry operates and the changes that are taking place.
9 The problems of overfishing and the national and international steps taken to conserve stocks – these may lead to political differences between states and the contraction of fishing fleets.

SECONDARY INDUSTRIES

These are concerned with the processing of raw materials into manufactured goods.

FACTORS INFLUENCING THE LOCATION OF INDUSTRY

There are numerous factors influencing industrial location and their relative importance varies from area to area and industry to industry. Many of the present locations are a reflection of conditions operating many years ago and may not necessarily be the most favourable in the current circumstances. It is, however, very expensive to close down a plant and move elsewhere and some industries remain in long-established locations rather than change to a more favourable site. This is called industrial inertia.

ENERGY

During the Industrial Revolution of the last century, energy sources were perhaps the most important location factor. Water power was initially important and the first textile mills located where machines could be driven by flowing water. When steam power became important, factories moved to areas on or near coalfields. As electricity became a major source of energy, it allowed industry to locate in areas which were more advantageous as this source of energy could be transferred easily by cable.

RAW MATERIALS

Costs of raw materials are an important consideration, particularly for heavy industry. They do, however, exert less of an influence on modern industrial plants as bulk cargo can now be moved cost effectively by large ocean-going vessels or by train. Some industries using large amounts of bulky raw materials, such as modern steel mills, seek waterside sites; others who use raw materials which lose bulk during processing, for example, pulp mills, tend to locate near their source of supply; a gain in bulk during processing tends to lead to a market location, e.g. automobile assembly.

Raw materials used in light industries tend to be smaller in scale and quantity and allow the industry to locate on the most advantageous site, perhaps adjacent to a motorway.

LABOUR AND LABOUR COSTS

The availability of a pool of labour, whether skilled or unskilled, is an important consideration for a company. Heavy industries tend to consider mainly male employees; light industries, such as the assembly of televisions or the clothing industry, tend to employ more female labour.

Wage differences between countries, or regional wage variations within a country, are a factor in location decisions. High rates of pay are an important contribution towards product cost and can only be absorbed by high productivity.

MARKETS

Market locations are a particular attraction to light industries. They tend to produce consumer goods and it is obviously advantageous if they can locate within easy reach of large urban centres as this reduces transport costs.

COMMUNICATIONS

All industries are dependent on efficient communications in order to reduce transport costs of either raw materials or finished products. Access to navigable water may be important for importing raw materials and exporting manufactured goods – steel plants and chemical works for example. Port industries, which process oil seed or agricultural products, may develop at importing centres.

GOVERNMENT

Government influences industrial location in a variety of ways. State-owned industries are sometimes located in an area for reasons other than pure economics. They may, for example, be a way of reducing unemployment in a region or may be placed there for strategic purposes. The location of privately owned industries may be influenced by: (a) planning legislation formulated in such a way that local authorities can refuse planning permission; and (b) incentives provided by them which encourage companies to locate in a particular area.

In the UK, grants and susidies became available to industry in less prosperous areas during the 1960s. Economic decline in inner cities, increasing problems within regions (particularly in the North and Scotland), the decline in industries such as steel and shipbuilding, all contributed to the proliferation of state aid. In the 1970s and early

Fig 2.13 Regional aid in
the UK

Assisted areas
[ ] Development areas
[ ] Intermediate areas

Scotland

GLASGOW   EDINBURGH

NEWCASTLE UPON TYNE

Northern
Ireland
BELFAST

North

Yorkshire &
Humberside
LEEDS

North
West

MANCHESTER

East
NOTTINGHAM

West Midlands
NORWICH

Wales   BIRMINGHAM

Midlands   East Anglia

LONDON

CARDIFF
BRISTOL

South East

South West   SOUTHAMPTON

PLYMOUTH

Source. Department of Trade and Industry

1980s, there was a three-tier structure for regional aid: Special
Development Areas; Development Areas; and Intermediate Areas.
All were operated by the Department of Trade and Industry. In
November 1984, britain adopted a two-tier structure: Development
Areas, concentrated around the heaviest unemployment areas; and
Intermediate Areas which qualify for less assistance. Development
Areas offer equipment, machinery and building grants equivalent to
fifteen per cent of the value while Intermediate Areas have no special
incentives for investment. Both qualify for additional help based on
the capital, location and job needs of the project. There is also help
with factory rents, worker relocation expenses, training and research
and development grants.

In addition to these regional strategies there is also a multiplicity of
other assistance available through, for example, Enterprise Zones,

Fig 2.14 Enterprise Zones and Development Corporations – some examples

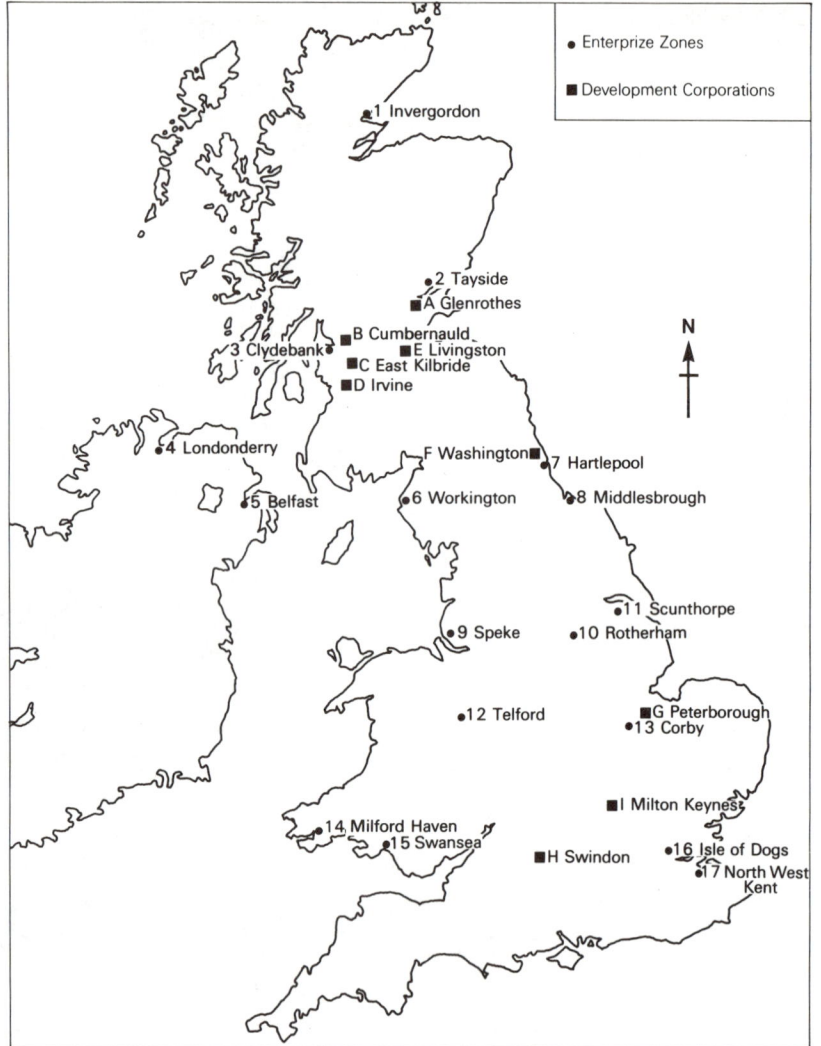

Steel Opportunity Areas, the New Town Development Corporation, the Highland and Island Development Board, and the decision to create Freeports.

Corby, for example, can run the advertisement in Fig 2.15 to attract industry.

Enterprise Zones were first created in 1981. They aim to provide areas within which there are simplified planning regulations. They are also exempt from local rates and receive 100 per cent allowances on capital expenditure for ten years. They appear to be relatively successful: Clydebank, for example, has developed an 80-acre site into a business park which has attracted some 200 new companies which employ over 3,000 people.

Local government also attempts to encourage industry to locate in

If you're planning to develop your business you need look no further than Corby.

Corby is a **Development Area** so your business gets the help of Development Area benefits. For most companies this means the better deal for them of either 15% grants on plant, machinery and equipment or £3000 per job created. There is also selective assistance for some job creating projects.

Corby is also a **Steel Opportunity Area,** and this means even more incentives.

Corby is **England's first Enterprise Zone.** There are factories off the peg, from 500 sq.ft. to 50,000 sq.ft., some of which are rates free until 1991. You can also choose from offices, warehouses, and high tech buildings.

Corby has **EEC aid for small businesses.** £1m is now available to aid efficiency.

Above all, Corby is right in the heart of England. Within 80 miles of London. 50 miles from Birmingham. Strategically placed for any business that needs fast, inexpensive, easy access to the big South East and Midland population centres.

However far you look, you will find that, as a total package for the success of your business, nowhere else comes within miles of Corby.

Development Areas

as defined by
The Department of
Trade and Industry
to take effect from 29.11.84

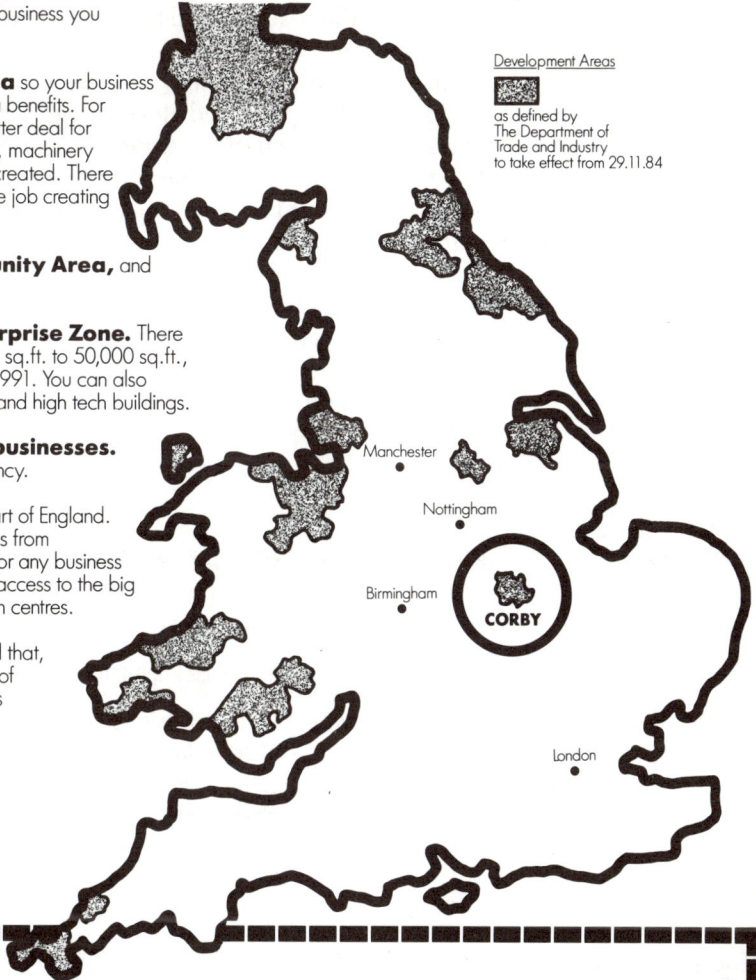

Manchester

Nottingham

Birmingham

CORBY

London

Name: _____

Company: _____

Position: _____

Address: _____

_____

_____ O 26/10

For more information, send to Fred McClenaghan,
Director of Industry, Corby Industrial Development Centre,
Douglas House, Queens Square, Corby, Northamptonshire
Telephone Corby (05363) 62571 Telex 341543
Prestel. Key ✴ 20079 #

CORBY WORKS

Fig 2.15 Corby's advertisement

its area by building industrial estates, offering rate reductions and looking favourably on planning applications from companies.

Many parts of Europe are adopting similar strategies to those of the UK. North-eastern France is attempting to encourage new industry to locate there to offset the economic impact of the industrial decline of the traditional large employers of labour, steel, textiles and coal. The

French government, in addition to offering large incentives, is improving the road and rail links in the area while the Calais Economic Development Corporation is offering loans for capital investment and grants for each job created. The French believe that these measures, along with the proposed development of the Channel Tunnel, will regenerate this region by attracting companies from all over Europe, including some from Britain. The European Economic Community attempts to provide financial assistance to areas experiencing difficulties through its Regional Development Fund, through the European Social Fund now particularly geared to helping the young unemployed, and through specific monies directed to providing relief for areas suffering from mine and steelwork closures. Britain has obtained almost £2,000 million from the Regional Development Fund alone including over £30 million to aid developments in the motor car industry on Merseyside.

CHECKLIST ♦

FACTORS INFLUENCING LOCATION OF SECONDARY INDUSTRIES

Factors influencing industrial location include:

1 Energy ⎫
2 Raw materials ⎭ becoming less important.
3 Labour availability and costs – differences between countries and regions may be significant.
4 Markets – a particular attraction to light industry.
5 Communications – transport costs of materials and manufactured items.
6 Governements – through state-owned industries; planning legislation; development area status enterprise zones.

THE STEEL INDUSTRY

Local supplies of iron ore were the basis of the early smelting industry (using charcoal) in countries such as the UK, USA, Brazil and Germany. As the industry's technology developed, coal became important as a source of power and new works tended to concentrate on the coalfields of the UK, the eastern United States and Germany.

As demand for steel increased, local ore began to be worked out and it became necessary to seek supplies elsewhere. In Europe, for example, the high grade iron ore deposits of Kiruna and Gallivare in Sweden became important for the industry of both the UK and Germany; in the USA steel works on the Appalachian coalfields began to purchase iron ore excavated from extensive deposits around the shores of Lake Superior.

The necessity to move vast quantities of ore in bulk began to change the location of new steel plants. In Europe, investment tended to be concentrated on constructing large plants at coastal locations. In the USA, steel making began at sites on the Great Lakes, e.g. Cleveland and Gary (which could obtain Appalachian coal cheaply and had waterway connections with the Superior deposits) and on the east coast, e.g. Sparrows Point, where tidewater sites meant that huge ore carriers could bring ore relatively cheaply from, for example, Schefferville, Venezuela and Brazil.

Steel producing capacity eventually proved to be too great. Many countries now produce in excess of their national demand and their export potential. The consequence has been a rationalization of production and a restructuring of the industry. Jobs have been lost and production concentrated at the more economic location. Older inland plants in the UK, in the Appalachians of the USA and in Europe have closed or drastically cut back production, while newer tidewater plants have generally survived. Governments have sometimes moved to protect their own industry and prevent more job losses by cutting back on imports: the US government in 1983 introduced measures to reduce the imports of certain specialized steels from Europe.

Export markets for the traditional producers have declined as many developing countries regard a domestic steel industry as a necessity in their move towards creating an industrial base. Some countries even regard a steel industry as a prestige project and a mark of their development; the demand for self-sufficiency in this commodity led at one time to the proliferation of backyard furnaces in China – an error the government quickly rectified.

NIGERIA

Nigeria is an example of a country attempting to develop its own steel industry. When its proposed programme is complete it will still not be in a position to meet demand but will cut back significantly on the four million tonnes of steel it must currently import.

Planning began in the 1960s, but it was not until the 1970s when the country had large revenue surpluses due to oil exports, that the strategy to develop two integrated plants and three rolling mills was finalized.

The first integrated plant at Aladja in Bendel state uses the direct reduction steel process but this needs imported iron ore from Brazil and Liberia which is of better quality than Nigerian ore. The other integrated plant at Abedkuta is almost complete and is planned to open in 1988. Its site in Kwara state was chosen because of its proximity to the Itakpe ore deposits and the Lafia/Obi coal deposits. The problems are that the Itakpe ore deposits discovered in the 1970s and exploited since 1980 are low in quality and therefore unsuitable for some steel processes. In addition, Lafia coal is high in sulphur content and may not be wholly suitable for use in steel production. Solutions are possible but may be expensive.

Itakpe ore will certainly need to be enriched before use and the plant to do this is yet to be constructed. Coal reserves are large (1.5 billion tonnes) but their exploitation has not been a priority for successive governments, and in consequence, output has plummeted.

When the new steel industry is fully operational, it will require more power than that generated at the moment to meet all of the country's needs and it is therefore vital that the mining industry becomes effective and efficient.

Even if the political will and the revenue exists to develop the plants, improve ore quality and improve coal production, problems will still remains for the new industry. Inter-dependent plants and mills will be hundreds of miles apart in some cases, transport will be a difficulty – a rail network needs to be built from the iron ore mine to the plant at Abedkuta – and Nigerian steel will be competing with that of other efficient producers for a share of a smaller internal and external market.

BRAZIL

Brazil is an example of a developing country which has successfully built its own steel making capacity. Iron ore and limestone were obtained from the state of Minas Gerais and the industry initially located in this area, particularly around Belo Horizonte. In 1946 a new plant was built at Volta Renonda, north-west of Rio de Janeiro, which was a move towards a more market orientated location. Although the state of Minas Gerais continues to be important, market orientation now dominates and new plants have been constructed, mainly in the Sao Paulo and Rio areas. These use ore from Minas Gerais and coke imported from the USA. More than forty plants now produce steel but Brazil has begun to experience the problems of other major producers as demand declines and competition increases (see also Book 1, Chapter 5).

USA

The most important early iron smelting area in the US was in New England where local iron ore and charcoal were used. As coal became an important source of power, the industry migrated to two coalfields of the Appalachians where good coking coal, limestone which acts as a flux and iron ore were available. Cities such as Pittsburgh, standing on the west Pennsylvanian bituminous field, therefore became important steel centres. When local iron ore was worked out, the extensive deposits at the western end of Lake Superior in, for example, the Marquette and Mesabi ranges were used. The Great Lakes provided a convenient and cheap means of bulk transport across the continent for this ore.

Iron ore destined for Appalachian plants was transferred from Great Lakes ore carriers to the railway network at ports along the shore of Lake Erie. The logic was obvious – to develop steel centres at these 'break of bulk points' where coal and ore could both be obtained. Steel companies could obtain land cheaply to build large integrated plants, the Lakes provided an unlimited supply of water for processing purposes, and industries which used steel were

Fig 2.16 Steel centres in the Great Lakes region

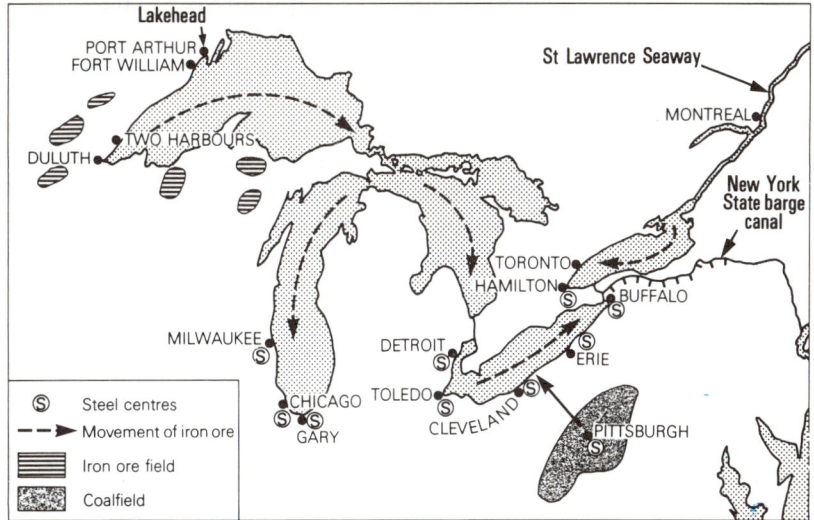

developing locally a ready market for any production. Cities such as Cleveland, Erie and Toledo became important centres and were quickly followed by others sited on both Lake Erie and Lake Michigan (including Chicago and Gary).

As ore imported from overseas became both necessary and economically viable to obtain, production began at a number of east coast sites. The best known of these is at Sparrows Point, the largest tidewater plant in the world. Large bulk carriers bring ore from Venezuela, Brazil and Schefferville to the plant's own docking facility. Coal is obtained from the Appalachian fields and its products can be marketed locally.

There are centres within the US which do not fit neatly into this pattern. The Fontana plant near Los Angeles in California was built during the Second World War and was sited for strategic reasons; the Birmingham plant in Alabama obtains all its raw materials locally, serves the developing southern markets and has been assisted by the construction of canalized river links with Mobile on the Gulf which allows it to import higher grade ores.

While the industry in the USA is facing the same problems as other world producers, it is the old-established Appalachian centres which are under greatest threat. The plants here are generally outdated and have little room for expansion in the narrow valleys. The scale of decline can be seen by the following statistics for one Pittsburgh plant:

1981 – 10,000 employees; 1985 – 700 employees. 14,000 further jobs in the area are threated by the problems of the Wheeling Pittsburgh Co-operation. Some of the smaller steel companies in the Appalachians are attempting to make their concerns more viable by reducing their wages and benefit rates from 21.40 dollars per hour to 17.50 dollars per hour. If their workers accept, it may lead to wage cuts at the large corporations, such as US Steel, Bethlehem Steel, LTV Steel and Inland Steel.

UK

As in the USA, local iron ore was the basis of the industry along with proximity to coal and limestone. Plants therefore tended to concentrate on coalfields in Wales, Central Scotland and in north and north-east England. As local ore was worked out, it became necessary to develop sites on the Jurassic limestone belt running in an arc from Scunthorpe to Corby and to import ore from overseas, e.g. Sweden, Spain and Venezuela.

Because of cost advantages, new investment tended to concentrate on or near coastal locations but inland works continued to produce because of continuing demand and factors of industrial inertia.

As demand fell, a cutback in capacity occurred. Many inland steel works and older works near the coast closed, e.g. Consett, Bilston, Ebbw Vale, Corby and Shotton, and production is now concentrated at Port Talbot, Llanwern, Redcar, Scunthorpe and Ravenscraig. These last two use deepwater terminals at Immingham and Hunterston, respectively.

Rationalization has still to be completed and the future of one of the British Steel Corporation's three ship mills which are currently operating at only seventy per cent capacity (Ravenscraig, Port Talbot and Llanwern) is in doubt. Ravenscraig's closure, for example, would add to the unemployment problems in Scotland but its future will be considered in 1988 and is probably more uncertain following the closure of the Gattcosh finishing mill which processes about twenty per cent of its output.

The EEC forecast of a further decline in demand, along with its call for an end to all state aid by 1987, do not augur well for the industry.

WEST GERMANY

The traditional location of the industry is on the coalfields of the Ruhr and Saarland. The Hanover area of the North German Plain is also important, using local low grade ore from the Salzgitter region and Ruhr coal. As in other states, coastal sites have developed, particularly at Bremen and Hamburg, both of which have access to imported ore and coal, along with local markets for steel in the shipbuilding and engineering industries, which has seen production decline from 17.4 m tonnes in 1977-8 to 11.7 m tonnes in 1986-7.

Duisburg is a good example of the traditional steel making region. Power and coking coal are provided by Ruhr coal, originally mined by open cast and adit mines but now shaft mined. Limestone is obtained from the Sauerland Plateau and iron ore is imported from Sweden (Kiruna/Gallivare area) and lower grade ore from Lorraine in France. Cheap water transport of imported ore has been the key to this area's survival – the River Rhine–Herne canal and the Dortmund–Ems canal

Fig 2.17 Steel at Duisburg

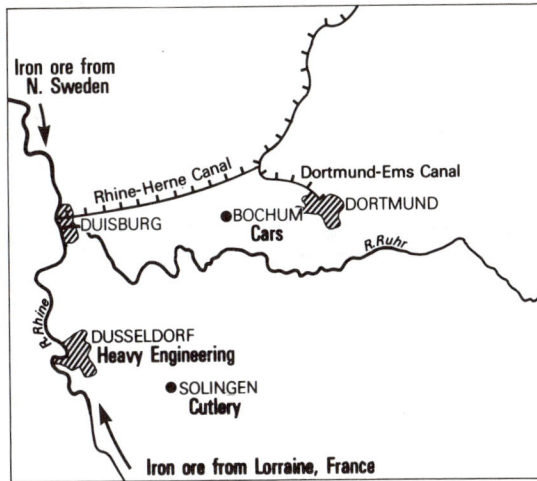

all connect the area with the sea; the canalized river Moselle is used to transport Lorraine iron ore to the Rhine system.

Overproduction of steel meant a large loss in labour in 1975 and again in the early 1980s. The Federal Government has accepted assistance from the EEC Regional Development and Social Funds to alleviate the worst effects of the industry's decline and the state government has also tried to attract new industry by providing grants and making the environment more attractive. Spoil heaps have been levelled, areas of waste replanted, lakes and river walks cleared for recreational use.

FRANCE

The traditional areas are the coalfields of Lorraine, the Nord and the small fields of the Massif Central. Low grade Lorraine one is used in the steel plants of the Lorraine coalfield at Nancy, Thionville and Longwy and on the coalfields of the Massif Central, while the Nord field uses imported Swedish ore. The newer developments are based on the highly integrated plants at Dunkirk (North Sea) and Fos-sur-Mer (Mediterranean). Both were able to develop on cheap, flat sites; their coastal location was ideal for importing raw materials, particularly high grade non-phospheric ore.

CHECKLIST ◗

THE STEEL INDUSTRY

1 The steel industry was originally located where coal and black band iron ore were found.
2 As ore ran out, more had to be imported or moved from elsewhere in the country.
3 Tidewater and break of bulk points became important, particularly where large amounts of cheap, flat land were available.

4 Overcapacity meant that production was concentrated at large integrated plants on coasts or lakes.
5 Many traditional steel making areas have now lost their plants and steelworkers their jobs.
6 Increasing competition for markets as the Third World begins to produce steel.

SHIPBUILDING

Shipbuilding has been an important industry in many countries for centuries. Peter the Great of Russia in the seventeenth century used British expertise to improve the quality of his ships. Countries which had a maritime tradition, because of their use of the surrounding seas for fishing or because they developed trading links overseas through their colonization of other areas, needed to have large fleets.

During the nineteenth century, technological advances resulted in wooden ships being replaced by iron and steel vessels and the industry then tended to concentrate in those coastal areas near or on coalfields which had access to steel.

Britain, with its maritime tradition, dominated the commercial production of ships: before the First World War (1914–18) it built 60 per cent of the world's merchant vessels. That situation changed gradually at first, but after 1945 its share of the world market declined rapidly (1951 – 38 per cent) and now (1986) under 2 per cent of the world's ships.

One of the major problems facing all producers is the volatility of demand. World trade varies enormously from decade to decade, and with it the orders for new ships; the nature of the demand changes rapidly – bulk carriers at one time, oil rigs and support vessels at another. Forward planning is therefore extremely difficult and in addition to these problems, there is increasing competition between nations and shipyards for the work available. Price is therefore important, as is the ability to deliver on time. Nations who have become interested in commercial shipbuilding relatively recently have the advantage of newer, more technically advanced yards which have had a great deal of capital investment, and a labour force which is prepared to be flexible in terms of doing whatever job needs to be done. Competition is such that many governments have been prepared to provide subsidies to their own yards in order to obtain orders.

UK

The UK is typical of an old established shipbuilding area which is declining. For over 100 years it was a shipbuilder for the world and its industry, despite problems in the 1920s and 1930s, experienced boom times during the Second World War, the Korean War and the Suez Crisis of the early 1950s. During the 1950s and 1960s, however, many companies did not take the opportunity to invest money in order to modernize their yards and the industry was also hindered in its attempts to obtain better productivity by workers insisting on doing only one particular job. This meant that sometimes they had to wait several days while other tradesmen completed a section of work before they could restart exercising their particular skill. Two reports, the Geddes Report of 1965 and Commission on Industrial Relations in 1972, both commented on the adverse effects of these long-established attitudes.

These two facts gradually meant that shipbuilding yards in Britain, rightly or wrongly, got the reputation of not delivering on time, and not pricing as competitively as others. It is a fact that it takes twice as many man hours to build a ship in the UK as it does in the *best* yards in West Germany, France and Denmark.

Many overseas companies placing orders were concerned at the dispute record in British shipyards. Disputes are, however, not the problem that many suggest; certainly since 1977 they have been infrequent and local. The major problem is illustrated by the following statistics which show the cut back in the world demand for shipping and the increasing competition from other countries for available orders. In 1973, 130m tonnes of ships were ordered, the UK obtaining 7m tonnes. In 1985, 30m tonnes of ships were ordered, the UK obtaining 0.8m tonnes. In this situation even British companies will not necessarily buy British – they seek the best commercial deal on offer.

Competition, lack of investment, and the changing nature of demand which could sometimes not be met by British yards (particularly those sited on narrow estuaries or rivers), has meant that the state-owned British Shipbuilders, formed in 1977, has cut back capacity. Yards have closed with many people being made redundant; in 1986 an additional 3,500 jobs have gone, some in areas of high unemployment like the North East and Scotland. British Shipbuilders merchant ship building activities are now concentrated at Govan on the Clyde and at Wearside. Its workforce in total will number 6,500. It appears that only the specialist naval yards, e.g. Vickers at Barrow, Vosper Thorneycroft on the Solent, have a relatively secure immediate future. Many former BS yards now in private hands will face increasing difficulties, although BS itself is likely to continue even if it trades at a loss.

EUROPE

Europe is facing similar problems to those of the UK. Denmark, Sweden, Norway and France have all been affected by the decline of their shipbuilding industry. The natural advantage of deep-water sheltered sites, e.g. Norway, Sweden and the Loire in France; availability of steel products from a domestic industry; and an engineering tradition, have all been offset by competition from Japan and Korea. In order to alleviate the problems of unemployment, the EEC has provided heavy subsidies to its member states which can be worth between 20 and 25 per cent of the final cost. This is still proving insufficient to halt the decline.

GERMAN EXAMPLE: BREMEN/BREMERHAVEN

This area has the advantage of a deep sheltered estuary (Weser), easy and cheap access to raw materials (e.g. steel from the Ruhr via the Dortmund–Ems–Weser canal), steel plate from within the Bremen/ Bremerhaven conurbation, and marine engines from Bremen. It has a ready market, particularly for bulk carriers which are used to transport iron ore from north Sweden to Germany.

Candidates are advised to make their own notes on France.

JAPAN AND KOREA

Together these account for sixty-six per cent of the world's merchant fleet construction. Until 1945, the Japanese were a strong imperial nation and this encouraged the industry. After the Second World War, Japan progressively became an important industrial and trading nation and this meant developing a strong merchant navy, particularly large vessels to import raw materials in bulk. Shipyards were extended (cheap land along the coastal plain was available) and modernized for this purpose and the Japanese were therefore in the ideal position to take advantage of the emerging world demand for large bulk carriers. An efficient steel and engineering industry had evolved which could meet their demands. The industry was also helped by the paternalistic nature of their major manufacturing companies; the company looks after its workers both economically and socially, and in consequence, industrial unrest is virtually non-existent. This attitude of flexibility has allowed the Japanese to react quickly to emerging demands and at present they are moving away from constructing bulk carriers towards constructing smaller more specialist vessels.

The Japanese government has also given its shipyards tremendous support and protection. The Japanese currency, the yen, is under-valued which helps exports; specialist banks provide the customer with large, long-term, cheap loans; companies are encouraged by the government to share technical expertise. The main yards are at Tokyo, Yokohama, Nagoya and Kobe/Osaka.

Korea is emerging as a major threat to Japanese supremacy. In 1974 it was unimportant as a world producer; by 1983 it had captured nearly one fifth of the world market. Its advantage lies primarily in its recent development; shipyards are modern with every technological aid; they are flexible enough to build whatever the customer requires, although production is concentrated on only four large supertanker yards including the world's largest shipyard owned by the Hyundai Company; labour relations are good; prices are competitive as their industry evolved in a competitive era. For example:

Lighthouse tender contract 1986
BS   Hyundai
£14.5m (£13.5m with subsidy)   £9.5m

CHECKLIST ▶   SHIPBUILDING

1   The reasons for the decline of Britain which once dominated the industry.
2   The need for flexibility as demand is volatile and unpredictable.
3   Many nations are chasing available orders.
4   The reasons for the emerging dominance of the Far East.
5   Governments subsidize their yards so that they can compete on world markets.

THE CHEMICAL INDUSTRY

The Industrial Revolution of the nineteenth century marked the start of the commercial and industrial production of chemicals. The raw materials of this industry include such things as coal, petroleum, natural gas, salts and sulphur, along with the by-products of industrial processes such as the manufacture of steel.

The major European producers are the UK, France, the Netherlands, Italy and Switzerland. Switzerland is particularly important as a manufacturer of pharmaceuticals (medicines and drugs) and major companies based there, such as Hoffman la Roche, spend millions of pounds annually on the research and development of new products.

UK

The nineteenth-century chemical industry was centred on the Cheshire/South Lancashire area and the Tees estuary. Both these areas had access to local salt fields, local coal, large amounts of river and estuary water and Pennine limestone. Their coastal location meant that they were in a position to continue to develop their product range by importing other raw materials such as vegetable oils and potash.

During the present century, the production of petrochemicals has become increasingly important. Both these traditional areas could import oil easily via the Mersey and Tees estuaries. With the development of Britain's offshore oil and gas fields, the Tees was again in an ideal situation. Imperial Chemical Industries (ICI) uses North Sea gas from the Ekofisk field (see page 40) at its Billingham plant. It has built the largest gas conversion complex in Europe and the methane gas is transformed into ammonia for fertilizers and into methanol to make a wide range of petrochemicals.

Other centres in the UK reflect the distribution of oil refineries, for example, Furley in Southampton Water, the Thames Estuary and the London area, South Humberside.

Between 1979 and 1982 the industry in Britain experienced problems and despite a recovery in the mid 1980s, it is likely that more jobs will be lost, imports will increase, and large companies will attempt to expand into the more flourishing European and American markets.

FRANCE

The geographical distribution of the industry is widespread but a pattern can be identified based upon raw materials, power and markets. Raw materials are provided by:

1 Coalfield locations, e.g. the Nord coalfield, using hydrocarbons and the by-products of steel production.
2 Oil refineries along the Lower Loire Valley, the Seine and the Marseilles/Fos-sur-Mer area of the Mediterranean. Fos-sur-Mer, for example, manufactures chlorine and polyethylene.
3 The salt deposit of Lorraine which is used by the chemical works of the Meurthe valley.

Power

The cheap production of hydroelectricity has attracted the chemical industry to both the Alps and the Pyrenees. An area south of Lourdes, for example, has become a centre of the industry and the French government hope that developments in more remote areas will act as a growth pole to stimulate other industrial developments.

Market potential has attracted the industry to cities such as Bordeaux, Marseilles and Paris, areas which contain the companies involved in the industrial processes which use chemicals.

WEST GERMANY

The industry is mainly concentrated in the Rhine–Ruhr region, particularly at Düsseldorf, Cologne and Mannheim/Ludwigshafen.

Cologne
1 **Power** Electricity is provided by the lignite burning power station at Frimmersdorf near Cologne.

2 **Raw materials** The basic raw material is imported oil from the Middle East and the North Sea. This can be brought cheaply by using either the Rhine (barges of up to 6,000 tons can reach Cologne) or by the extensive pipeline network which crosses Germany; the north-west pipeline from Wilhelmshaven to Cologne is particularly important. Lignite is moved from the Ville field and coal gas piped from the Ruhr coke works.

3 **Markets** The textile centre of Wuppertal provides a market for dyes.

NORTH AMERICA

The same factors (raw materials, power and markets) can be used to account for the distribution pattern:

1 Raw materials and power

The coalfields of the Appalachians were an early centre for the industry providing coke oven by-products from the steel industry.

The Edmonton area of Canada has local supplies of oil and natural gas from the Athabaska Valley; the Gulf Coast plants at Houston, Corpus Christi and Beaumont-Port Arthur have access to the salt, sulphur, oil and natural gas deposits of the South; the Eastern Seaboard and Great Lakes cities can obtain raw materials cheaply because of their break of bulk location.

2 Markets

(*a*)   In cities of the North-East, Mid-West and California, chemicals have a huge market potential in, for instance, plastics, drugs and motor car manufacturing.

(*b*)   The Gulf Coast works and Edmonton service the Cotton Belt and prairies, respectively.

CHECKLIST ◆

THE CHEMICAL INDUSTRY

1   The major European producers are the UK, France, Netherlands, Italy and Switzerland.
2   The importance of petrochemical production.
3   Location is determined by three factors: raw materials, power and markets.

DEVELOPING TECHNOLOGIES

At the same time as the more traditional industries such as steel, engineering and shipbuilding were declining, the economically and technically advanced nations had begun to develop industries based upon new technologies, particularly micro-electronics. For more than a decade, American-based companies dominated the industry but gradually other nations developed their own capacity, either through American investment and expertise or by the efforts of their own manufacturers.

USA

The largest concentration of high technology companies in the USA is found in the Santa Clara Valley of California which stretches from Stanford to San Jose. Developments in this valley, south of San Francisco, are centred around Palo Alto and some 3,500 companies employ over 500,000 people.

Fig 2.18 Silicon Valley, California

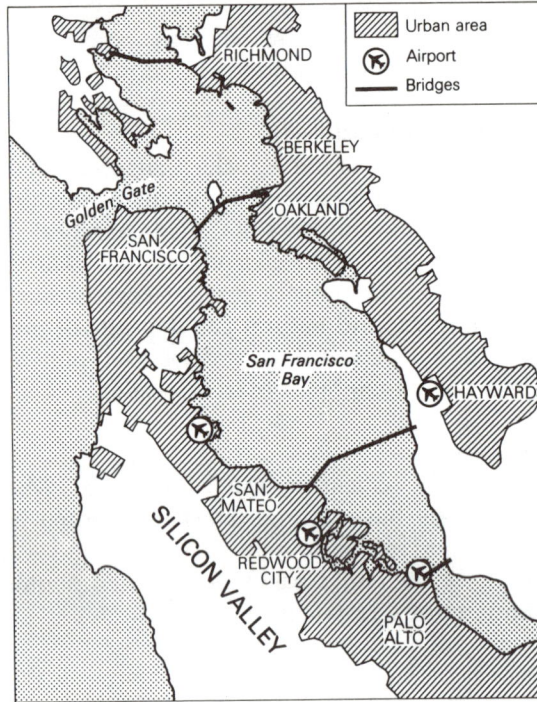

The attractions of this area to the industry were:

1 Stanford University with its research and development facilities.
2 The availability of well-trained and skilled personnel.
3 Access to airports – the products are high value and not bulky.
4 The pleasant environment and climate.

For over a decade the industry expanded but in the mid-1980s there was a tremendous slow down in demand for the products of those companies manufacturing personal computers. Forecasts indicate that by 1987, only 75 of the original 350 companies will still be operating. Two domestic factors appear to have contributed to falling sales, which have led in turn to fierce price cutting;

(a) Publicity.

(b) Technological advances. Home computers were oversold by the manufacturers, and their promises of more and more advances in technology encouraged the business community to delay purchasing.

The third factor is increasing competition from the Japanese – some of their microchips cost one-seventh of those manufactured in America – coupled with an inability to obtain greater access to Japanese markets. The situation is such that there is a distinct danger of a protectionist lobby in the USA which will seek to limit Japanese imports.

Silicon Valley has become a victim of its own success. Expansion has meant development on agricultural land in the Valley; house prices are high because residential land has become scarce; high house prices have encouraged people to commute to work from further afield; commuting, plus job stress, have led to a poorer quality of life which in turn has meant that companies and individuals are tending to look for locations or jobs elsewhere.

The industry's growth potential, however, remains enormous for those companies at the forefront of technology or producing the right product at the right time. Compaq, a new company, illustrates this: three executives left a major manufacturer in 1982 to set up their own company. They concentrated on business computers rather than home computers in anticipation of a demand for portable and desk top machines for business people, and the table below shows the company's rapid growth:

	1982	1983	1984	1985
Employees	3	750	1,400	1,600
Installation, sq ft	–	10,000	650,000	1,000,000
Units delivered	–	53,000	144,000	200,000

UK

The Central Valley of Scotland between Edinburgh and Glasgow (often called 'the Silicon Glen') has the largest concentration of silicon chip manufacturing in Europe. The reasons for its development partly mirror those responsible for the development of California's Silicon Valley:

1 Access to local higher education institutions.
2 The availability of well-trained and skilled personnel.
3 Access to a good communications network including Prestwick International Airport.
4 A pleasant environment within easy commuting distance.

Other different but equally important factors are that overseas companies wanted access to Commonwealth and European markets in the 1960s, and Britain's subsequent membership of the EEC gave foreign companies, particularly American and Japanese, an even wider market. Financial incentives from the Scottish Development Agency and the EEC also encouraged them to locate in the Central Valley. It is estimated that the SDA has over a number of years helped to bring 300 electronics firms to the area which employ some 45,000 people. These companies have received over £41 million in grants.

The roots of the industry stretch back to 1943 when Ferranti located at Edinburgh producing gyroscopic gunsights for aircraft. This company now has electronics factories in Livingstone and Dundee.

The first large-scale developments came in the 1960s with American investment and by 1970 some 49,000 people were employed in the electronics industry. The recession in the mid-1970s, due to world overproduction in microcircuits, saw Plessey and ITT leave and other companies, such as Burroughs and WCR, cut back.

1982 saw an upturn in the industry with IBM investing in a personal computer plant at Greenock, Wang Laboratories developing at Stirling and ACT at Glenrothes.

One recent example of a new development in the area is the Digital Equipment Corporation's £82m plant on the Forth near Edinburgh. It decided to build this new microchip plant because of the availability of massive amounts of water from the Forth and the highly developed chip industry in the area which is able to supply raw materials, components and equipment worth some £12m annually. Most of this new plant's output will go to the DEC factory in Ayr.

In addition to hardware (machines) the area is developing a software (programme) expertise, e.g. Office Workstations Ltd (OWL) in Edinburgh, and the Turing Institute in Glasgow.

All these developments have in combination attracted other 'high-tech' industries. An American company is building a £30m biotechnology plant to manufacture monoclonal antibodies which are used in the diagnosis and treatment of serious illnesses.

Future US investment in the Silicon Glen is likely to be in semiconductor technology, and other important developments are likely to be in cellular radio and electronic health care: machines for both diagnosis and treatment.

NORWAY

Norway is an example of a small European country which has developed a technology industry. In 1967, Norsk Data was founded at Skullerund near Oslo. The company designs, develops and manufactures a wide range of super minicomputers and information retrieval systems with high speed scientific and technical applications. Some 2,500 staff are employed and all of them own shares in the company.

WEST GERMANY

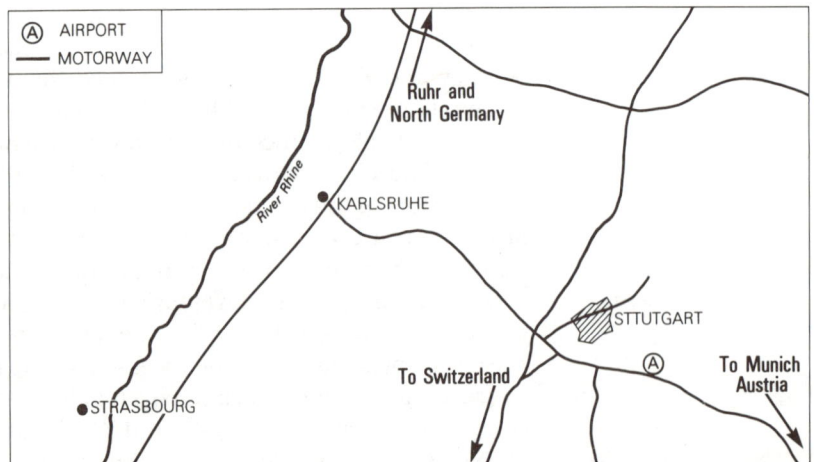

Fig 2.19 The position of Stuttgart

The state of Baden-Wurttemberg with its capital, Stuttgart, is becoming the centre of West Germany's computer and micro-electronics industry.

This industry is linked with a tremendous research drive at the state's eleven universities and in its other major industrial concerns. It is following the US's example by creating technology parks which positively encourage the type of links described. Active encouragement by the state government is also an important factor.

Success in creating this industry, along with its well-established car and machine tool industries, has meant that the state has one of the lowest unemployment rates in the Federal Republic (5.9 per cent).

JAPAN

The Japanese economy is one of the strongest in the world. Output is expanding by an average 10 per cent per year; there is a positive trade surplus; inflation remains low at 2.2 per cent; and unemployment, despite an increase in the labour force, is only 2.4 per cent. As traditional industries have declined, and Japan experiences competition from countries like Korea and the Philippines who can underprice her on labour, intensive heavy industrial products and capital goods, her great need is to stay one step in front of the rest of the world in improving her technology.

The Japanese have refined other people's inventions and mass-produced them for the world market. They have become the main producer of memory chips; the Nippon Electric Corporation (NEC) have begun to market their own development: the world's largest and fastest general purpose computer; innovative ideas are emerging from the Tsukuba Science city created by government funding some twenty years ago; and the Japanese are pushing forward with research into biotechnological products.

SPAIN

Spain entered the European Community on 1 January 1986, and is likely to become an important centre of this industry. The Spanish State Telephone Company (Telefonica) is a central part of the government-sponsored strategy to develop the electronics industry. It has entered into a partnership with Fujitsu, a Japanese computer manufacturer; with AT and T to produce microchips; and with Sweden's Ericsson Company to produce telephone equipment. The AT and T agreement will mean that Spain will have the largest microchip factory in Western Europe, located just outside Madrid. The main markets for production are likely to be the EEC and Latin America.

DEVELOPING TECHNOLOGIES

1   Factors encouraging the development of the industry – access to universities, airports, skilled personnel and a pleasant environment.
2   Encouragement of the industry by grants from central government or state agencies.
3   The growth potential of the industry.
4   The multinational nature of developments, e.g. American and Japanese companies in Britain and Spain.

REGIONAL VARIATIONS IN MANUFACTURING INDUSTRY

NORTH-WEST ENGLAND: TRADITIONAL INDUSTRY IN DECLINE

North-west England has high levels of unemployment – a consequence of the decline in the area's traditional industries such as textiles, shipbuilding and coal mining – and large scale redundancies in industries which have located in the area more recently, such as motor car manufacturing.

TEXTILE INDUSTRY

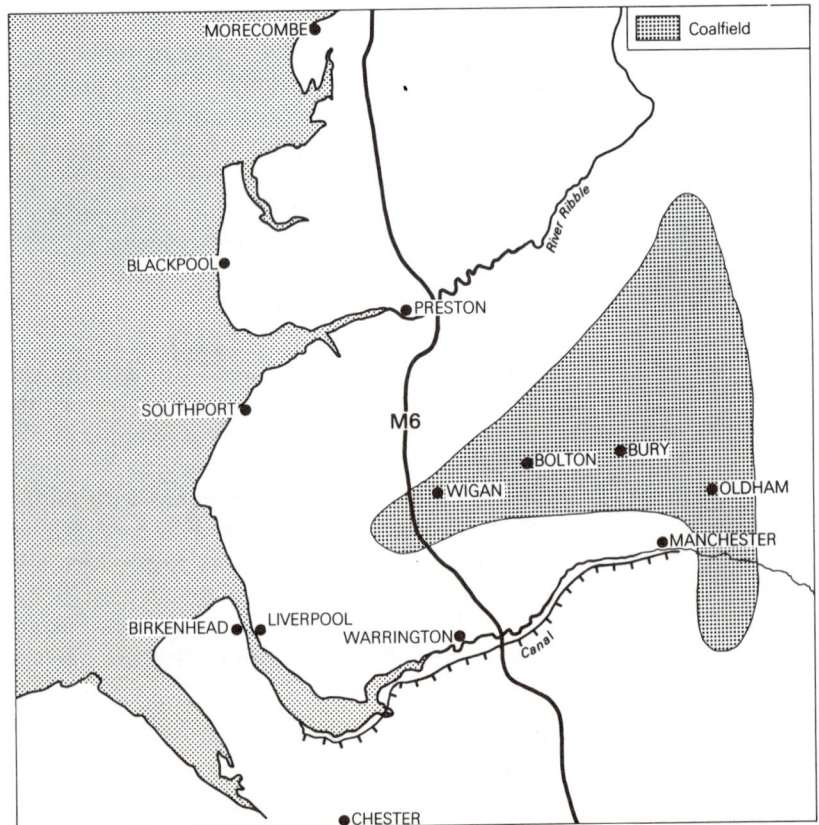

Fig 2.20 North-West England

The Lancashire textile industry was based on the making of woollen goods in Pennine valleys and the working of linen. This cottage industry was often the responsibility of farmers' wives who obtained adequate light by having mullioned windows in their cottages.

The use of water power to work machines, technological developments such as Arkwright's water frame, and the availability of imported cotton, led to cotton manufacturing on a commercial basis. Gradually, steam power replaced water power and the industry moved to coalfields or near coalfield sites. The movement of people from rural to urban areas provided the labour force the new industry needed; the population expansion and the development of the Empire provided the market.

The industry's problems began in the mid-1950s. Other countries, particularly those in the Far East, were developing their own textile industrial base using cheaper labour, thereby depriving Lancashire of some traditional markets. As their own home markets then provided a secure financial base, they began to export to the UK and gained an increasing market share by undercutting prices. In combination with a lack of investment in new machinery, which would have allowed Lancashire mills to compete more efficiently, the industry declined. Attempts have been made to halt the decline by restructuring the industry and moving into man-made fibres but this has not prevented further job losses. The textile engineering industry, at one time an export earner, has also shed jobs as both cotton manufacturing in Lancashire and the woollen industry of the West Riding cut back production and factories closed.

The EEC is attempting to assist and the multi-fibre arrangement it has negotiated with 36 countries has limited their exports to the UK. It has also given grants from its Social Fund to assist workers made redundant and has helped finance retraining schemes.

SHIPBUILDING

Birkenhead was an important shipbuilding centre based upon its proximity to Liverpool, access to a deepwater channel, availability of coal and steel, and the development of industries servicing its requirements locally. It has been affected by the problems of the shipbuilding industry nationally and internationally, and the Cammel Laird Yard has drastically reduced its labour force, currently employing under 3,000 people.

COAL

The Lancashire coalfield is no longer a significant employer of labour. Early exploitation worked out its most productive seams and those which remain are faulted and dip steeply, increased mining costs.

PORT WORK

Liverpool Docks were an important source of employment until the 1960s. Liverpool's site, situation, and industrial hinterland, meant that it developed as an important port, trading particularly with North America. As traditional industries declined in the North, and new industry began to experience problems and methods of handling cargo changed, the port's labour force contracted.

THE PROBLEMS OF RECENTLY DEVELOPED INDUSTRIES

In the 1960s, the motor car industry moved to the area because of government encouragement, a plentiful supply of labour and cheap land on which to develop the large assembly plants. Financial assistance from the European Regional Development Fund in 1980 assisted further developments. The motor car industry is, however, experiencing increasing competition, and although it is still a large employer in the area, some of the jobs initially created have now been lost.

A number of other national and international companies involved in a wide variety of enterprises which were attracted to the area, are now rationalizing production, concentrating their efforts elsewhere and closing down their factories.

HOPES FOR THE FUTURE

Modern industries usually require access to a good communications network. The national motorway network serves this region and Manchester airport has developed as an international airport. The area enjoys development area status, has enterprise zones, and the Greater Manchester Economic Development Corporation is successfully attracting industry to its region. It has been directly involved in the development of four major industrial estates in Stockport, Wigan, Atherton and Bolton and is encouraging small businesses through its village workshops at Prestwich.

The government's designation of Liverpool as a Freeport in 1984 is another attempt to boost the economy of the area by allowing goods to be imported, processed and exported without payment of customs duty.

THE GULF COAST OF NORTH AMERICA: AN EXPANDING INDUSTRIAL AREA

The Gulf Coast is an important industrial area, and Texas in particular has experienced a large increase in its manufacturing base since the mid-1960s. Initially, industrial developments were those associated with the availability of minerals, energy (coal and oil) and chemicals but since that time, investment has diversified into other industries such as electronics and engineering.

Industry has been attracted to Texas by geographical factors such as the pleasant climate and deepwater ports, and by economic factors such as the availability of cheap energy, an expanding population creating a large market, tax advantage from the state, and lower wage costs because of the tradition of a non-unionized work force.

THE MEZZOGIORNO: AN INTEGRATED PLAN FOR AGRICULTURAL AND INDUSTRIAL EXPANSION

The Mezzogiorno is the name given to the southern part of peninsular Italy and the islands of Sicily and Sardinia. It includes seven of Italy's administrative regions, contained over 40 per cent of the country's population and generated only 20 per cent of its wealth.

Fig 2.21 Mezzogiorno

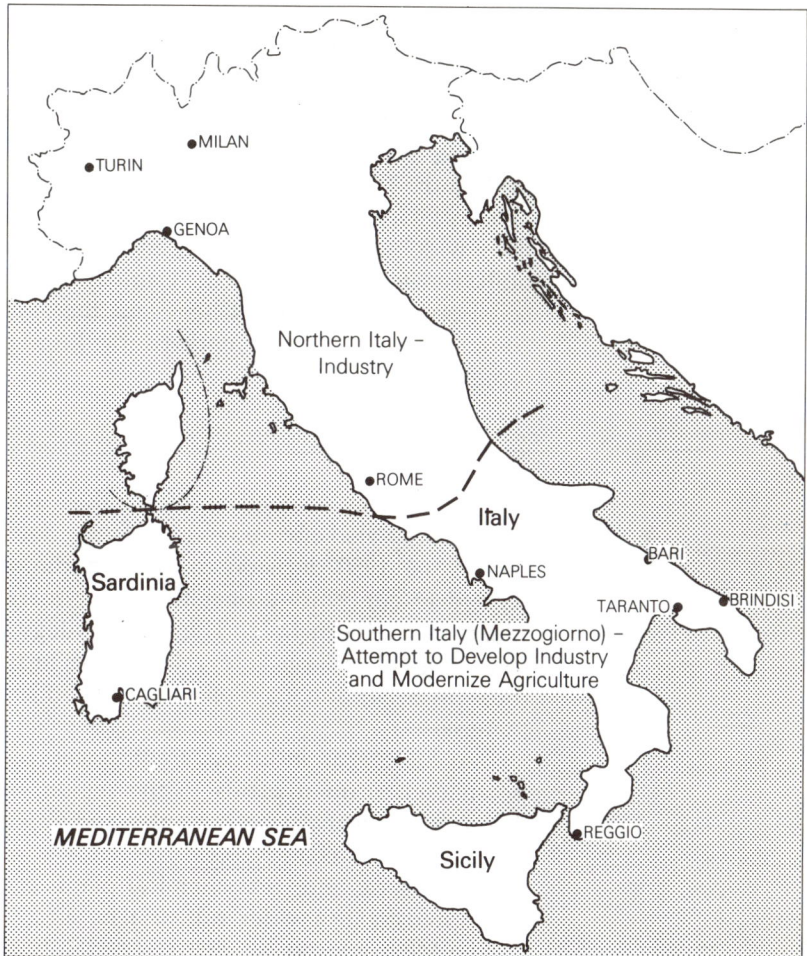

In 1950, the Italian government decided to set up the *Cassa per Il Mezzogiorno* (Fund for the South) and the *Enti di Reforma* (Reform Agencies) with the intention of expanding agricultural and industrial production in the area and creating more jobs. In addition to government funds, the World Bank and the EEC have also made significant financial contributions to this project.

AGRICULTURE

Land was mainly owned by absentee landlords who farmed large estates. This system, *latifundi*, depended upon share cropping. One-third of the estate was allocated to share croppers who in return for working their piece of land, often fragmented into holdings all over the estate, had to farm the remaining two-thirds for the benefit of the owner. The share croppers and the labourers they employed (*bracci-anti*) made a very poor living in return for their hard work, and the *braccianti*, because of the seasonal nature of their labour, were often unemployed during the winter months. During the last century, many of these seasonal labourers spent each winter in Argentina working on large estates; because of this seasonal movement between hemispheres they were known as *golandrinas* (swallows).

Using their powers under the new law, the *latifundi* were broken up and the land transferred to peasant farmers. Holdings previously held by share croppers were consolidated (made into one piece rather than widely separated strips) and irrigation and drainage schemes built. Fertile areas such as the Campanian plain (volcanic and alluvial soils) are now highly efficient and the small farmers have formed co-operatives to can and market agricultural produce such as fruit and tomatoes.

INDUSTRY

As part of the strategy to tackle the problems of the south, the government also encouraged industrial developments in the region. Before the 1950 decision to develop the south, Italian steel mills tended to concentrate near the major markets for steel: Turin and Milan in northern Italy. The new strategy was responsible for the development of large integrated works at tidewater sites at Taranto (built in 1964) and Bagnoli (Naples), both of which rely upon raw materials.

The motor car industry, traditionally located in the north, was persuaded to open plants in the region, and as a result, Fiat has extensive capacity at both Naples and Palermo (on Siciliy) and Alfa Romeo has located at Naples.

Oil refining and petrochemical plants have also been built in an attempt to create a wider industrial base.

The Mezzogiorno Scheme has certainly changed agricultural pro-duction in southern Italy and has assisted three particular areas, Naples, parts of Sicily and the Bari–Brindisi–Taranto triangle, to develop industrially. It has not, however, brought jobs to many areas of the south, and Naples (the main city) continues to attract people from all over the region with the result that it has large areas of greatly overcrowded housing and a developing unemployment problem.

BRAZIL: INDUSTRY IN THE DEVELOPING WORLD

Brazil's industrial development early this century was founded on processing agricultural productions such as wheat, coffee and cotton. The iron and steel industry (see page 88) provided the breakthrough into a more advanced stage of industrial development and its products had a ready market in the economically buoyant states in which it located. The government was keen to develop and protect industries by offering financial incentives and discouraging imports through high import duties. The motor car industry, which now produces over one million cars per year, thrived because of this policy and attracted investment from major American and European producers. Petrochemicals and the aerospace industry received the same encouragement. In conjunction with these advances, the government developed the necessary communications and service infrastructure demanded by modern industry. This strategy of encouragement, protection, and concentrating industrialization on certain growth points has been successful in creating economic growth and employment, but at the same time it has also reinforced regional inequalities within the country: almost seventy per cent of Brazil's manufacturing industry is located in the states of Rio, Sao Paulo and Minas Gerais (see also Book 1, Chapter 5).

CHECKLIST ▶

REGIONAL CONTRASTS IN DEVELOPMENT

1 Areas dependent on traditional industries, such as coal, steel, textiles and shipbuilding, are in decline despite recent changes to their industrial base.
2 New industry will not absorb all the labour shed from traditional industries.
3 It is important to diversify the industrial base and use whatever natural and economic advantages an area can provide to create economic expansion, e.g. Texas.
4 Government money will assist an area to develop but cannot guarantee that growth will be equal throughout that region, e.g. Mezzogiorno.
5 Given favourable conditions, Third World countries can develop a successful industrial base, e.g. Brazil.

EFFECTS OF INDUSTRIAL GROWTH

The effect of industrial growth is to highlight the imbalance between the developed and developing world. Economists calculate that approximately 25 per cent of the world's population account for in excess of 90 per cent of the world's manufacturing capacity. Developing nations cannot rely on producing agricultural products and minerals to increase living standards for their people, but need to undergo the industrial revolution which raised living standards elsewhere. By so doing, they may well create problems for peoples who do not at the moment appreciate that many of the advantages they possess and take for granted are not shared by all.

Within the Developing World, industrial growth tends to widen the gap between those areas and people who benefit and become more prosperous, and those who do not. Brazil, which is making rapid strides industrially, still has a problem in that 90 million out of population of 137 million live in extreme poverty. What is needed in their case, and in the case of the poorer regions of the developed world like the Mezzogiorno of Italy, is the development, probably through government incentives, of more labour intensive rather than capital intensive industries. The drift of population from rural to industrial areas needs to be stemmed by land reform and the development of small industries in rural areas.

In both the developed and developing worlds, multinational corporations play an increasingly significant role in the industrial life and therefore the economy of any particular state. The new technological industries demonstrate this: US and Japanese companies have been vitally important in developments in the UK and Europe. Well-established industries, such as motor car manufacturing, also illustrate the significance of these corporations. Brazil's production (it is Latin America's major car producer) is based upon Ford, General Motors, VW and Fiat; Spain, which produces 1.4 million cars per year (twice as many as the UK) and is Europe's major car exporter, relies heavily on the presence of Ford, General Motors, Renault, Peugeot Talbot and Nissan. (For additional details on multinationals see Book 1, Chapter 5.)

Although multinationals do create employment in a particular country, they can also create problems. Their decisions as to production are taken on commercial grounds (they want to make a profit) and if a subsidiary company in a particular country is not making sufficient profit, it may be closed, whatever effect there may be locally. A multinational presence does not always stimulate local research and development (so vital to creating or improving existing products) within that country. Spain, which has many multinational corporations operating within it, spends less on this aspect of industry than any of the other European states except Portugal and Greece.

Unemployment, where it is a problem, is not drastically reduced by a multinational presence; heavy industrial manufacturers are needed to produce that result. New developments, such as the Nissan plant at Washington in north-east England, use modern production techniques which demand a much smaller work force, and therefore, if closed could not have the devastating effect on the whole area which the closure of Bedford plants in Luton and Dunstable is likely to produce.

Industrial growth provides jobs, and when manufacturing industry cuts back production and has problems, governments try to help alleviate the unemployment which follows. The mechanism for this assistance varies and political decisions taken as to which areas or regions will benefit create anomalies. Experience suggests, however, that aid of whatever type does not create sufficient new jobs to compensate for losses in the more traditional industries.

Manufacturing industry while providing a better standard of living for people and creating wealth which can be used to help the less fortunate in society through the provision of better health care, pensions and social security systems, also has the effect of pressurizing resources. Many of these are finite. It also creates large urban areas which are now starting to generate their own particular problems, and pollution which can have an adverse effect on the environment, e.g. acid rain and the polution of the Mediterranean Sea. (See Chapter 1 above and section on leisure below.)

TERTIARY INDUSTRIES

These are sometimes referred to as the service industries. They range from large corporations and banks who provide a financial service, and the tourist industry which may provide a significant contribution to the economy of a region at one end of the spectrum to the small corner shop competing with the supermarket or hypermarket at the other end of the spectrum.

BANKING AND INSURANCE

The invisible earnings for Britain from insurance and banking amounted to £6.1 billion in 1984 and help to illustrate just how important this one particular sector of the economy is to our nation. The main world financial centres are London, New York and Tokyo.

THE LEISURE INDUSTRY

The leisure industry is an important and growing contributor to the income of many regions and countries. The UK government views tourism as a real growth area in terms of providing additional employment, particularly since the number of visitors to the UK has doubled since 1975 to over 15 million and they bring £4 billion into our economy. At present, one million people are employed in the tourist industry in the UK and experts project that this could rise by approximately 52,000 per year, provided the government is prepared to create the conditions for expansion by, for example, the recent relaxation of our licensing laws and encouraging the development of better hotel facilities.

REASONS FOR THE GROWTH OF THE TOURIST INDUSTRY IN THE UK

Early development

The industrial revolution of the last century attracted people into towns which expanded as the transport systems, the horse bus, the tram and the railway became more efficient. People in these emerging industrial areas had more leisure time; factories did not work seven days a week; and the railway network allowed access to seaside areas locally where they could relax. Resorts like Blackpool, Bridlington, Scarborough and Brighton therefore began to develop as centres for the industrial areas of the north and south-east.

Their growth accelerated with the idea of an annual paid holiday: factories closed for one or two weeks and their employees, if they could afford, went to the seaside where they stayed in boarding houses or hotels.

After the Second World War (1939–1945) the pattern of holiday-making for the majority of the population began to change. As holiday entitlement lengthened, people had more money to spend and motor car ownership became more common, attractive areas distant from industrial regions (such as Devon and Cornwall) became popular. People also began to holiday abroad as package tours became more numerous and cheap. This basic pattern became firmly established in the 1960s although there have been changes of note.

Recent changes

These have involved both the type and timing of holidays. Increasingly, many people have been able to take their holiday entitlement at any time during the year and this has encouraged the development of winter sports holidays, either in Scotland or abroad. Autumn and spring breaks have also become popular as a result of their added flexibility. Hotels have encouraged this type of development as a means of lengthening their season and therefore their potential profitability, as many people are now looking more towards self-catering holidays in flats and caravan and camping holidays. Hotels are also facing increased competition from people interested in activity holidays such as riding, sailing and fell walking which are provided by specialized centres.

The development of the motorway network in particular has dramatically changed access to certain resorts. The M5, linking the Midlands and Bristol areas with the south-west, has meant that resorts such as Exmouth and Torbay are now within easy driving distance (one to three and a half hours) for a day visit. On Easter and Whitsuntide holidays, these areas have become as popular with day trippers as Margate and Blackpool were in the early part of this century.

All areas are actively promoting tourism through Regional Tourist Boards while some towns or groups of towns have their own publicity material. The Scottish Tourist Board and the Highlands and Islands Development Board have both been instrumental in increasing the number of visitors to Scotland, and the EEC have helped by being prepared to finance tourist projects in the region which create additional jobs. The UK government has also helped by offering financial assistance under the Development of Tourism Act 1969, section 4: the English Tourist Board may provide finance to assist with the development of tourism-related projects.

THE IMPACT OF TOURISM

The south-west of England has six million visitors annually and these bring both problems and benefits to the region. People visit the south-west because of its climatic advantages (mild winters and warm summers), its contrasting scenery (sandy bays, cliffs and highlands) and its coastline which is an important sailing area. They spend large amounts of money in hotels, camp sites and shops, and by doing so, provide employment for local people. It is calculated that in Devon alone, approximately £350 million is spent. They do, however, create problems in the area which the majority of locals accept as the price they have to pay for the prosperity the industry brings. These problems are similar to those faced by tourist areas everywhere.

Traffic

At weekends during the holiday season, roads are congested with vehicles entering or leaving the region. The M5 motorway ends just south of Exeter and three lanes of fast motorway traffic move on to dual carriageway as far as Plymouth and then on to a normal road network. Traffic going northwards is often held up at Okehampton where the main road goes through the town centre. Attempts to build

Fig 2.22 South-West England

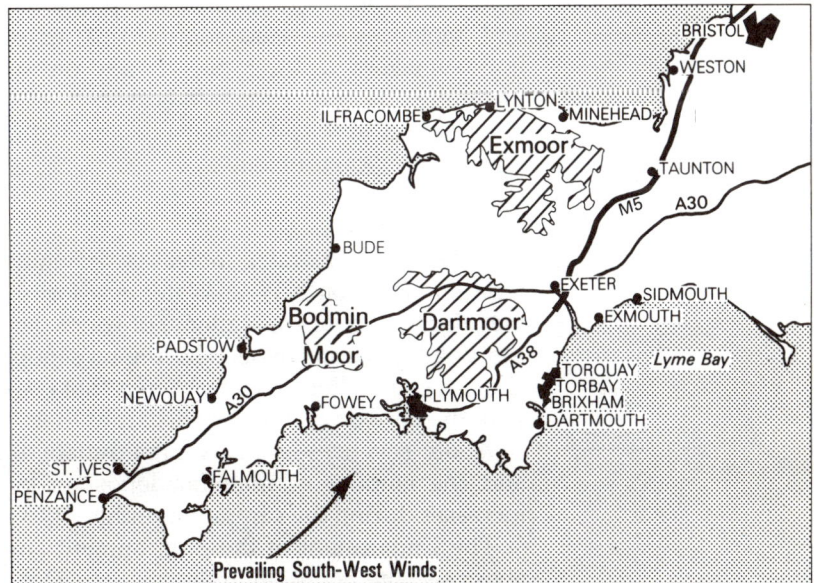

a bypass have met with strong resistance because it may encroach into the Dartmoor National Park.

In both coastal and inland towns, centres are congested by traffic and relief roads have had to be built, e.g. Helston. Cars create a pollution problem in these areas and cause inconvenience to local people wishing to shop, visit or carry out their normal business and commercial activities.

Overcrowding

Resorts become overcrowded at certain times of the year and facilities may be inadequate to cope. Distribution of visitors is not uniform within a tourist area, e.g. Devon has found that its visitors tend to concentrate between Westward Ho! and Ilfracombe in North Devon and from Brixham to Seaton in South Devon. Poor weather usually means people do not go on the beach but tend to visit towns to shop or go to the cinema, adding to overcrowding in the major inland towns.

Seasonal unemployment

Many businesses employ people during the holiday season to cope with the additional rush; these people, however, are then made redundant for the winter months when demand is much lower. Holiday regions generally have high levels of winter unemployment, partly because there are few alternative sources of employment and partly because some people migrate to the area, preferring to be unemployed in a pleasant environment rather than in an inner city area.

Emergency services

Huge numbers of additional people create problems for the emergency services. Each summer the police have to deal with accidents and violence; the coastguards and air–sea rescue services with holidaymakers drifting out to sea on sunbeds, trapped by the incoming tide or on cliffs. Medical services, both doctors and casualty departments at hospitals, have to cope with the influx of visitors who develop medical problems.

Water and sewerage

The demand for water increases dramatically during the summer months. The South-West Water Authority has to provide over 450 megalitres (100 million gallons) of water per day during the height of the holiday season when the region's population has increased by about half a million. The problem is that peak demand often coincides with the period when reservoirs are at their lowest level.

About seventy-eight sewerage outfalls drain directly into the sea and the amount of material deposited by this method obviously increases during the summer months.

The Department of the Environment and the EEC are concerned about sewage pollution in the UK. The DoE are to conduct a national survey of Britain's leading holiday resorts to discover how many beaches fall below the EEC safety standards. Only twenty-seven beaches are currently designated EEC beaches; these do not include resorts such as Brighton, Great Yarmouth, Blackpool and Llandudno. The problem is that too much untreated or partially treated sewage is pumped into the sea along outfall pipes which are too short. This can result in the presence of infectious microorganisms in material washed up on beaches, in bathing waters and concentrated in shell-fish.

No direct link has yet been established between catching disease and bathing in polluted waters but scientists and doctors believe that in some cases, typhoid and paratyphoid could have followed swimming in affected water.

Adverse effects on the things visitors come to enjoy

Kynance Cove is a beauty spot on the Lizard Peninsula. Large numbers of visitors on their way to the beach were trampling all over the cliffs creating problems of erosion. Much work has had to be done to create well-defined walks in order to protect the area from the effects of the very people who come to enjoy its beauty.

The effects of foreign holidays on the south-west

Because of their experience overseas, people are no longer prepared to accept what they regard as inferior facilities in either hotels or their resorts. These facilities are becoming increasingly important, particularly if the area is subject to 'poor' summers. In Devon alone, between 1978 and 1983 over £70m was spent on improving hotel facilities (e.g. provision of heated indoor swimming pools and leisure complexes) and the local authority and the private sector are promoting leisure complex and marina facilities.

OVERSEAS HOLIDAYS

Longer holidays, more affluence, curiosity about other countries and improved communication, particularly by air, encouraged travel companies to offer package holidays to overseas destinations. These packages may involve hotels (full-board or part-board), apartments or villas and the cost includes air fares and accommodation. Italy, Spain, Portugal, Greece and Southern France are popular destinations for those who prefer sun and sand; Switzerland, Austria, Scandinavia and West Germany are popular with those who prefer a less warm but perhaps more scenic holiday.

Increasingly, people who can afford are looking further afield than traditional European destinations. Yugoslavia is developing both its skiing industry and its summer tourist industry; North Africa, North America, the West Indies and Sri Lanka are becoming increasingly popular.

South-western France

Fig 2.23 South-west
France – tourism

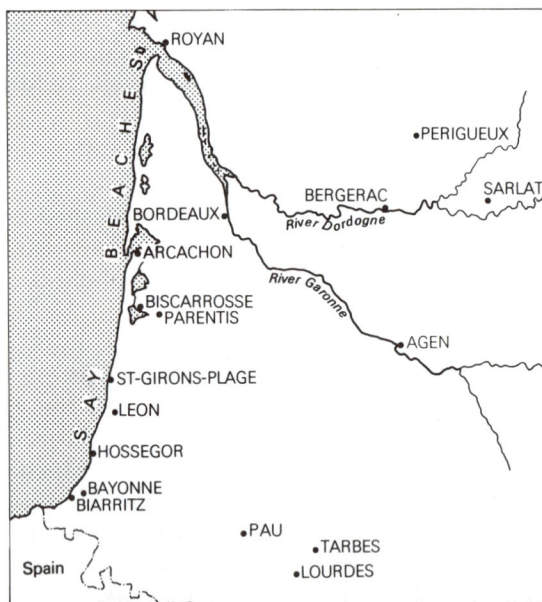

South-western France is becoming increasingly popular as a destination for both British holidaymakers and those from the Netherlands and Germany. Its climate is not as excessively warm as that of
the Mediterranean but its summers are hot; the beaches are less
crowded and cleaner, waves are heavier. There are a number of lakes,
e.g. Lake Parentis, which are warm and shallow (ideal for younger
children or windsurfing) and extensive pine forests. The area is
within easy driving distance of two other regions favoured by tourists: the Dordogne and the western Pyrenees. The latter have beautiful mountain scenery, they are ideal walking country, e.g. Cirque de
Gavarnie, and are the site for towns such as Lourdes.

Good quality accommodation is available in towns such as Arca-
chan and Biarritz, and the pine forests and lakesides are the site for
good quality camping and caravanning sites.

Bars, discos, nightclubs and casinos provide nightlife while there
are numerous shops selling a variety of goods for people who wish to
escape from the beach.

The area has good fast road connections northwards via the N10
and autoroute. Bordeaux is a motor-rail centre of the SNCF (French
railways). British visitors can therefore transport their car by motor-
rail from the Channel ports.

Costa Brava

The Costa Brava (the north-east coast of Spain) has hot, dry summers
and mild, wet winters: a Mediterranean climate which appeals to
Northern Europeans, as do the sandy beaches of its headland coasts.

France, Portugal, Germany, the UK, Scandinavia and Benelux provide most visitors. It gains from its location on the French border and its proximity to the airports of Barcelona and Gerona. Its towns are a blend of the old settlement with narrow streets and small shops, and the new multi-storey hotels with their own swimming pools and bar facilities. Most towns are an attractive balance between the two; the one major exception is Lloret de Mar. In addition to the attractions of sea and sand, the area also has the historical remains of the settlement at Ampurias where both Greeks and Romans built on the same site, and the real Spain in the countryside stretching towards Andorra. Bars, discos, restaurants and nightclubs are found in towns such as Estartit and La Escala.

The tourist industry, which is facing increased competition from other areas, is of vital importance to Spain's economy (43 million visitors providing ten per cent of the national income). Adverse comments in the British Press about hooliganism by British tourists brought a swift response from the Spanish authorities who deployed additional police officers. Attempts by ETA, the Basque Separatist Organization, to disrupt the tourist trade by planting bombs at resorts along the Mediterranean, have also resulted in a heavier police presence. Despite these efforts, bookings did decline but the problem is nowhere near as serious as that experienced by the French Mediterranean coast.

In an effort to diversify away from the Costas, the Spanish National Tourist Office is devoting much of its resources to promoting inland holidays to see the real Spain: the Moorish cities of Granada, Seville and Cordoba; the magnificence of Madrid itself; and the unspoilt beauty of the countryside. They are also stressing the attractions of western and northern Spain where beaches are kept clean by Atlantic tides, scenery can be spectacular, the climate reasonable and villages and towns unspoilt.

Problems of the Mediterranean resorts

The French Mediterranean resorts typify the emerging problems which are being experienced by many of the long established tourist areas of the northern Mediterranean coast. Bookings are declining (estimates range from 2 per cent to as much as 10 per cent) because the reputation of the area is declining. Beaches are polluted, there are increasing traffic problems and development is virtually unchecked. Steps to combat these problems will be necessary if Mediterranean France is to continue to attract 36 million foreign visitors each year who contribute £3 billion to the French budget.

Recent developments have tried to recreate the original character of small French fishing villages, rather than create uninspiring although luxurious concrete blocks. At Cap D'Agde, the largest purpose-built resort in Europe, planners have created eight man-made harbours surrounded by traditional type villages, each of which has its own character and each concentrating upon one aspect of holiday life, e.g. a naturist village; a seventy-two-court tennis village.

This attempt contrasts quite sharply with other developments which while providing what the tourist wants, have tended not to blend in well with the surrounding area.

An attempt has been made to minimize traffic problems by creating pedestrianized areas (especially in new developments), building multi-storey car parks, and enforcing existing parking regulations more rigorously.

Pollution

Humans have made the Mediterranean one of the worst polluted seas in the world. Britain discharges some untreated sewage directly into the sea through outfalls (see page 114) but this is insignificant when compared with countries bordering on the Mediterranean which dispose of over ninety per cent of their sewage in this way. The enormous yearly influx of tourists, about 150 million in the region as a whole, merely add to an already existing problem of major proportions. In addition to sewage, industrial and chemical waste is discharged into rivers which flow into the Mediterranean (some 30,000 tonnes per year), and despite legislation in individual countries under which pollutants can be heavily fined, this continues. However careful refineries are, accidents happen and materials are discharged – Mediterranean refineries unfortunately are no different from those elsewhere – and a small number of oil tankers add to the problem by washing out their empty tanks during the night while in transit for the Suez Canal and the Middle East oil fields.

All these pollutants tend to wash around the tideless Mediterranean causing embarrassment and a potential health hazard to those who live in and visit the area. Ingesting polluted water can cause gastro-enteritis and bathing in polluted water, skin problems. The tideless nature of the sea means that it takes much longer (80 years) for pollutants to disperse.

International concern, and years of discussion and negotiation under the auspices of the United Nations, has brought agreement on what action needs to be taken, but so far effects have been minimal because poorer countries cannot afford to implement some of the proposals, as they will be an enormous drain on their finances.

Other countries have made some attempts: Barcelona, where the first conference was held in 1976, began to clean sewage from beaches each day, but has now spent £9 million on a sewerage plant with the result that the bacteria count on its most popular beach fell dramatically. Until other areas are prepared to adopt Barcelona's approach, it is likely that tourists will continue to bathe in a warm but polluted sea.

Despite all these problems, the map illustrates why visitors still flock to the Mediterranean area in autumn.

Winter resorts

Austria, the French and Italian Alps and Switzerland are the well-established and important winter playgrounds of Europe.

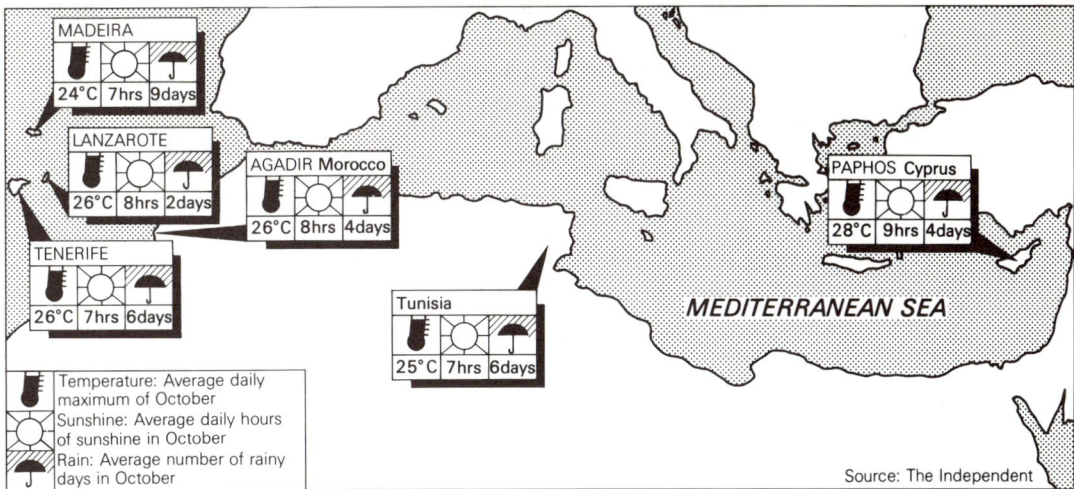

Fig 2.24 The attraction of Mediterranean areas for autumn holidays

Individual resorts within one country may vary enormously in terms of what they offer to the prospective tourist. Saas Fee, for example, contains no luxury hotel complex and retains its village identity; Grachen, however, a village of only 1,250 people for most of the year, has extensive hotel and apartment developments which can accommodate 5,000 people during the winter season; Zermatt, an important ski complex, also attracts day visitors who come to view the Matterhorn. The following statistics illustrate the type of facilities available for those taking a winter holiday:

	SAAS Fee	Grachen	Zermatt
Resort at	1,817 m	1,635 m	1,635 m
Top station	3,538 m	2,932 m	3,856 m
6-day lift pass (approx)	180 S Fr	150 SF	210 SF
Marked runs	80 km	35 km	150 km
Longest run	9 km	5.5 km	18 km
Largest vertical descent	1,716 m	1,009 m	2,224 m
Suitable for skiers	of all levels	Beginners to advanced intermediates	Second year skiers to advanced
Lift capacity/hour	20,000	10,700	29,630
Mountain railways	1	—	2
Ski school instructors	80	40	175
Ice hockey	Yes	Yes	Yes
Ski bobbing	Yes	Yes	—
Curling rinks	1	2	10
Mountain restaurants	10	2	30

Source: The Guardian

Other regions are trying to break into what is a very lucrative market. The 1984 Winter Olympics were held at Sarajevo in Yugoslavia and tour companies are realizing exactly what the country has available for the winter sports enthusiast: good snow, beautiful countryside and low costs. Developments have been rapid but the following statistics illustrate the gap between the new resorts of Yugoslavia and the long-established resorts of Switzerland.

	Bled	Bohinj	Kranjska Gora
Resort at	509 m	531 m	818 m
Top station	1,276 m	1,905 m	1,615 m
Marked runs	16 km	14 km	22 km
Longest run	2.5 km	8.5 km	3.5 km
Largest vertical descent	383 m	974 m	807 m
Suitable for		Beginners to intermediates	Beginners to advanced intermediates
Lift capacity/hour	4,150	4,000	19 lifts
Ski school instructors	10	3	9
Ice hockey	Yes	—	—
Mountain restaurants	1	3	1

Source: The Guardian

Any change is likely to have both positive and negative effects on local people. Hotel developments at Kranjska are tending to over-shadow the former village and the new disco no doubt tends to raise a few eyebrows in this traditional area. The area will ultimately become more popular and more prosperous but this prosperity will no doubt bring the sort of problems referred to earlier which seem to affect all tourist regions.

Europe
The development of the tourist industry in Europe generally follows a similar pattern to that outlined for Britain. Northern Europerans tend to seek the sun: the Dutch and Germans in particular seem to appreciate Greece, Southern France, Spain and Italy. The majority of Spaniards, Portuguese and Greeks tend to have a lower standard of living and holiday locally. Britain attracts its foreign tourists principally from northern Europe and North America.

Migration as a result of holiday visits
Many people from areas which experience a colder, damper winter have decided, once they have spent holidays in a more pleasant environment, to buy property there for use either as a holiday or retirement home. Many northern Europeans have bought properties in southern France, Spain and Portugal, while many Americans have decided to purchase properties in Florida or California. The local economy therefore benefits from additional residents who purchase goods and pay taxes, but this is partly balanced by the need to improve services, particularly health care.

RECREATION

Countryside parks

The government felt that there was a need to meet the needs of people who lived in urban areas who wanted to spend a day in the countryside but who might not wish to travel large distances to National Parks. These areas, usually woodlands, parklands, heathlands or coastal areas, are normally found near urban centres and provide opportunities for walking, sailing, fishing and riding.

Devon County Council, for example, provides three country parks at Stover, Northam Burrows and the Grand Western Canal at Tiverton; commercial concerns provide two others at Farway (East Devon) and on the River Dart.

Other countries have made similar provision for recreation adjacent to large urban centres – parts of the reclaimed polders of the Zuider Zee have been given over to this purpose; land reclaimed from spoil heaps in the Ruhr Valley has been made into nature trails.

Fig 2.25 England and Wales – National Parks

NATIONAL PARKS
1 Northumberland
2 Lake District
3 Yorkshire Dales
4 North Yorkshire Moors
5 Peak District
6 Snowdonia
7 Pembrokeshire Coast
8 Brecon Beacons
9 Exmoor
10 Dartmoor

A.O.N.B.
A Lincoln Wolds
B Shropshire Hills
C Chilterns
D East Devon/Dorset
E Downs + Surrey Hills

National Parks
Area of Outstanding Natural Beauty

National Parks

North America led the way in creating National Parks, areas where the scenery, flora and fauna (plants and animals) are protected so that they can be appreciated by all and enjoyed by future generations. the first, the Yellowstone National Park, was created in 1872. The United Kingdom created National Parks under the 1949 National Parks and Access to the Countryside Act. Ten areas of great natural beauty were designated so that their beauty and natural and historical features could be protected and public enjoyment of them promoted. The essential difference between parks in North America and those in the UK is that North American parks are usually owned by Federal or state agencies while the land in the UK parks is owned mainly by individuals.

The UK parks are administered by local National Park Committees which have powers granted to them under the 1948 Act, the 1968 Countryside Act and the 1981 Wildlife and Countryside Act. It has a statutory duty to preserve the natural beauty of the area, to promote its enjoyment and to have regard for the social and economic well-being of its residents. It also arranges for ranger and visitor services.

The parks in both North America and the UK are faced with similar problems:

1   Easy asccessibility because of car ownership and better roads means that many thousands of visitors crowd into the parks each year, usually at weekends or during holiday periods. This puts pressure on car parks and other facilities: Dartmoor receives eight million visitors each year.

2   Those visiting do not spread themselves throughout the park but tend to congregate at particular spots, especially those accessible by car, which then become overcrowded. A recent Devon County Council report states in relation to Dartmoor 'changes in activity on Dartmoor have, however, been detected such as more car-borne visitors appearing at heavily used sites and areas and fewer using the high moorland access points'.

3   Encroachment or attempted encroachment by other potential users: reservoir construction, quarrying, new roads (Okehampton bypass into Dartmoor National Park).

4   Accommodation. Many people want to stay in the parks but building is strictly controlled. The management objective on Dartmoor is 'to control holiday development and other facilities so that local residents are not inconvenienced by them; to support the established policy of discouragement in the bulk of the Park but encourage development near the edges and outside it'. Caravans and campers are attracted to these areas but in both North America and the UK their sites are strictly controlled, both in terms of location and number of pitches; in consequence they are soon full.

The management objective in the Dartmoor National Park is 'to provide for touring caravans near the edge of the park and tents at other appropriate sites'.

5   The more visitors who arrive in parks, the more potential danger to

plants, animals and land. They may ultimately destroy the very things they have come to see.

6 Pollution from car exhausts, and litter.

7 The inability of wardens or the ranger service to supervise adequately the parks, e.g. summer drought can lead to fires because of carelessness, winters usually bring problems for emergency services because people venture into the parks ill equipped.

Areas of Outstanding Natural Beauty

In addition to National Parks, which are mainly in highland areas, the UK has also designated certain areas as being of Outstanding Natural Beauty, e.g. the New Forest, parts of the Isle of Wight and the Lincolnshire Wolds. Planning applications are strictly monitored as the local authority can exercise tighter controls in these areas which are more convenient for day visitors than most National Parks.

Local facilities

The provision of recreational facilities so that people can enjoy their leisure time has become increasingly more important. Local authorities (councils) and private developers have provided sports facilities which cater for both minority and popular sports and pastimes. In addition to providing a public service they also provide employment.

Exeter Leisure Centre

The site chosen for the building of the new leisure centre was on a piece of derelict land. Some of the houses on this site were damaged during the Second World War and subsequently knocked down. Houses and a number of shops were eventually purchased from their owners and a car park created. After a number of years, two ideas were discussed: industry or recreational facilities; eventually it was decided to build a leisure complex along with shopping facilities. The £7.5m scheme was started in June 1984. It is ideally placed relatively near the city centre, can serve the rapidly expanding residential area west of the Exe, and is easily accessible to surrounding rural areas and small country towns.

CHECKLIST ▶

THE LEISURE INDUSTRY

1 Stages in the growth of the industry in the last century: post-1945; 1960s–80s.

2 The contribution tourism makes to the economy of a country or an area may be significant: UK £4 billion; Spain 10 per cent of the country's wealth.

3 The impact of tourism on a region, e.g. overcrowding, water and sewerage disposal, traffic problems.

4 Overseas holidays in winter and summer in France, Spain, Switzerland and Yugoslavia.

5 The problems of the Mediterranean resorts: pollution, traffic, new resorts building and the attempts to tackle them.

6   Other recreational provision at a local (leisure centres) and a national level (parks, countryside parks and Areas of Outstanding National Beauty).
7   The problem of National Parks in North America and the UK.

SHOPPING FACILITIES

LOCAL SHOPS

These tend to be family concerns staffed by the owner and relatives and provide little, if any, additional employment. They have survived mainly by working long hours, including weekends, and stocking convenience items. Their prices may be slightly more expensive than supermarkets as they do not buy in the huge quantities which attract large discounts. Some have attempted to compete by joining small consortiums which buy and wholesale in large quantities. This type of shop may serve an inner urban area or perhaps a section of a large estate.

LINEAR DEVELOPMENTS ALONG MAIN ACCESS ROUTES

These are often a mixture of privately owned shops and those owned by local or national companies. They have the advantage of accessibility for both local people and those commuting into town from further afield and therefore provide a wide cross-section of service.

THE CENTRAL BUSINESS DISTRICT

This area normally contains shops owned by large national department stores, chains and other major retailers. Land values and rates in this area are high and many developments are in multi-storey buildings. It is an area where banks, building societies and estate agencies tend to locate and where locally owned shops tend to specialize in selling more expensive items such as jewellery, furniture, photographic equipment and expensive clothes.

The CBD is often an area which has undergone quite significant changes in terms of rebuilding and pedestrianization. From time to time, 'traffic-free' is not wholly accurate as park and ride schemes have meant that if shoppers are to be encouraged to leave their cars away from city centres, minibuses must be allowed access to these precincts.

Many CBD traders are finding that they are facing increasing competition from out of town shopping centres which cater for the vast majority of shoppers' requirements and have the advantage of large car-parking facilities around the complex. Many stores in the CBD are now opening for late-night shopping on at least one occasion per week and are attempting to price goods very competitively.

CHANGES IN EMPLOYMENT

The manufacturing industry is no longer the major employer of labour. As the industrial recession has bitten into British industry, companies have closed down uneconomic plants, cut back output to bring it more in line with demand, and rationalized their production, sometimes concentrating their operations on factories in Europe. The traditional industries, e.g. motor vehicles, textiles, steel, coalmining, shipbuilding, machine tools, have shed enormous numbers of employees since the late 1970s. The growth industries have also fared badly, apart from computer manufacturing. This pattern has been repeated in many developed nations, e.g. Germany, France and USA, to a greater or lesser extent.

While manufacturing industries have experienced problems, the service industries, insurance, banking, finance and business services; health; education; hotels, restaurants, catering; entertainment and recreation; public administration, have been going through a period of expansion.

The problem is that job losses have not been equally spread throughout the British Isles (the North has been particularly badly hit) and the jobs created in the tertiary sector have tended not to be in areas experiencing these heavy job losses.

Future trends project further large-scale job losses in the non-service sectors of the economy and further growth within the service sector. Many economists and politicians believe that attempts must be made to revitalize our manufacturing capacity as a basis for future growth and that traditional industries must be encouraged to survive the present economic difficulties in order to take advantage of any future economic recovery, and alleviate the problems associated with unemployment.

Unemployment rates have risen everywhere in Britain. The idea that the more pleasant counties escape is false, although their problems are nowhere near as desperate as the traditional industrial heartlands where 16 per cent is common, and within which black spots of 18 and 19 per cent may occur. Devon illustrates the type of rise experienced by a south-west county:

	March	June	December
1980	7.8	7.5	10.5
1981	11.4	11.4	13.5
1982	13.7	13.5	14.0
1983	14.1	12.0	13.4

The problem for many people is that they have been without work for considerable periods of time, and as manufacturing industry continues to decline, there is every prospect of more experiencing the particular types of hardship this brings.

INDUSTRY – GLOSSARY

adit mine shafts excavated at a shallow angle to a mineral seam.

acid rain rain containing pollution, particularly industrial. **Appalachians** mountain range along the east coast of North America.

Areas of Outstanding Natural Beauty (UK) attractive areas, e.g. New Forest, which provide facilities for people and enjoy some protection from developments.

bituminous coal a type (or rank) of coal.

British Shipbuilders state-owned shipbuilding company operating a number of shipyards in the UK.

Central Business District area of a city or town centre where land values and rates are high and where banks, specialist shops and department stores are located.

chemical pulp wood is broken down chemically to produce pulp.

countryside parks areas of woodland, parkland or coast, adjacent to urban areas in Britain.

Development Areas (UK) grants are available to encourage industry to locate in these regions which are chosen by the UK government.

Enterprise Zones (UK) created in 1981 to attract industry to an area.

freeports (UK) areas in which goods may be imported, processed and exported without payment of customs duties.

Highlands and Islands Development Board an organization to promote economic development, e.g. tourism, in the Highlands and Islands of Scotland.

hypermarket large shopping development in the UK, Europe and North America, usually located outside towns near good communication networks.

industrial estates areas specially built for occupation by light industries.

integrated steel plant the whole process of steel making is carried out in these sites; minerals are brought in for the plant and steel goes out.

Jurassic limestone type of limestone formed during the Jurassic period of the Earth's history.

Klondykers the name given to Eastern European 'factory' vessels which buy fish caught off the British Isles.

latifundi large estates in southern Italy owned by absentee landlords. These estates are now being bought and divided.

leaching the term given to the process by which plant minerals are washed out of the soil by rainwater percolating through it.

London Metal Exchange where minerals from all over the world are traded.

Massif Central a highland area in France.

mechanical pulp wood is crushed by machines to form pulp.

Mezzogiorno southern part of peninsular Italy and the islands of Sicily and Sardinia which is the subject of agricultural and industrial development.

multinational companies these operate in a number of countries.

National Parks areas designated by governments where the landscape, plants and animals are protected.

North Atlantic Drift a current of warm water which flows across the Atlantic and along the north-west coast of Europe, raising winter temperatures in coastal areas.

Norrland the sparsely populated northern region of Sweden.

oasis a place where water-bearing rocks (aquifers) reach the surface.

open cast mining minerals near the surface are obtained by removing the top soil.

overfishing the removal of too many fish from a particular fishing ground.

plankton microscopic organisms on which fish feed. Where these are particularly abundant, the fishing industry is likely to be important.

primary industry agricultural activities, extraction of minerals, and the use of natural resources, such as forests and fishing.

Regional Development Fund (EEC) an organization created by the European Economic Community to provide financial help to those areas of the EEC requiring it.

Ruhr a tributary river of the Rhine in Germany along which mining and industry have become important.

rural depopulation the movement of people away from rural areas.

secondary industry processing raw materials into manufactured goods.

shaft mine minerals excavated by sinking a shaft to the seam.

Silicon Glen the areas fo the central lowlands of Scotland important for computer and associated equipment manufacturing.

Silicon Valley an area in California important for the production of computers and associated equipment.

soft woods coniferous trees.

supertanker extremely large vessel (250,000 tonnes plus) for carrying oil.

tertiary industry service industries, e.g. tourism, banking and insurance.

THE PHYSICAL ENVIRONMENT AND HUMAN ACTIVITY

CONTENTS

Contents

Fig 3.1 Structure of the
Earth

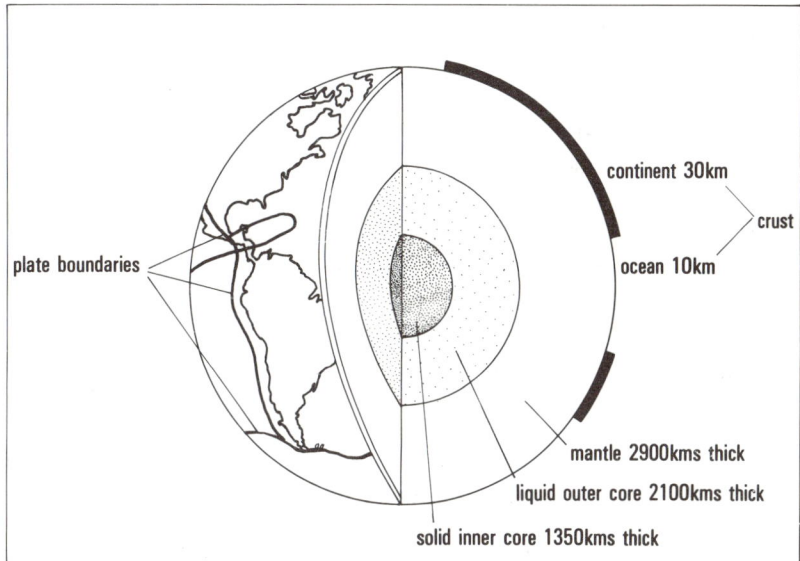

The earth is composed of three parts.

1 The core The core is subdivided into two parts.
> (i) the inner core – a solid sphere composed of very dense rocks.
> (ii) the outer core – an area of molten iron and nickle at a temperature of between 2,000°C and 5,000°C.

2 The mantle Composed of semi-liquid rocks at temperatures up to 1,500°C.

3 The crust Thin layer of brittle rocks which comprises the continents and ocean floors. The latter are composed of silica and magnesium (SIMA) but the continents are composed of silica and aluminium (SIAL) lying over the sima.
    The crust has been fractured into many parts which are called plates. It is at the margins of these plates that the earth's crust is at its weakest.

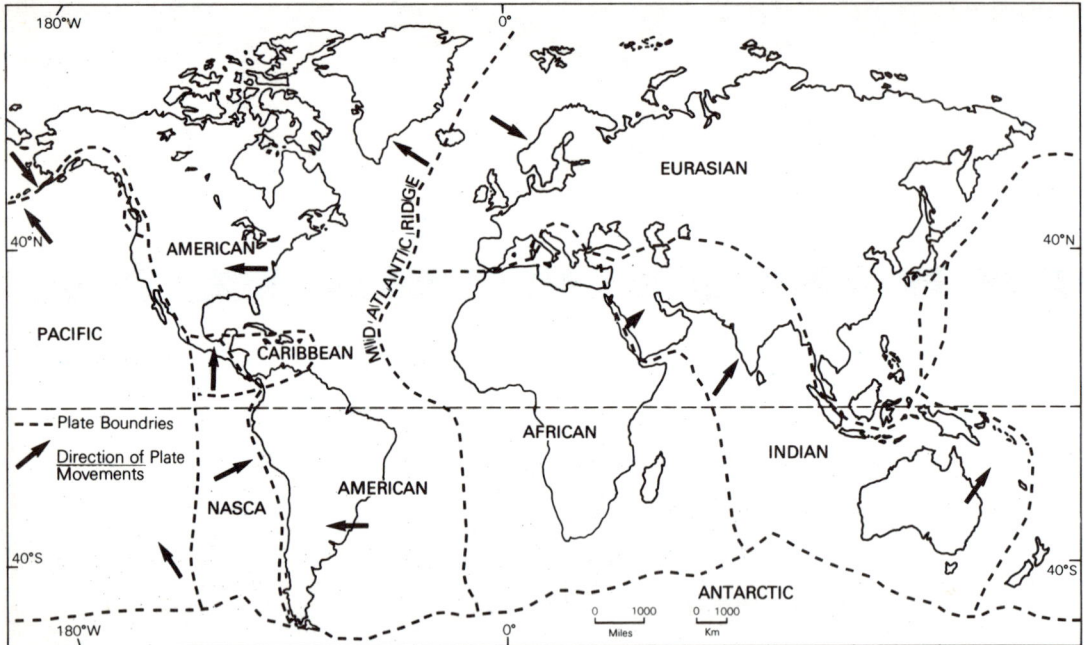

Fig 3.2 Crustal plates

PLATE TECTONICS

The solid plates which compose the earth's crust are constantly moving. At present it is thought that the major force causing these movements is convection currents within the mantle created by the core's high temperatures. At certain places molten magma is rising through the mantle, spreading horizontally beneath the crust, creating a great strain on this thin, rigid layer. This pressure drags plates apart. At other places, plates are being pulled towards each other, and at others they pass/slide by (see Fig 3.2 above.)

PLATE MARGINS

There are three types of plate margin, classified according to the direction in which the plates are moving.

1 Where plates are colliding: destructive margins
The oceanic plate is forced down into the mantle, melting as it descends. This creates a deep oceanic trench. The less dense continental plate rides over the oceanic plate and crumples, forming fold mountains. The collision between these two plates causes earthquakes. Molten rock from the mantle may escape at the plate boundary on to the earth's surface, creating volcanoes.

2 Where plates are diverging: constructive margins
As two plates move apart, magma from the mantle fills in the gap, and solidifies to form new crust. Each time the plates move, this

Fig 3.3 Fold mountains

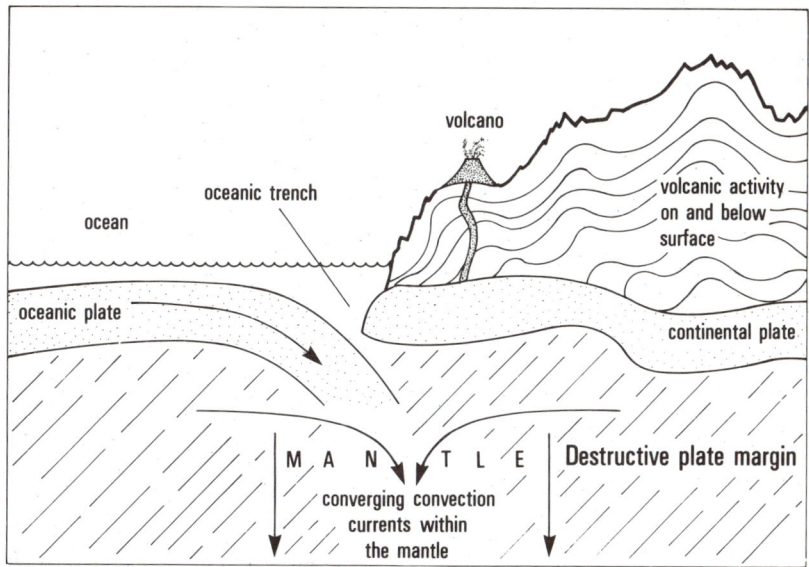

Fig 3.4 Constructive plate margin

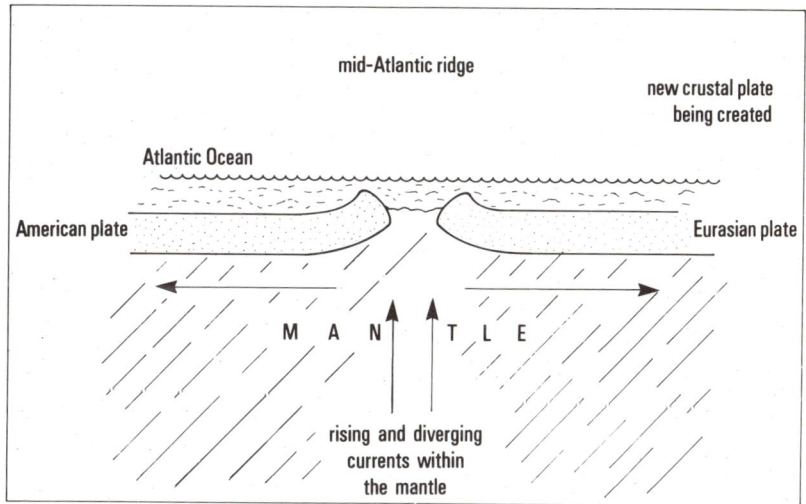

process is repeated, creating a series of ridges. When a constructive margin occurs beneath an ocean, an oceanic ridge is created, taller parts of which are volcanoes which may protrude above sea level to form islands.

3 Where plates slip alongside each other: passive margins

At passive margins opposite moving plates slide past without significantly parting or riding over each other. If this movement is slight/steady little harmful effect is caused; but if there is a build-up of pressure and sudden movement, major earthquakes and/or volcanic eruptions will occur. This is clearly evidenced in California where the

Fig 3.5 Passive plate
margin

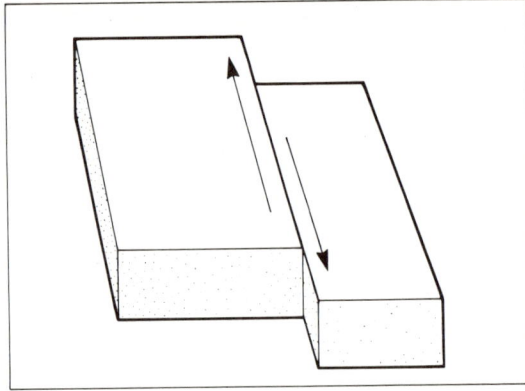

Pacific Plate meets the North American Plate at a major fault line called the San Andreas Rift. The sudden movement of the plates in 1906 created a massive earthquake which destroyed San Francisco. More recently the build-up in pressure caused the Mount St Helens volcanic eruption.

EARTHQUAKES

Earthquakes are a series of shock waves caused by movements within the earth's crust where stresses have been built up to breaking point. The point at which the earthquake starts is called the **focus**. The **epicentre** is the point on the surface of the crust directly above the focus.

An earthquake produces three types of shock wave, each of which is recorded by seismographs (instruments used to record earthquake activity).

1 Primary waves These are the most rapid moving, will pass through solids or liquids (crust, core and mantle), and cause rocks to move backwards and forwards in the direction in which the wave is moving.

2 Secondary waves These will only pass through solids, being reflected from the core back to the surface. These cause the rocks to pass from side to side.

3 Long waves These are the slowest waves travelling on the surface of the earth. These waves create the greatest damage as they cause rocks to move up and down.

EARTHQUAKE LOCATION

As earthquakes are caused by disturbances in the earth's crust, they are most frequent and most violent on or near plate boundaries.

Nevertheless, they may occur in other regions, even in the UK (but are usually weak and infrequent).

EARTHQUAKE MEASUREMENT

Seismographs Earthquakes are recorded on instruments called seismographs based at various centres throughout the world. They are capable of recording the intensity of the earthquake and the time at which each of the shock waves arrives at the recording station. The location of the earthquake can be calculated by comparing the arrival times of the different seismic waves.

Richter Scale Charles Richter devised a scale for describing earthquake intensity by measuring the amplitude of waves recorded on a seismograph. Minor earthquakes have a magnitude of 5 or less and major earthquakes have a magnitude of more than 7.

THE EFFECTS OF EARTHQUAKES

1 Cracking of the earth's surface (see Book 1, Chapter 4).
2 Vertical and/or lateral displacement either side of the crack.
3 Landslides.
4 Shaking of the ground.
5 Sagging or raising of parts of the sea bed causing tsunamis.
The results of these movements may cause human devastation on a massive scale. The extent of the damage is dependent on the magnitude of the earthquake, its location and its degree of unexpectedness.

As a result of earthquakes, buildings may collapse burying many people in residential areas, fires are created, gas explosions may occur, sewerage and fresh water pipelines are severed leading to the development of diseases such as cholera. Access to the devastated area may be difficult due to the cutting of communications. Many people, not killed initially, may die as a result of exposure (loss of shelter), starvation, disease, or due to being trapped in collapsed buildings. Some may be drowned by tsunamis (massive tidal waves) crashing on to coastal zones.

Ways in which the effects of earthquakes are being reduced

1 An early warning system based on seismograph readings.
2 Planning controls preventing the construction of residential areas in high risk zones, such as on the San Andreas Rift in California.
3 The building of 'low-rise' housing in areas of frequent earthquake.
4 The use of ferro-concrete in construction of buildings.
5 The storage of emergency supplies in 'earthquake-proof' buildings in high risk areas.
6 Regular practices for trained teams so they may act swiftly and decisively at the time of an earthquake.
7 A network of tsunami recording stations around the Pacific Ocean.

8 Constructing houses on solid rock or, if this is not possible, on concrete rafts which 'float' during an earth tremor.

FOLD MOUNTAINS

Young fold mountains such as the Andes and the Himalayas have been created by converging plates. Sediments are laid down by rivers creating coastal waters and by waves creating very thick layers of sedimentary rock (sometimes over 10,000 m). These deposits occupy a depression (a geosyncline) created by colliding plates. As the plates approach each other, it is the sedimentary rocks which buckle and are forced upwards creating fold mountains. Intense volcanic activity occurs creating surface landforms such as volcanoes and lava flows, as well as intrusive volcanic features such as batholiths.

FAULTING

Movements within the earth's crust may cause cracks or factures (faults). Along the lines of these faults rocks may be displaced by being uplifted, moved horizontally, or the land between parallel faults may sink.

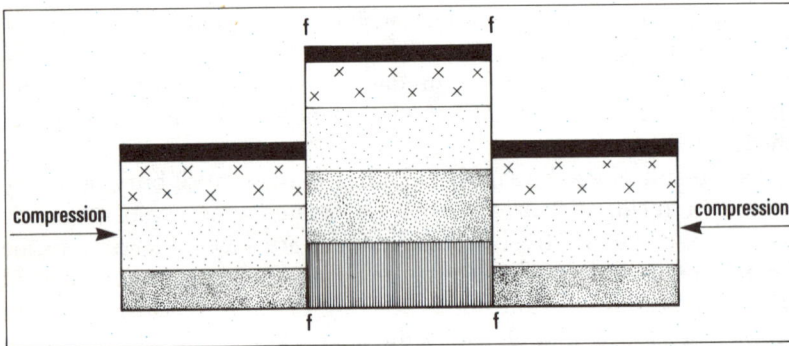

Fig 3.6

A horst created as the central block is forced upwards along the line of the two faults.

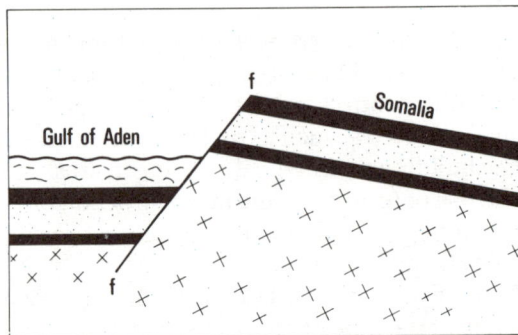

Fig 3.7

A tilt block is created where the uplifted block is tilted from the horizontal.

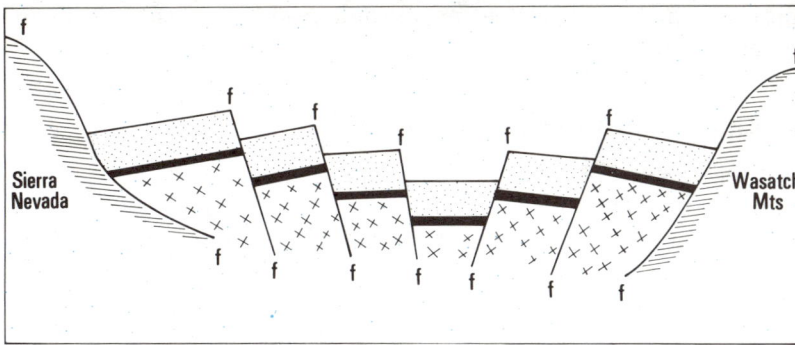

Fig 3.8 Great Basin of USA

Block mountains may be created where a series of faults occur producing many tilted blocks.

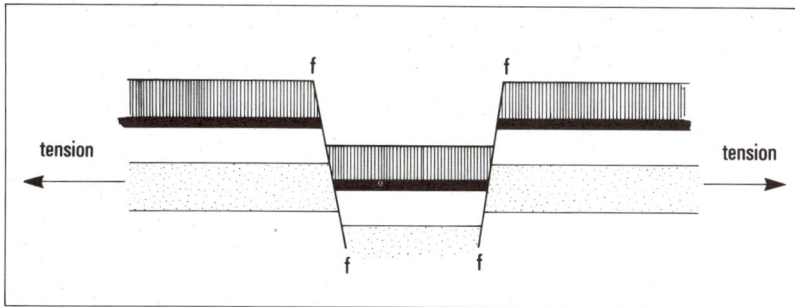

Fig 3.9

A rift valley may be created where land slips between two or more parallel faults.

Not surprisingly, many of the above landforms are found in close association and are often accompanied by volcanic activity as magma escapes along the fault lines, creating volcanoes and lava plateaux.

Fig 3.10 The Rhine Rift Valley

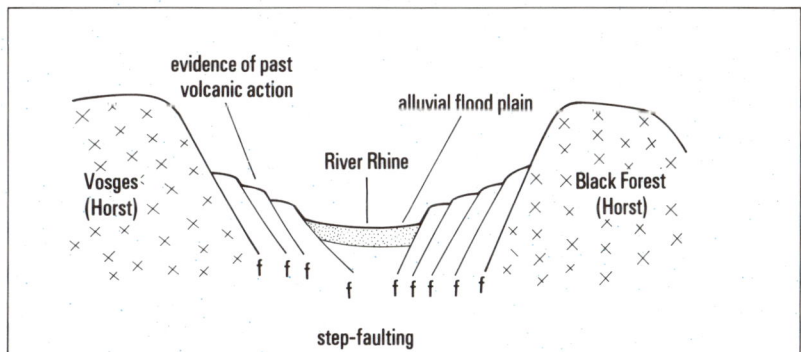

THE GREAT RIFT VALLEY

The largest rift valley system in the world extends for some 5,000 km from Syria, through the Dead Sea, and through much of East Africa to the Zambesi River. It comprises a series of rift valleys, many of which are occupied by major lakes (such as Lake Tanganyika). Evidence of volcanic activity is displayed by volcanic peaks such as Mt Kiliman-jaro and Mt Kenya.

INFLUENCE OF FAULTING ON HUMAN ACTIVITY

1 Rift Valleys Rift Valleys generally attract settlement as they provide natural routeways, are more sheltered, and contain fertile alluvial soils deposited by the rivers that occupy these depressions. If the valley is step-faulted, the benches created on the sides provided settlement sites above flood level, as well as being good defensive positions. In the Rhine Rift Valley these terraces are use for viticulture (see also Book, 1 Chapter 2).

2 Block mountains Block mountains such as those in the Western Cordil-lera of USA create major communication barriers. As they are often sandwiched between taller mountains, they are frequently in a rain shadow and are hence arid. Nevertheless, where irrigation is prac-tised or where workable mineral veins occur, small dense pockets of settlement may arise.

VULCANICITY

Molten rock (magma) from the mantle of the earth forces its way through weaknesses (faults, plate boundaries, rifts) towards the sur-face. At locations of great pressure in the crust, parts of the crust may melt, forming molten rock.

1   If the magma (molten rock) cools beneath the surface it forms **intru-sive** volcanic features, which will only be found on the surface when the overlying rock is eroded or weathered away.
2   If the magma cools on the surface it forms **extrusive** features, com-posed of rocks with small crystals.

Fig 3.11

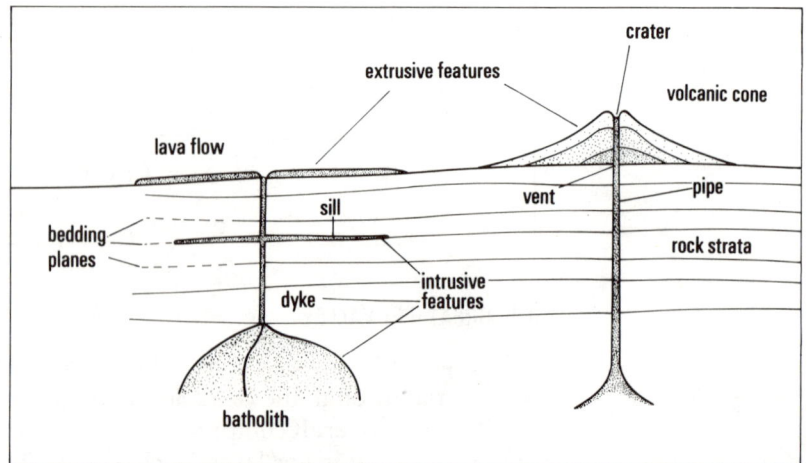

INTRUSIVE FEATURES

Dykes

Dykes are sheets of solidified rock where magma has forced its way across bedding planes. Where dykes are composed of material more resistant than surrounding rock, they form wall-like features, such as ridges or escarpments. Where dykes are less resistant, they may form shallow depressions or troughs. Dykes do not occur singly, but occur in great numbers. It has been estimated that the Isle of Arran has been stretched several miles by the intrusion of these dykes. In north-east Yorkshire the Cleveland Dyke is a major local feature influencing the drainage pattern.

Sills

Sills are sheets of solidified rock where magma has forced its way along the bedding planes of sedimentary rocks. As sedimentary rocks are often folded or tilted the sills may appear on the surface as a tilted sill.

Fig 3.12

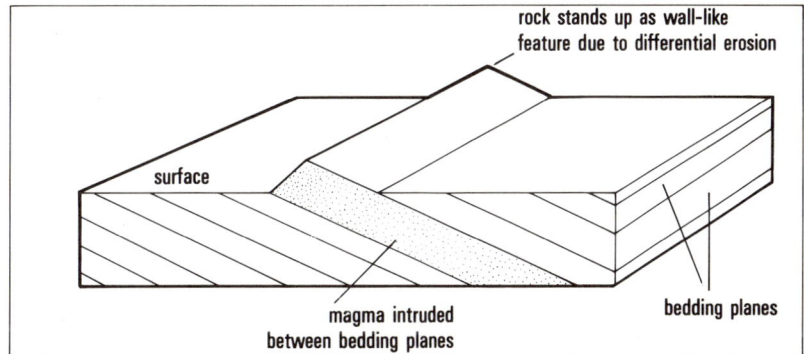

rock stands up as wall-like feature due to differential erosion

surface

magma intruded between bedding planes

bedding planes

Hadrian's wall is built upon the Great Whin Sill taking advantage of the fact that in some places it forms a low, north-facing escarpment.

Batholiths

Batholiths are masses of solidified rock where great cauldrons of magma have cooled slowly. When erosion of the overlying rocks brings these features to the surface they create very resistant, infertile granite uplands such as Dartmoor in south-west England and the Wicklow Mountains in Ireland.

Laccoliths

Where dykes or sills force up the sedimentary beds a dome shaped laccolith may form. This may create blisters on the earth's surface.

EXTRUSIVE FEATURES

Where magma reaches the surface of the crust it solidifies quickly, but the rate at which it solidifies depends largely on the chemical nature of the lava.

1 Where the lava is **basic** it has a low melting point, is a less sticky mixture and consequently flows further before solidifying.

2 Where the lava is **acid** it has a higher melting point, is very sticky and will not flow far before solidifying. The chemical nature of the lava partly accounts for the differences in the type of extrusive volcanic landform.

Lava flows

Where large quantities of basic lava well up from fissures in the earth's crust, they smother the existing relief before they solidify into thick sheets of volcanic rock. Successive eruptions result in the formation of lava plateaux of enormous thickness (e.g. the Deccan Plateau of India is nearly 2,000 m) and covering vast areas (the Snake–Columbia Plateau of Western USA covers nearly 300,000 sq. miles).

These basic lava plateaux (rich in iron and magnesium) may weather to form fertile soils as in the north-western part of the Deccan which produces commercial cotton. They may form tourist features because the basalt solidifies into hexagonal columns as in Fingal's Cave on the Island of Staffa in west Scotland or the Giant's Causeway in Northern Ireland. They may be carved by rivers into impressive gorges or canyons affecting communications such as those created by the River Snake in north-west USA. These gorges may be dammed to conserve water for irrigation of the arid intermontane plateaux, for HEP generation and for general water supply as well as for recreational purposes.

Volcanoes

When material issues from a crack in the earth's crust (vent) it may build up into a core. Volcanoes may be classified according to the shape and the constituents of these cones.

1 Acid lava cones These are composed of thick silica rich acidic lava which issues slowly from the pipe. As this type of lava has a high melting point it does not flow far from the crater before solidifying. Consequently these cones are tall, steep-sided and convex in profile. The eruption is generally explosive as lava frequently solidifies in the pipe, causing blockages which are blasted clear. An example is Mont Pelee in Martinique.

2 Basic lava cones These are composed of thin, runny iron and magnesium: rich basic lava which flows readily from the vent. As this type of lava has a lower melting point, it may flow far from the crater before solidifying. Therefore the cones are more gently sloped (less than 10°) and may be convex in profile – **shield shaped.** Despite their gentle gradients, they are often tall as vast volumes of lava pour out of the crater. As the pipe is rarely blocked eruptions tend to be non-explosive. An example is Mauna Loa, Hawaii.

3 Ash and cinder cones These cones are built of ash and cinder persistently exploded out of the crater. As the cinder is heavier it falls to the ground nearer the crater but the lighter ash travels further from the vent, often carried by the wind. Therefore, the cone may be tall, steep sided (30°) and concave in profile. An example is Mt St Helens in western USA.

4 Composite cones These are the commonest type of volcano consisting of alternate layers of ash and lava. Great pressure blasts a hole in the earth's crust, throwing ash and cinders high into the air. Acid lava flows from the vent solidifying quickly. The ash and cinder settle on to the lava, forming a layer called **tephra** or **tuff.** The volcano may go dormant before exploding again, repeating the above process. Consequently these volcanoes are often tall and steep sided (20°). An example is Mt Etna in Sicily.

The life cycle of a volcano

In the beginning eruptions are frequent and the volcano is **active.** This stage eventually gives way to a period of infrequent eruptions separated by long periods of inactivity. Volcanoes are said to be **dormant** (sleeping). When volcanoes have not erupted in historic times and there appears to be no activity they are said to be **extinct.** As extinct acidic volcanoes are weathered and eroded away only the resistant pipe or plug may remain. This may form steep-sided hills, ideal defensive sites. Edinburgh Castle is built on one of these 'plugs'. In central France these plugs are called 'puys', being used as sites for monasteries and/or medieval castles.

The location of volcanoes

Volcanoes are generally found in narrow bands along plate margins (see Fig 3.13 and 3.5 above). Consequently, they are mostly found on continents within a few hundred miles of the sea where continental plates meet oceanic plates. This is clearly evidenced by the **Pacific Ring of Fire** where a ring of volcanoes encircles the Pacific Ocean. As continental plates contain much silica the type of lava produced is acidic resulting in the formation of acid lava cones, composite cones, as well as ash and cinder cones. Volcanoes occur at these destructive margins as crust is melted and escapes to the surface.

   Most of the basic lava cones are found at constructive margins beneath the oceans where oceanic plates are pulling apart allowing the upwelling of lava forming submarine volcanoes which may grow until they break surface creating islands such as Iceland, Tenerife and so on.

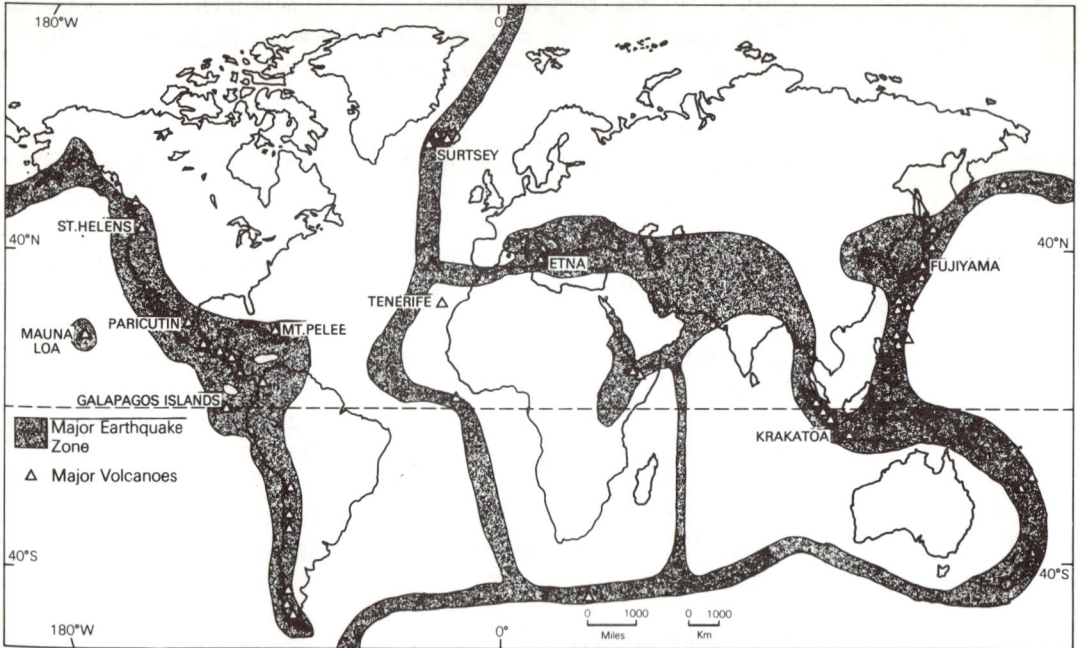

Fig 3.13 World distribution of the major volcanoes and earthquakes

THE EFFECTS OF VULCANICITY

1 Great loss of life The 1902 Mont Pelee eruption killed 30,000 people in the town of St Pierre on the island of Martinique.

2 Great destruction The Mount St Helens eruption buried massive areas under tons of fine volcanic dust; forests were totally destroyed; tons of melted snow, mixed with mud and ash, destroyed homes, timber camps and camp sites; roads were blocked; railway lines snapped; electric cables brought down; sewers blocked by ash and mud; rivers dammed creating flooding; shipping lanes on the Columbia River were clogged with mud; wildlife killed; and river water heated killing fish.

Constructive effects

1   Basic lava weathers into fertile soils, e.g. around Etna and on the island of Java. The dense agricultural production is largely due to the fertility of the soil.
2   Water heated by volcanic action is used to heat homes in Iceland.
3   Fresh lava from volcanic islands creates new land, such as Surtsey in Iceland.
4   The formation of precious stones and minerals, occurring in some igneous and sedimentary rocks, such as tin deposits in Cornwall. Others include copper, borax, sulphur, diamonds and quartz.
5   Geothermal power stations in Wairaki, New Zealand. Here water is

pumped down into the hot rocks, is heated into super-heated steam and is used to generate electricity by means of steam turbines.

METHODS OF REDUCING DAMAGE BY VOLCANOES

1 The diversion of mud or lava flows by the use of explosives (Etna 1983), channels, barriers.
2 The rapid cooling of lava to speed up solidification (use of sea water on Helgafell lava in 1973).
3 Early warning – use of **tiltmeters** to detect at an early date the bulging of volcanic cones, the forerunner of an eruption.
4 Planning controls – control of building construction in areas of high risk.

CHECKLIST ▶

THE STRUCTURE OF THE EARTH

1 There are three types of plate margin: destructive, constructive and passive.
2 Folding and faulting are associated with crustal plate movement.
3 Faulting produces a number of landforms: horsts, tilt blocks, block mountains and rift valleys.
4 Features produced by vulcanicity may be classified as intrusive or extrusive.
5 Intrusive features include dykes, sills, batholiths and laccoliths.
6 Extrusive features include volcanoes and lava plateaux.
7 Volcanoes are often classified according to their shape and the constituents of which they are composed: acid lava cones, basic lava cones, ash and cinder cones and composite cones.
8 Volcanoes are frequently found at plate boundaries.
9 Vulcanicity may bring advantages as well as disadvantages.

WEATHERING AND MASS MOVEMENT

WEATHERING

Every day the land is worn away, broken debris is removed to alternative locations and deposited. This is part of the process of landscape formation and is the result of numerous different agents and processes.

The general wearing away of rocks is called denudation, which itself is classified into weathering and erosion.

Weathering is the break-down of rocks where they stand. The weathered material stays where it is worn away or it falls, slides, rolls or creeps down a slope due to gravity.

Erosion is where material is broken down and transported away from its area of origin by some agent such as water, wind or ice.

TYPES OF WEATHERING

Weathering is normally classified into physical, chemical and biological weathering, each of which is subdivided. The extent to which one type is more active than another is largely a product of the prevailing climate and as a result of the rock type being weathered.

Physical weathering

Exfoliation In hot desert areas the alternate expansion (due to intense daytime heating) and contraction (due to rapid cooling at night) causes the outer layers of rock to peel off. This eventually creates rounded boulders or exfoliation domes. Despite the fact that this process is associated with arid locations, exfoliation is more rapid when moisture, such as dew, is present, because then chemical reactions will also occur.

Fig 3.14

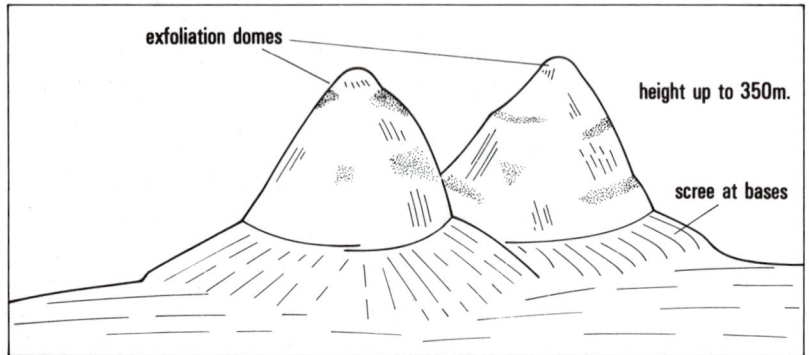

Frost shattering This process occurs in a variety of climatic zones, but is most active during the winter in temperate latitudes where temperatures oscillate either side of freezing point.

During the day water enters small cracks in rock faces. At night this water freezes and expands forcing the crack wider. Each day this process is repeated dislodging angular rock fragments from the rock face. These particles may fall or roll down the hillside creating **scree** slopes.

Block disintegration As a result of frost-shattering and exfoliation, certain types of rock may break up into towers or piles of rectangular-shaped blocks. These blocks themselves may continue to weather into piles of rounded blocks such as the granite **tors** on the granite moors of south-west England.

Chemical weathering

Carbonation As rain falls, carbon dioxide in the atmosphere is absorbed creating a weak solution of carbonic acid. Dilute carbonic acid converts the insoluble calcium bicarbonate of limestone rocks into soluble calcium carbonate. This is dissolved and carried away in solution by percolating water.

Oxidation Certain minerals when exposed to the oxygen in the earth's atmosphere oxidize. This frequently results in a weakening in their composition.

Hydration Certain crystals grow in size due to the addition of water creating stresses within the rock which may eventually disintegrate or crumble.

Hydrolysis Water mixes directly with other compounds, especially feld-spars, causing disintegration into basic clay minerals.

Biological weathering

Plant roots may widen cracks in rock faces and burrowing animals may dislodge soil and help to break up rock.

Rotting plants may create humic acid helping to disintegrate rocks chemically. Animals may do the same by means of ureic acid.

MASS MOVEMENT

This is the movement of waste material downhill under the force of gravity. It may be slow (such as soil creep) or very rapid (such as landslides). The type of process involved and its velocity are dependent on many factors including the angle of slope, the amount of water present in the waste material, the degree and type of vegetation and the interference of mankind.

SOIL CREEP

Soil moves slowly down the slope as a result of processes of weathering such as frost heave where soil is forced up by soil water

Fig 3.15 Evidence of soil creep

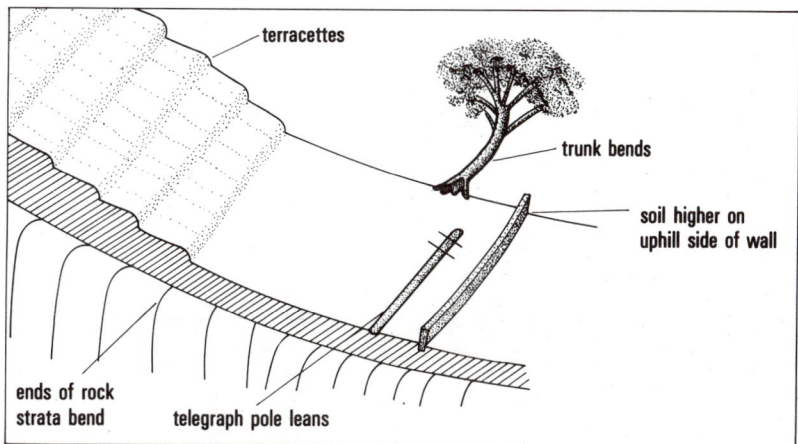

freezing and expanding. When the soil water thaws, the soil is moved a few millimetres downslope. Burrowing animals may dislodge downslope-displaced soil. Farmers ploughing land will steadily force soil downhill.

ROCK FALLS

Frost shattering may cause rock to fall from free faces often creating a scree slope protecting the foot of the free face.

Fig 3.16

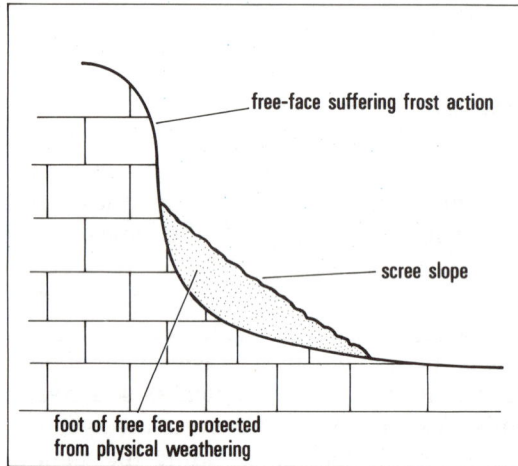

LANDSLIPS/LANDSLIDES

Waste material on a slope may become unstable and slide down a slope. This movement may be due to the saturation of a slip plane by persistent rainfall producing a slippery surface on which the overlying material may slide. This slipping may result in rotational slip due to the angle of the slip plane(s).

Fig 3.17

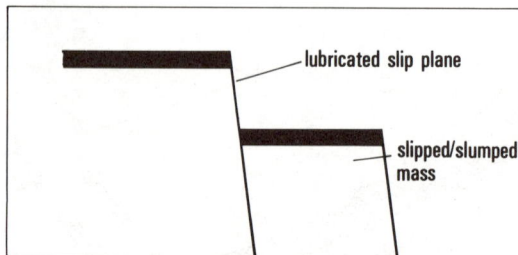

Fig 3.18

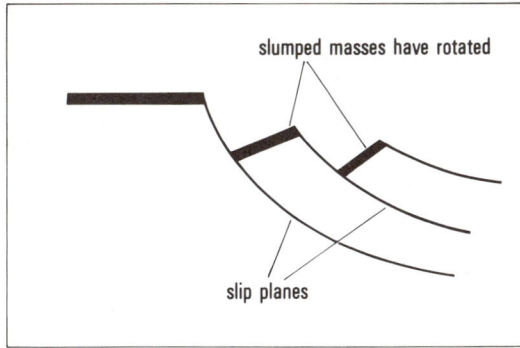

EARTHFLOWS/MUDFLOWS

Where earth is saturated with water it may flow down even relatively gentle gradients. Unlike slumped/slipped masses the moving material changes its shape due to its fluid nature, creating great tongues of liquid material. This process is closely associated with tundra regions where meltwater is trapped in the top metre of the soil by the permafrost.

ROCK TYPES

Rocks are the materials of the earth's crust. They are usually composed of small pieces or minerals compressed together. The earth's crust is made up of three rock types: igneous, sedimentary and metamorphic.

IGNEOUS ROCKS

These are the initial source of all rocks as sedimentary and metamorphic rocks are simply altered or refashioned igneous rocks. They are formed from molten magma from the mantle cooling and solidifying in or on the crust. They are normally classified into two groups.

Intrusive igneous rocks These are formed where magma cools slowly in the crust, creating rocks with large crystals. They include granite, which contains three common minerals: feldspar, mica and quartz. They form very strong rocks which resist erosion and weathering. Consequently, they are used for major construction such as the making of bridge piers and for roads as well as headstones for graves.

Extrusive igneous rocks These are formed where magma cools rapidly on the surface of the crust creating small crystals. They include rocks such as basalt and obsidian. Basalt is often crushed and used to surface roads while obsidian, because it is glossy in appearance, may be used for jewellery.

SEDIMENTARY ROCKS

There are a great variety of sedimentary rocks each of which is composed of small fragments or individual crystals from previous existing rocks. Generally they consist of layers or strata laid down and compressed under water. They may contain the remains of plants and animals (fossils). There are three main groups.

1 Chemically formed, e.g. rock salt and potash.
2 Organically formed – from animals, e.g. limestone
                    – from plants, e.g. coal.
3 Mechanically formed by the wind – loess
                      by ice sheets – boulder clay
                      by the sea and river – alluvium, gravels, clays.

The uses of these sedimentary rocks are numerous but include **construction** (limestone as a building material, as a base for cement; sandstone and gravel for concrete; some clays for bricks; shale for tiles), **fertilizers** (potash, nitrates, lime), and **chemical industry** (rock salt, mineral oil, coal, lignite, limestone, etc.).

METAMORPHIC ROCKS

Where igneous or sedimentary rocks are affected by intense heat and/or pressure they may alter. Their minerals may be realigned, new crystals may be formed or new minerals may be formed.

An increase in heat on chalk creates new crystals which make up marble. An increase in pressure on shale realigns the minerals into parallel sheets which produces slate; but if there is also extreme heat as well as pressure involved the shale will be converted into schist, which includes new minerals such as mica.

Marble is used as a decorative building material as well as for statues. Slate is an important roofing material. Anthracite is a valuable smokeless fuel.

CHECKLIST ▶

WEATHERING AND MASS MOVEMENT

1 Weathering breaks down material which remains in situ; erosion breaks down material and transports it out of the area.
2 Weathering is classified into physical, chemical and biological.
3 The relative importance of any type of weathering is largely dependent on the local climate.
4 Mass movement may be rapid (flows, slides) or slow (creep).
5 Rocks are classified into igneous, sedimentary and metamorphic.

THE HYDROLOGICAL CYCLE

Fig 3.19 Hydrological cycle

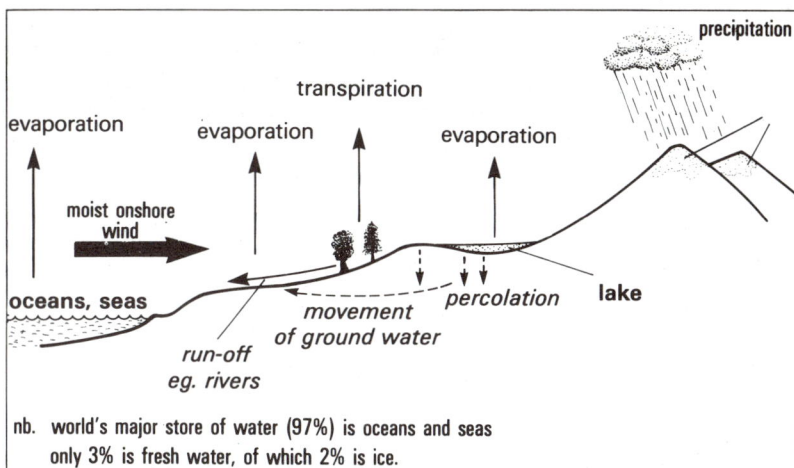

precipitation

transpiration

evaporation   evaporation   evaporation

moist onshore wind

oceans, seas

run-off eg. rivers

movement of ground water

percolation   lake

nb. world's major store of water (97%) is oceans and seas
only 3% is fresh water, of which 2% is ice.

The earth's total amount of water is constant, although it is continually being moved in liquid, solid or gas form from one store to another. It is this movement which comprises the hydrological cycle.

Water is evaporated from oceans and seas, creating moist onshore winds. These cause precipitation (inputs) over continents as the water is condensed into clouds and droplets are enlarged by coalescence and collision. Much of the rain runs directly into the sea via rivers, lakes and streams (flows). Some moisture percolates (flows) later to become the source of many streams. Some moisture is absorbed by vegetation and is transpired directly back into the atmosphere (outputs). Some water is directly evaporated from water surfaces such as lakes or inland seas (outputs). Ice sheets thaw in summer adding to the volume of water in the sea (outputs). This is replaced in winter by snow (inputs) which is frozen into ice (storage).

FACTORS INFLUENCING HYDROLOGICAL CYCLE

1 **Amount of precipitation.**

2 **Seasonal distribution of precipitation** In wet seasons there will be higher amounts of run-off as the land will already be saturated.

3 **Temperature and humidity levels** When temperatures are low water may freeze into ice seriously slowing run-off, reducing evaporation levels, and if vegetation is dormant there will be little, if any, transpiration. Percolation may not occur because joints and pore spaces are frozen. Where sea ice occurs evaporation from the sea will be very low and cold winds will have low humidity levels as they are incapable of holding much moisture. Where/when temperatures are high evaporation and transpiration will be high, percolation will be rapid as the

ground is so dry, dry winds will cause little precipitation and high evaporation, ground water may be drawn to the surface by capillary action or by vegetation with deep tap roots.

4 Wind directions Onshore winds will bring higher humidity levels and more chance of precipitation. Offshore winds will reduce precipitation and decrease humidity. Wind direction will affect temperatures.

5 Relief of the land Areas of high relief are likely to have higher rainfall figures, have lower temperatures which will reduce evaporation and may create ice sheets. Rain shadow areas may reduce precipitation levels. Relief will also influence the type and density of vegetation thereby affecting transpiration levels.

6 Vegetation Sparsity of vegetation will increase run-off, reduce transpiration and increase percolation rates.

7 Rock type Impervious rocks reduce percolation and increase run-off. They will also encourage the formation of lakes increasing storage and allowing increased evaporation. Pervious and porous rocks will greatly increase percolation reducing run-off and evaporation. They may also reduce vegetation levels, reducing transpiration.

8 Mankind Man can radically affect the water cycle in numerous ways either by influencing the above factors or by direct interference.
(a)   Artificially creating rainfall by dry-ice seeding.
(b)   Affecting temperature levels by the consruction of industry and towns.
(c)   Removal of natural vegetation by clearance of forests, and ploughing of grasslands (see Book 1, Chapter 3).
(d)   Construction of reservoirs, diversion of river flows, extensive irrigation systems, dry farming techniques, contour ploughing, artificial drainage, embanking of rivers, extraction of water from rivers or ground water stores, development of drainage and sewerage systems, transfer of water from one drainage basin to another and desalinization schemes (see Book 1, Chapters 2 and 3).

THE DRAINAGE BASIN OF A RIVER

A drainage basin is an area of land drained by a river and its tributaries. Smaller drainage basins rest inside larger basins. Each basin is separated by a watershed or river divide of higher land – the high land from which water will run into the major river of the drainage basin.

THE RIVER BASIN HYDROLOGICAL CYCLE

The basin hydrological cycle in an open system consisting of the following:

Fig 3.20 The river basin
hydrological cycle

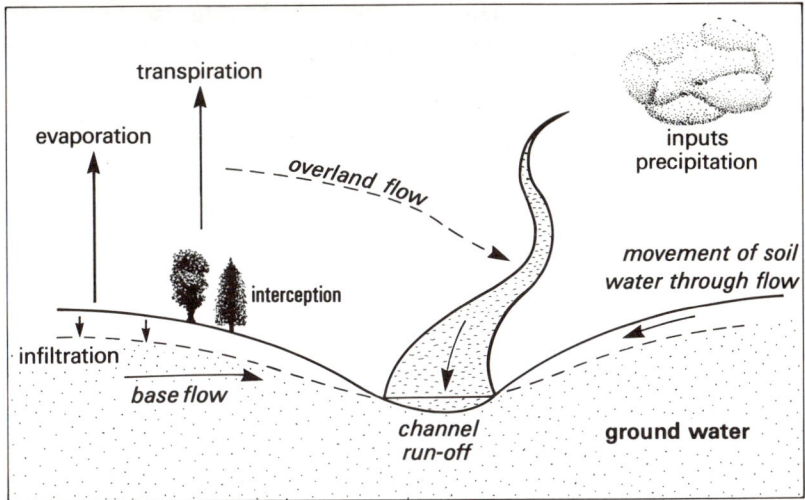

(a)   Inputs
      (i) precipitation.
(b)   Storage
      (i) by plants which intercept imputs when precipitation is
      caught on leaves and branches;
      (ii) at the surface in puddles;
      (iii) in the soil;
      (iv) within rocks beneath the surface (ground water);
(c)   Flows (throughputs)
      (i) channel flow – precipitation falling directly into the river
      channel;
      (ii) overland flow – precipitation running quickly on the sur-
      face in the form of sheetwash or in rills or gullies;
      (iii) throughflow – water moving generally slowly through
      the soil using the soil pores and cracks;
      (iv) base flow – the very slow seepage of ground water into
      the stream.
(d)   (i) evaporation   ⎱
      (ii) transpiration by plants ⎰ evapotranspiration;
      (iii) river outflow or discharge.

   It is base flow that maintains a river's flow during periods of
drought, because it varies little. But it is the fluctuations in overland
flow which result in major variations in the volume of water found in
the river channel.

RIVER REGIME

This is the variations in the amount of water the river is carrying over
a measured period of time. This involves obtaining the **discharge** of
river. It is recorded by obtaining the cross-sectional area of a stretch of
river channel × the depth of water × speed of flow (m^3/sec). Consequently, the discharge is the measurable output of a drainage basin.

The variations which comprise a river regime are a product of the changes in input, storage and flow to be found within a drainage basin over a period of time. These changes depend largely on the following factors:

1 The amount and intensity of rainfall. Regular heavy rainfall or heavy rainstorms will result in very little infiltration and much overland flow as the soil soon becomes saturated. This rapid run-off can lead to 'flash-floods', which may be very destructive.

2 The types of rock and soil found in the drainage basin. Impervious rocks will result in surface storage as well as higher run-off figures but porous or pervious rocks will increase rates of infiltration leading to more base flow (considerably slower) and greater storage in the soil and as ground water.

3 The nature of the vegetation cover. This influences the degree of transpiration, interception, soil water flow.

4 Other factors such as the shape of the drainage basin, the number of streams in the drainage basin.

Fig 3.21 Influence of basin shape on regimes

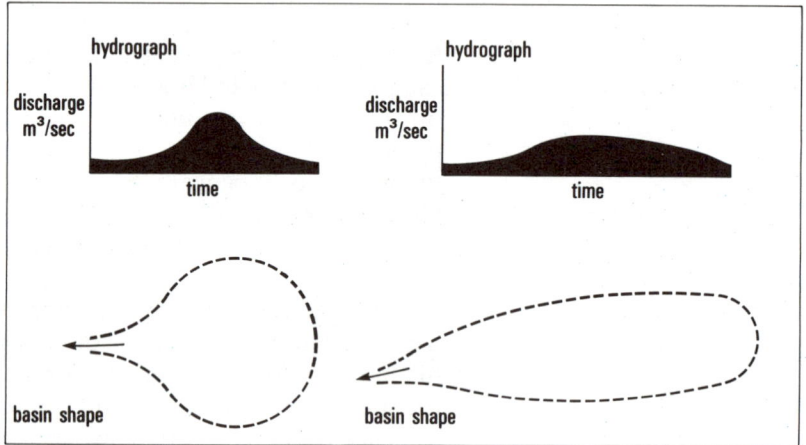

Fig 3.22 Influence of stream density on regimes

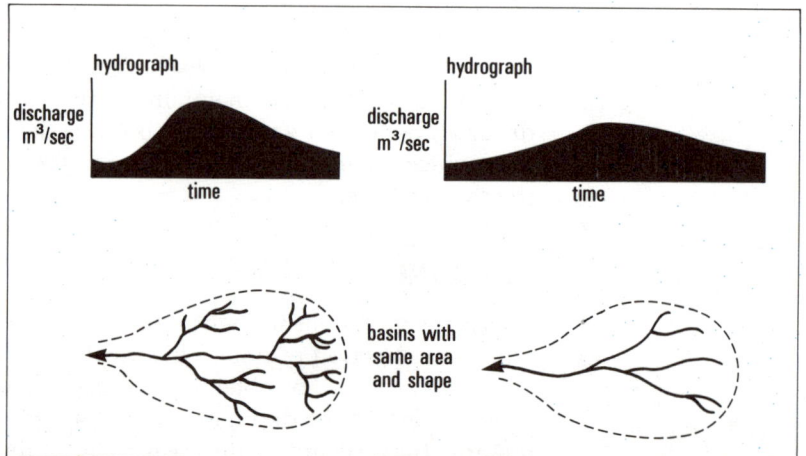

WATER BUDGET

It is possible to calculate the water budget, by comparing the amount of precipitation falling within the basin, with the amount of run off. The difference between the two indicates storage and evapotranspiration. Generally, this figure is higher in the wetter west of England and Wales than in the drier east.

RIVER CHANNELS AND VALLEYS

THE ENERGY OF A RIVER

Rivers require energy to erode their beds and banks and to transport the eroded material (the load). Moving water creates **kinetic energy** which is a product of the volume of the water and its velocity. If either of these two factors increases, so will the ability of a river to do its work. However 98 per cent of a river's energy is used in simply overcoming friction within its channel.

ENERGY LOST TO FRICTION

Internal friction
This is created where turbulence causes currents to work or rub against each other.

External friction
1   Contact between the moving water and boulders, stones found on the river bed or protruding from the river banks.
2   The winding or meandering course of a river increases friction between the river and its banks.
3   The shape of the river channel. Where a volume of water has least possible contact with its bed and banks there will be less friction and a more efficient channel slope. This is best achieved where the width of the channel is twice the depth.

Fig 3.23 Influence of channel shape and water level on friction

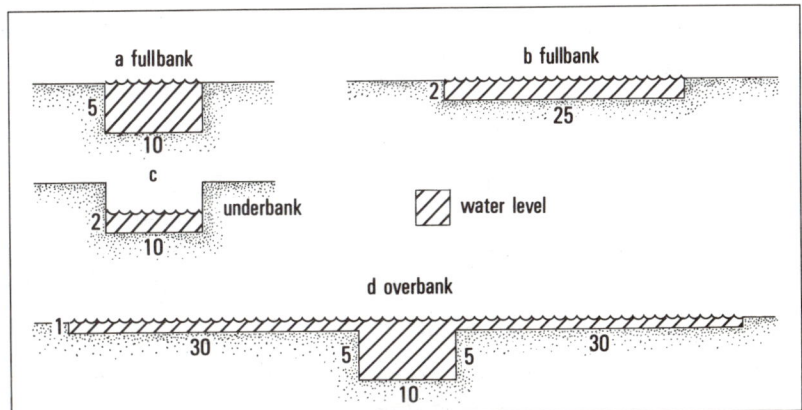

Referring to fig 3.23 on p. 153:
At A. The river is at full bank (totally occupying the channel). The amount of contact with the beds and banks is 20 m. The (wetted perimeter) cross-sectional area of water in the channel is 50m². The efficiency of the shape of the channel is

$$\frac{50}{20} = 2.5$$

Also at full bank with the same cross-sectional area of water.

At B. It is

$$\frac{50}{29} = 2.08$$

Calculate the efficiency of the river in overcoming external friction when it is underbank (C) and flooding (overbank D). Which is the more efficient water level?

METHODS OF RIVER EROSION

1 Corrosion – where river water dissolves rock such as chalk.
2 Corrasion – where debris moved by the river is used as a cutting tool against its bed and banks.
3 Scouring – where moving water acts like a high pressure hose washing away loose material.
4 Cavitation – the sudden release in pressure (explosion) of air trapped by turbulent or falling water.
5 Attrition – the reduction in calibre of the load by persistently striking the banks, beds or itself.
    The amount of erosion done by the river is dependent on surplus energy and varies with the river's regime. Many other factors play a part including rock type, vegetation and mankind.

METHODS OF RIVER TRANSPORT

1 Solution load – material dissolved in water.
2 Suspension load – very light material carried within the river but not dissolved.
3 Traction load – large calibre material rolled along the river bed.
4 Saltation load – material bounced along the river bed.
    The volume and calibre of the load are dependent on the amount of surplus energy available. For large calibre loads the energy required for initial movement of the bouler must be very high. Consequently, flash floods are associated with traction.

DEPOSITION

A river drops part of its load when it loses energy:
1 Where it slows.

2 When the volume of water is reduced.

The coarser, heavier material is deposited first but finer material (alluvium) is deposited later. Consequently, a river is said to grade its material.

THE UPLAND COURSES OF RIVERS

THE UPPER COURSE VALLEY

In the upper course, the river concentrates on vertical erosion lowering its channel bed; but the river does not only transport the material it has eroded but also removes weathered material moved downslope into its channel by the processes of mass movement (see p. 145–6 above).

Fig 3.24

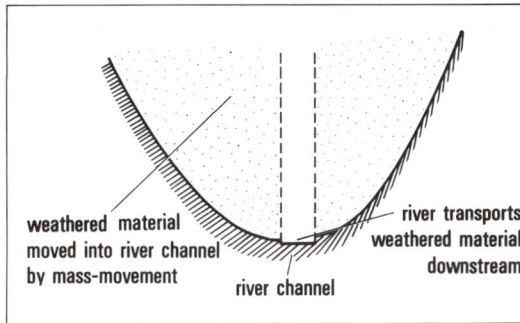

Consequently, upland valleys are steep sided and have narrow valley floors, largely occupied by river channels. The river bed is occupied by large calibre material as there has been little chance for attrition to reduce it. The river channel winds around spurs of high land projecting across the valley. These are interlocking spurs.

Upper course features
Potholes These are shallow holes found in the rocky bed.
1 Stones are washed into natural hollows in the river bed.
2 Turbulence is created by the uneven nature of the bed.
3 This extra velocity generates extra energy so that the trapped stones are whirled around the hollows, acting like a drill.
4 The stoens corrode the bed, enlarging and deepening the hollow.
5 The potholes join up, so lowering the bed of the river channel.

Example The Strid on the River Wharfe near Bolton Abbey.

Waterfalls, rapids and gorges Waterfalls occur where there is an initial drop, possibly due to faulting.
1 The falling water forms a plunge pool.
2 The enlargement of the plunge pool and erosion by splashback undercuts the overlying rock.

3 The cap rock collapses into the plunge pool and is used to enlarge the pool further by means of corrasion.
4 As the waterfall retreats, a gorge is created.
5 As waterfalls retreat, their height is reduced and they may degenerate into rapids where tumbling rather than falling water occurs.

Example Niagara Falls between Lake Erie and Lake Ontario in N. America.

Fig 3.25

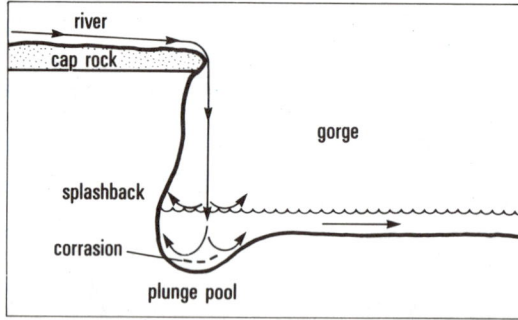

Fig 3.26

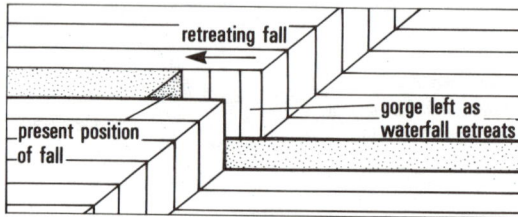

THE USES OF UPLAND VALLEYS

1 Hill farming – the growth of fodder crops and improved pasture for sheep and cattle during the winter.
2 Forestry – especially coniferous trees grown on upland slopes which give a quicker rate of return than deciduous trees. They also reduce soil erosion reducing sedimentation where HEP is being generated.
3 Tourism.
4 Hydroelectric power generation (see page 169).
5 Water supply.

THE MIDDLE COURSES OF RIVERS

THE MIDDLE COURSE VALLEY

In this section the river concentrates on lateral erosion and the transportation of its load. The river has a much greater volume of water due to the attraction of many tributaries and despite the reduction in the gradient of its long profile, the addition of extra volume more than compensates to produce much energy to transport very large loads. Middle course valleys tend to be wide with gentle valley sides and with a noticeable alluvial plain occupying the valley floor.

Fig 3.27

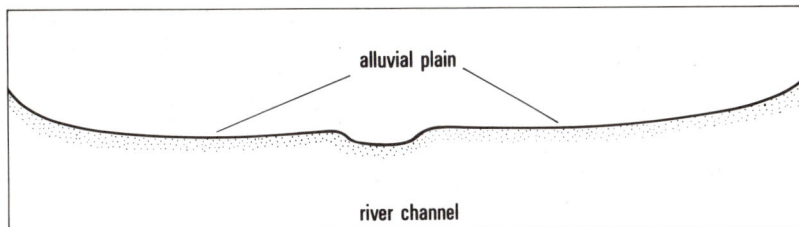

Middle course features

Meanders These are the bends of a river caused by reduction in velocity.

1   Faster-flowing water occurs on the outside of a meander causing the outside bank to be undercut.
2   Slower-flowing water is on the inside of a meander resulting in deposition on the inside.
3   Meanders move down stream – **down**-valley migration.

River cliffs and alluvial plains These are the result of down-valley migration of meanders.

1   As meanders move downstream they remove interlocking spurs.
2   This results in the river creating nearly parallel valley sides.
3   At certain points the outside of the meander will be actively undercutting the valley side, creating a steeper section called a river cliff.
4   Between the valley sides is a plain composed of alluvium formed by deposition on the insides of meanders.
5   This alluvial plain may frequently be flooded when the river discharge is so high that the river channel cannot contain all the water. The flood waters are slowed by increased friction and will deposit more alluvium on the alluvial plain.

Example On the Gloucestershire Avon, near Pershore.

THE LOWER COURSES OF RIVERS

THE LOWER COURSE VALLEY

In this section, despite the increased volume of water, the reduction in velocity leads to much deposition of silt. The river meanders extensively over a wide marshy flood plain, frequently taking changes of course. Individual sections of the river are cut off, flood water and tributary streams may have great difficulty entering the main river due to the presence of levees.

Fig 3.28

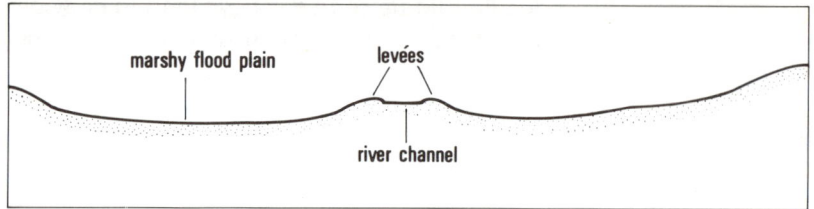

Lower course features
Ox-bow lakes/cut-offs

1   Meanders become very accentuated.
2   The outside of one meander may approach the outside of another.
3   Eventually the two meanders meet.
4   The river takes the shortest route, creating a cut-off.
5   The ends of the cut-off are sealed by deposition due to friction with the slack water. This creates an ox-bow lake.
6   The ox-bow lake is a temporary feature as there is no permanent influx of water.

Example The lower course of the river Mississippi, South of St Louis.

Fig 3.29

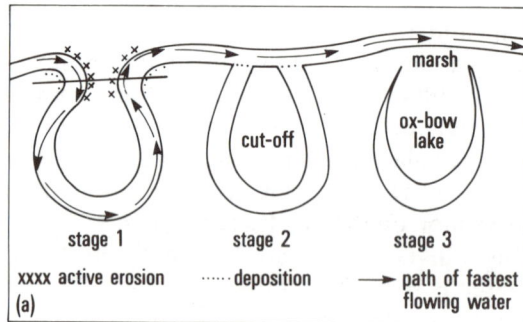

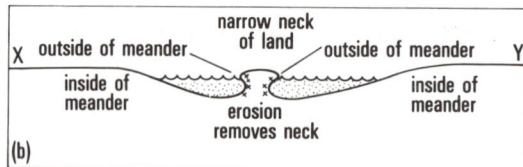

LEVEES AND FLOOD PLAINS

Levees are low natural walls of sand, silt and gravel on the banks of a river. They are higher than the surrounding flood plain.

1   When a river floods, the laden river-water overflows its banks.
2   The flow of this water is instantly checked by increased friction.
3   Consequently, the heavier, coarser material is deposited on the river

banks, creating low walls which are added to each time the river floods.

4 The rest of the laden floodwater spreads out over the flood plain.

5 As much of this floodwater is unable to return to the main river because of the levees, it either evaporates or percolates leaving behind a layer of silt.

6 Each time the river floods, the level of silt is increased, creating a flood plain.

Example The lower course of the river Mississippi.

BRAIDING

1 Deposition occurs on the bed of a river, creating many small, low islands of coarse, river gravel.

2 The river is forced to split into many sections to pass by these islands: braiding.

3 The positions of these islands and of the river channels are not fixed as the variations in the river's regime may result in the reworking of the deposited material and shifts in channel position.

DELTAS

These may occur where a river enters a sea or lake.

1 As the river enters the sea, its velocity is checked.

2 The river has less energy and therefore deposits much of its load.

3 With continual additions, the deposited material may build up to break above sea-level.

4 Therefore the river must split into distributaries to pass by these islands of material.

Where there are strong lake or sea currents, deltas will not form. Consequently, there are no significant sea deltas in Britain.

Example The mouth of the river Rhine in Holland.
The delta separating the lakes of Derwentwater and Bassenthwaite in the Lake District.

THE RIVER LONG PROFILE A river's source is in upland regions and its mouth is often the sea. The gradient of the route between these two points is its long profile. All rivers attempt to make this gradient a smooth curve, called the curve of water erosion.

The lowest point to which a river erodes is base level, which is frequently sea-level. If base level falls then the curve of water erosion at the mouth is not steep enough. If base level rises the gradient is too steep.

Fig 3.30

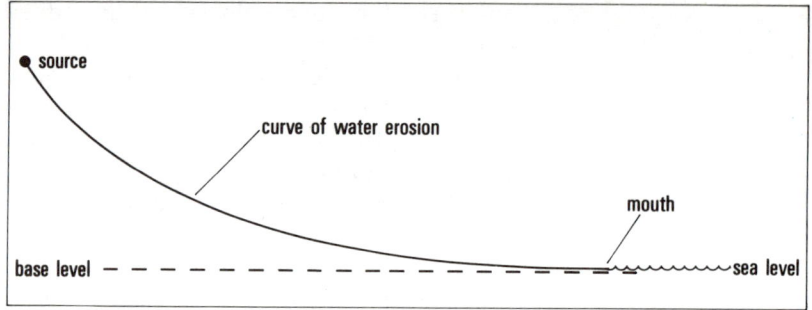

FEATURES PRODUCED BY CHANGES IN BASE LEVEL

A rise in base level This results in the sea flooding the lower stretches of the valley, creating a **ria.** The rivers velocity is checked so deposition occurs in the ria creating **marsh** or **salt-marsh.**

A fall in base level As the curve is no longer steep enough at the river mouth, the river actively downcuts its channel into the existing valley floor. This creates
(*a*)   a distinct break in slope in the profile, called a nick point. This may create a waterfall or rapids;
(*b*)   areas of floodplain abandoned above the river channel.
      These are called **terraces.**

RIVERS AND MANKIND

The life of the human race is inextricably linked with rivers and river valleys, as they provide so much that mankind requires:
1   Water supply.
2   Navigation.
3   Routeways.
4   Settlement sites.
5   Power sources.
6   Recreation.
7   Fertile soils for farming.
   But they can also bring serious dangers such as flooding, landslides, etc.

1 Water supply (see page 149).

2 Navigation Waterways provide major navigational systems as transport of bulky, non-perishable goods is cheaper than by any other system of transport. The Great Lakes–St Lawrence Seaway system and the Rhine Navigation are of great importance to North America and Europe respectively (see Book 1, Chapter 3).

3 Routeways Valleys provide natural routeways especially through upland regions. Consequently many railways and roads keep to the lower valley slopes as they follow the valley. At the same time valleys may make communications difficult when a canal, road or railway line needs to cross a steep-sided valley or wide river. Expensive bridges or viaducts or aqueducts have to be constructed, tunnels created, hairpin bends built (see Book 1, Chapter 3).

4 Settlement sites Valleys provide sheltered locations, flatter sites, easier access, focal routes (bridging points), more fertile soils, water supply and so on. Consequently, nucleation has occurred in valleys especially on terraces, at confluences of rivers, along spring lines, at bridging points (see Book 1, Chapter 4).

5 Power sources The development of water power encouraged the development of mill-races for mills and attracted textile mills to a bankside location. Hydroelectric power development is a further extension of the use of rivers for power generation (see page 44).

6 Recreation Man's enjoyment of rivers takes numerous forms including looking at them, painting, walking alongside, boating, canoeing, fishing, swimming.

7 Farming River valleys provide fertile alluvial soils, water for irrigation and drinking as well as more gentle slopes for mechanized farming. They are also nearer to settlements encouraging more intensive farming methods and easier access to communications for transport of market produce (see Book 1, Chapter 2).

CHECKLIST ▶   **RIVERS**

1   Many factors influence the hydrological cycle.
2   The basic hydrological cycle contains inputs, storage, flows and outputs.
3   The water budget shows regional variations in the British Isles.
4   Rivers possess energy, most of which is lost in overcoming friction.
5   Rivers erode by corrosion, corrasion, scouring, cavitation and attrition.
6   Rivers transport their load by solution, suspension, traction and saltation.
7   Deposition occurs where/when rivers lose energy.
8   Rivers may be classified into upper, middle and lower course sections, each of which has distinctive landforms.
9   Changes in base level produce district river land-forms.
10 Rivers are, and always have been, of great importance to mankind.

GLACIERS AND ICE SHEETS

Many high latitude and high altitude areas of the world receive their winter precipitation as snow. In many areas, these accumulations of snow completely melt away during the summer (ablation). But if the amount of snowfall exceeds the amount of melt, then each year greater and greater depths of snow will accumulate. The weight of overlying snow will compress lower layers to form nevée and eventually ice.

When ice and snow occupy vast areas of continents, then an ice sheet is formed; but if a river of ice is largely restricted to upland valleys, then a valley glacier is created. As these glaciers leave the confines of upland valleys, they may spread out and join up to form piedmont glaciers.

In the twentieth century ice sheets occupy Antarctica and Greenland; valley glaciers are found in mountainous regions such as the Himalayas and Alps. But the climate of Europe has been colder than it is at present. These cold periods are called the Ice Ages. They resulted in massive accumulations of ice in most upland regions, especially Scandinavia. From these uplands, glaciers and ice sheets moved to cover much of north-west Europe, including Britain (north of the Thames Valley). The result was considerable erosion, transport and deposition.

METHODS OF GLACIAL EROSION

1 Frost shattering During the daytime meltwater flows down rock faces, entering cracks and joints. At night, when the temperature drops below 0°C, this water freezes and expands, cracking the rock.

2 Plucking Occurs when loosened blocks are frozen into the base of sides of a glacier. As the glacier moves, these blocks are pulled away.

3 Grinding Any *moraine* which protrudes from the side or base of the glacier scrapes or gouges the valley floor or sides as the glacier moves along.

FACTORS INFLUENCING THE AMOUNT OF GLACIAL EROSION

1 Thickness of ice The thicker the ice, the greater pressure and the greater the erosion.

2 The type, calibre and shape of the moraine Resistant, angular material will make the glacier more effective at grinding.

3 The relative weakness or strength of the rock being eroded Rock more easily eroded may be:
(*a*)   soft;

(b)   weakened by previous faulting;
(c)   weakened by extensive frost shattering;
(d)   weakened by chemical weathering.

MOVEMENT OF GLACIERS

Ice moves by sliding along the valley floor (basal slip). This movement is aided by meltwater acting as a lubricant between the base and sides of the glacier and the valley floors and walls. Despite this lubrication the ice at the surface and in the centre of the glacier moves fastest as there is less friction.

Ice may also flow like a viscous plastic. This movement and the irregularities of the surface over which the glacier passes create cracks or crevices within the ice, when the semi-rigid ice is forced to bend.

Glaciers move downhill under the influence of gravity, but it is also possible for their bases to move some distance uphill, as long as the general slope is downhill.

TRANSPORTATION

Material is transported by glaciers in the form of moraine. This is material plucked from the sides and bottoms of valleys, as well as material which has fallen on to the top of the passing stream of ice as a result of frost shattering.

DEPOSITION

Glaciers deposit moraine where/when ice melts. The exact location of deposition will vary from year to year according to climatic variations. In a cooler summer a glacier may extend further down a valley before melting, than in a hotter summer.

When an ice sheet/glacier melts, the material it is carrying is deposited, covering the underlying relief with thickness of till (boulder clay). As the material carried by a glacier is not evenly distributed, then deposition is not even, causing a hummocky surface with long lines or walls of moraine. The material is often resorted by meltwater streams.

Fig 3.31

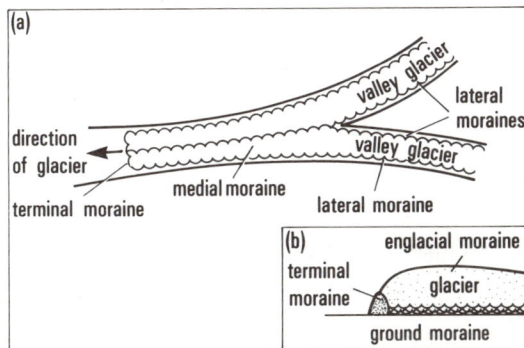

HIGHLAND GLACIATION

LANDFORMS

Corries and corrie lakes Corries, cirques or cwms are armchair-shaped hollows, from which glaciers originate. Snow accumulates in hollows on the north-east facing slopes of mountains. The snow is compressed into nevée and then ice. The hollow is deepened by chemical solution allowing for greater snow accumulation. During the summer the bergschrund crevasse opens, allowing meltwater to flow down the rock faces. Frost shattering weakens these rock faces, allowing the glacier to pluck out the loosened rock, to be used by the glacier as a grinding tool when the ice is forced to rotate slowly around the hollow. When some of the ice is squeezed out of the hollow a sill is formed. After the Ice Ages this sill may pond back water to form a lake.

Example Llyn Idwal in North Wales is a corrie lake overlooking the Nant Ffrancon Valley.

Fig 3.32

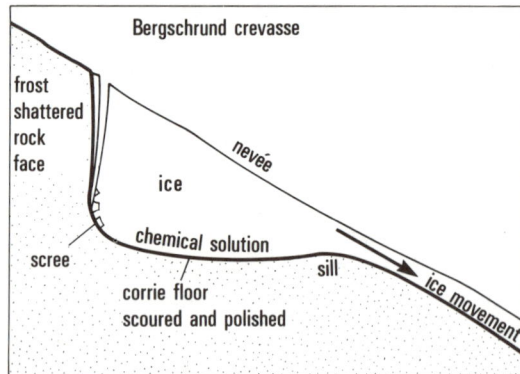

Arêtes These are knife-edged ridges which separate corries. They are created by the continued erosion of the spur of land separating the backs or sides of two corries.

Example Striding Edge in the Lake District.

Pyramidal peaks/horns These are pyramid-shaped mountain peaks created by three corries eroding backwards.

Example The Matterhorn in Switzerland.

Glacial troughs Troughs are steep-sided valleys with wide, flat valley floors. They are often bowl shaped (incorrectly described as 'U' shaped valleys).

During the Ice Ages river valleys were occupied by glaciers. As

Fig 3.33 Pyramidal peaks

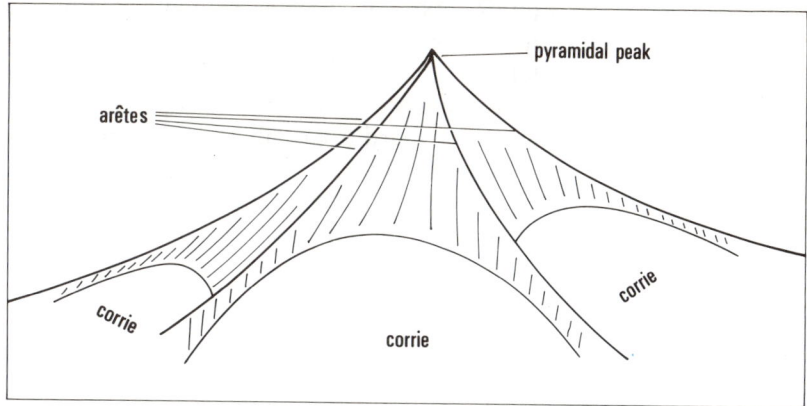

they are more powerful erosive agents than rivers, the valleys were widened and deepened. The valley floors and sides were previously weakened by frost shattering, allowing the glaciers to erode them by plucking and grinding. The ends of the interlocking spurs created by rivers were quickly removed to form **truncated spurs.** At the end of the Ice Ages, till was deposited on the floor of the trough creating a hummocky, impervious surface. Rivers re-occupied these troughs, but are obviously too small to have created such large valleys. These rivers, which may meander extensively over the floor of the trough, are called *misfits*.

Example Nant Ffrancon Valley in North Wales.

Hanging valleys These are the valleys of tributary glaciers which may end abruptly, high up on the valley side of the main glacial trough. They were formed because tributary glaciers were composed of a smaller depth of ice than main glaciers. Consequently, their valleys were not eroded as deeply as the main glacial trough. At the end of the Ice Ages, these tributary glacial valleys were left perched high up on the valley sides of the main glacial trough. The misfit streams that now occupy the hanging valleys may often fall or tumble on to the main glacial floors, creating glacial fans out of the material deposited when their velocity is checked.

Example The Valley of the Buckden Beck is a hanging valley. The small village of Buckden in Wharfedale, North Yorkshire, is built upon a glacial fan to provide a drier settlement site above the marshy floor of the Wharfe valley.

Mountain ribbon lakes and morainic dammed lakes These are long, narrow lakes occupying the floors of glacial troughs.
   Mountain ribbon lakes occur where glaciers have over-deepened part of the floor of a glacial trough. This may occur due to:

(*a*)   extra vertical erosion due to the addition of greater thick-nesses of ice when a tributary glacier joins the main one;

(*b*)   a softer band of rock forming the valley floor, sandwiched between more resistant bands upstream and downstream;

(*c*)   a hard rock sill crossing the valley resisting erosion and creating a dam.

Morainic dammed lakes are created by valley glaciers melting and depositing moraine at their **snouts.** This terminal moraine forms a crescent-shaped dam across the glacial trough, form one valley wall to the other. At the end of the Ice Ages misfit streams occupied the

Fig 3.34 Glacial highland featues in Snowdonia

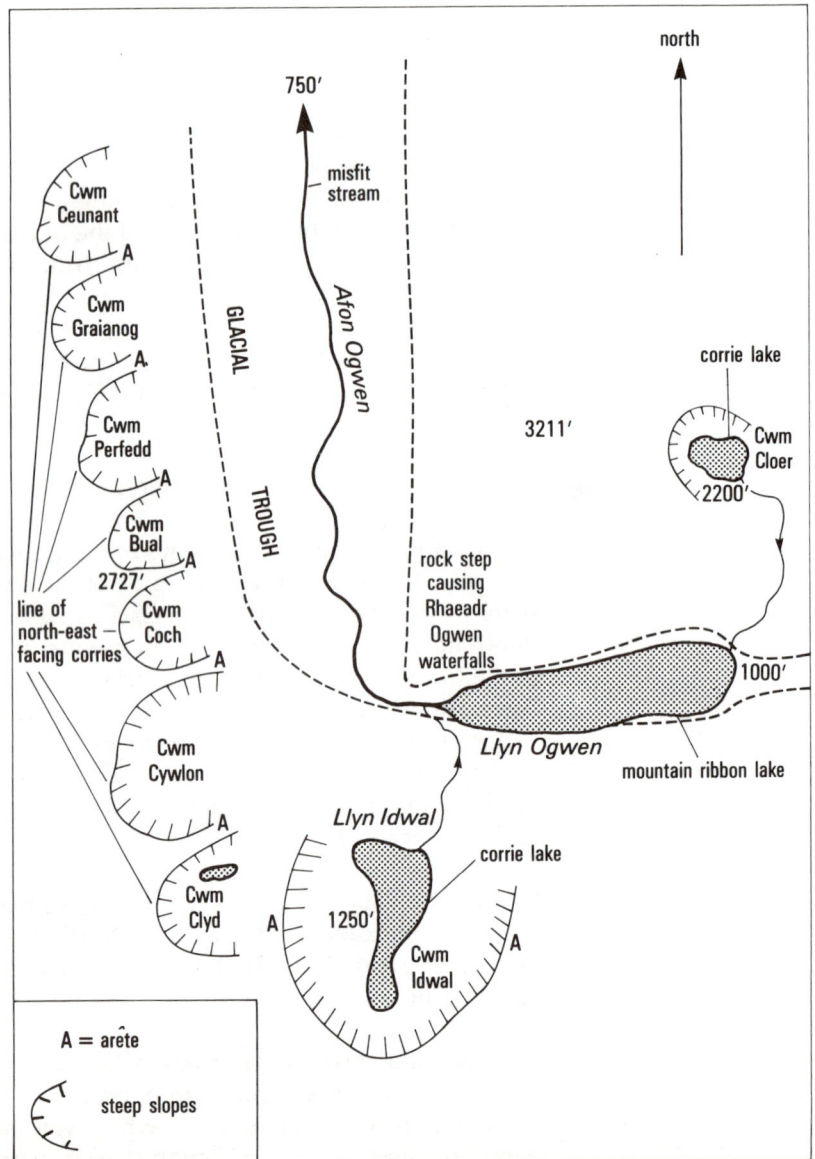

glacial troughs and created lakes by filling in the hollow or being ponded back by terminal moraines. Water cannot escape sideways due to the steep sides of the glacial trough.

Examples

1 Morainic dammed lakes – Lake Windermere, Lake District
2 Mountain ribbon lakes: Loch Ness, Scotland.

LOWLAND GLACIATION As valley glaciers leave the confinement of the upland valleys they spread out and join up to form ice sheets or piedmont glaciers. The ice is now at a lower altitude and is consequently more likely to melt. Therefore features created by lowland glaciation are more likely to be a result of deposition rather than erosion.

GLACIAL LANDFORMS

Roches moutonnées These are boulders or outcrops of rocks of varying size, but whose appearance follows a distinctive pattern. The upstream side of the rock is polished smooth by the process of grinding caused as the ice sheet passes over the rock. The downstream side is ragged due to the plucking out of shattering rock.

Crag and tail An ice sheet meets a massive obstruction of resistant rock such as a volcanic plug. This obstruction forces the ice sheet to divide, causing erosion in front of the crag but shielding the local rock behind the crag. This protected rock forms the tail.

Example Edinburgh Castle is built on a crag and the tail is the main street leading down from the castle.

Drumlins These are huge piles of deposited glacial material, many over a mile in length. Each pile has a distinct shape with a blunt nose and a tapered tail. Drumlins occur in groups called **swarms** forming a distinct **basket of eggs** topography.

Example Eden Valley in Cumbria.

Erratics These are rocks which are foreign to the areas in which they are found. They are of a different composition from the underlying bedrock, having been transported into the area by ice sheets.

Eskers These are long sinuous ridges of gravel transported and deposited by sub-glacial rivers. As glaciers can travel uphill so too do the tunnels erected by these rivers. Eskers are created by the deposition of gravel as the sub-glacial river emerges from the snout of the glacier. As the glacier retreats (ablation) a train of gravel will form where the snouts of glacier remain for a significant period, a greater thickness of gravel will be deposited causing **beaded** eskers.

OUTWASH PLAINS

When an ice sheet melts, vast volumes of meltwater transport glacial till beyond the terminal moraines. This glacial material is resorted and graded by rivers before being re-deposited as fluvio-glacial material. The coarser gravels and sands are dropped first and the finer clays dropped last. The area created by this deposited material is called an outwash plain.

At the end of the Ice Age some of these fine clays were picked up by strong winds, transported to other areas and deposited to form thick layers of very fertile soil called loess or 'limon' (France). Extensive deposits cover much of the Red Plain of China. In Britain, the nearest equivalent are 'brick earths' loess which has been reworked by rivers.

THE INFLUENCE OF GLACIAL ACTIVITY ON HUMAN ACTIVITY

1 Icebergs

These are floating lumps of ice which have been calved from ice sheets or glaciers. The direction in which they float is governed by ocean currents. In the North Atlantic many icebergs come from Greenland glaciers. They drift southwards carried by the cold Labrador current. The majority melt before they reach the major great circle shipping route between New York and Europe. But when they do not, they can be a major hazard to shipping, as was clearly demonstrated in 1912 when the *Titanic* sunk.

Nevertheless, icebergs could prove to be advantageous. There are adventurous schemes being proposed to tow icebergs to prosperous arid countries (such as those in the Middle East) for major fresh water supplies.

2 Avalanches

These are the tumblings of snow and ice moving rapidly down a steep slope. They are caused by vibrations such as those created by loud noises such as gunshots, or by movements such as passing vehicles. They may also be caused by rapid thawing such as that caused by the föhn effects – a warm wind which can suddenly raise temperatures on the leeward side of mountains. Their effect can be devastating: destroying villages, and burying people alive.

Various methods are used either to prevent avalanches occurring or reduce their effect. These include:
(*a*)   the construction of snow nets, fences and bridges;
(*b*)   the planting of shelter belts of conifers above the villages;
(*c*)   the construction of strengthened, wedge shaped buildings in high-risk areas;

(d)   the deliberate triggering of small avalanches before massive snow accumulations become unstable;

(e)   the use of sniffer dogs and heat-seeking detectors to find quickly people buried under the snow;

(f)   the greater use of tunnels to prevent blockages of roads and railways;

(g)   the greater monitoring of avalanche conditions to produce early warnings.

3 Skiing (see also pages 118–120)

With the increases in spare time, the rise in the standard of living of the Developed World, the reduction in costs brought about by package tours, and the massive improvements in speed and efficiency of transport systems (especially air), many more people take a winter holiday to specially developed skiing resorts, such as Aviemore in the Cairngorms, Scotland. Invariably areas such as these attract many people not only for skiing but also to rock climbing, fell walking, fishing, hunting, bird-watching (especially ospreys at Loch Garten). The result is the inevitable damage inflicted on the natural environment by large-scale tourism, albeit unwittingly.

LAKES

Areas largely denuded of soil, such as the Canadian Shield are often pock-marked by lakes. These can present barriers to easier land movement, but in other places they can greatly enhance cargo transport, reducing transport costs of bulky non-perishable goods. This is clearly evidenced by the Great Lakes in North America, where the transport of iron ore, coal and wheat have been of great importance to the towns on their banks. Tourism may also be attracted to water locations, whether it be for water sports, fishing or ornithology.

HYDROELECTRIC POWER

Glacial troughs and hanging valleys are invariably ideal sites for the generation of HEP. They are usually deep and steep sided. The construction of a single dam can produce an enormous **head of water.** Often the areas are remote with a low density of population and being upland areas have high precipitation figures and large catchments. They are also areas in which alternative methods of electricity generation would be costly. So for industries such as lumbering or the extraction of minerals on the Canadian Shield, glacial troughs are a great boon. Examples include Porjas Falls in Sweden, and the Churchill Falls in Canada (see also pages 44–6).

SOILS

The influence of glaciation on soils can be both advantageous and disadvantageous. Boulder clay plains, such as East Anglia may be fertile, thereby favouring agriculture (see Book 1, Chapter 2). Yet in other areas boulder clay may create poorly drained marshy plains, such as the Central Plain of Ireland. Some areas may be virtually devoid of soil (such as the Canadian Shield). Fluvio-glacial gravels and sands are used as aggregates in the making of concrete. Abandoned gravel pits are used as sites for sailing, water skiing and fishing. Loess deposits provide very fertile soil conditions.

FIORDS

Glacial valleys drowned by a rise in sea-level provide fine natural harbours, supplying deep water and sheltered anchorages, for large bulk carriers. The result has been the development of towns and industries, such as Narvik in Norway, for the export of iron ore from Gallivare in Sweden, the development of a pulp and paper plant at Annat Point on Loch Eil in Scotland, and the building of an aluminium smelter at Kitimat on the Douglas Channel in British Columbia.

Unfortunately, fiords may also be a barrier to land movement along the coast, lengthening journey times and costs of construction, making the development of ferry crossing or the building of expensive bridges a necessity.

EFFECT OF OVERFLOW CHANNELS AND DIVERSION OF DRAINAGE

Some glacial lakes have cut deep overflow channels where their normal exit route has been blocked by advancing ice sheets. These natural routeways have been exploited by mankind. They include the Hudson–Mohawk Gap through the Appalachians (see Book 1, Chapter 4) and Newtondale through the North York Moors. The former is used by road, rail and canal (New York State Barge Canal), while the latter is used by rail on route to the port of Whitby.

CHECKLIST ▸

ICE

1   Ice sheets cover vast areas of countries/continents; glaciers are largely confined to valleys.
2   Glaciers erode by plucking and grinding. These processes are assisted by frost shattering.
3   Highland glaciation landforms include corries, arêtes, pyramidal peaks, troughs, truncated spurs and hanging valleys.
4   Glacial lakes include corrie, morainic dammed and mountain ribbon.
5   Lowland glaciation landforms include roches moutonnées, crag and tail, drumlins, erratics, eskers and outwash plains.
6   The effects of glaciation may be both beneficial and a hazard to mankind.

COASTS

Fig 3.35 Coastal Zones

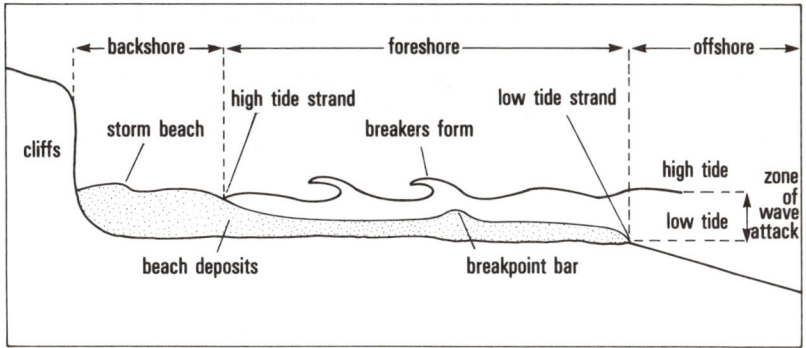

FACTORS AFFECTING
COASTAL FEATURES

1 Wave action.
2 Tides.
3 Ocean currents.
4 Climate.
5 Geology.
6 Vegetation and animal life (coral).
7 Changes in sea-level.
8 Other erosional and depositional agents: ice, rivers.
9 Volcanic activity.
10 Mankind.

WAVES

Waves are caused by winds. So it is winds that influence the direction, the wave length and the wave height.

Fig 3.36

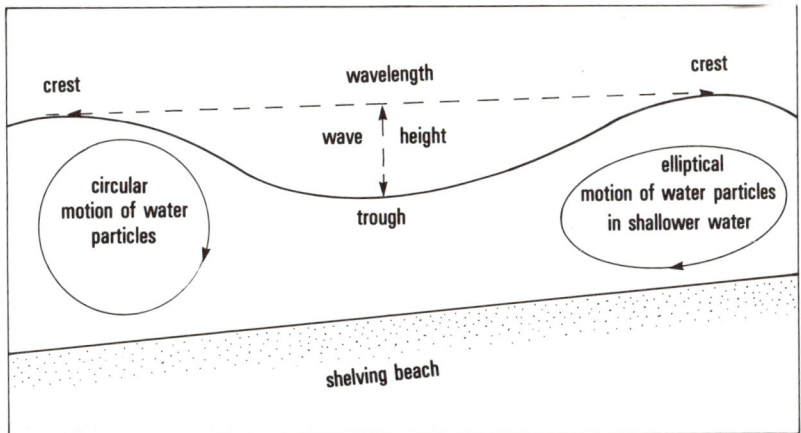

Three major factors influence the size of a wave: 1 wind speed; 2

the length of time the wind has been blowing; 3 the distance over which the wind/wave has travelled (the fetch). Areas of the world with large fetches are the areas of largest waves and best surfing, such as Hawaii, California, Cornwall.

Within each wave, water particles are circling in a vertical plane, each particle making little forward or backward movement, despite the apparent phenomenon of waves appearing to move. (Like 'flicking' a rope, waves appear to run to the end of the rope, yet all they have done is to move up and down!)

As a wave approaches shallower water, the circular motion of the particles is interrupted. At first the particle motion is flattened, the wave length is decreased and waves become steeper. Eventually even the elliptical motion is interrupted by more friction with the sea-bed, causing the waves to break. (This occurs when wave length is seven times greater than wave height.)

TYPES OF WAVE

Fig 3.37 Constructive waves

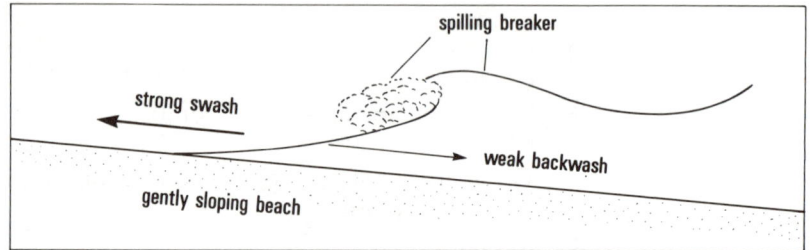

Constructive waves These are long, flat waves which break at a rate of less then ten per minute. Consequently, each swash (a wave's forward motion) is not checked by the backwash from the preceding wave and is capable of moving material up the beach. The backwash is relatively weak due to the shallower gradient.

Fig 3.38 Destructive waves

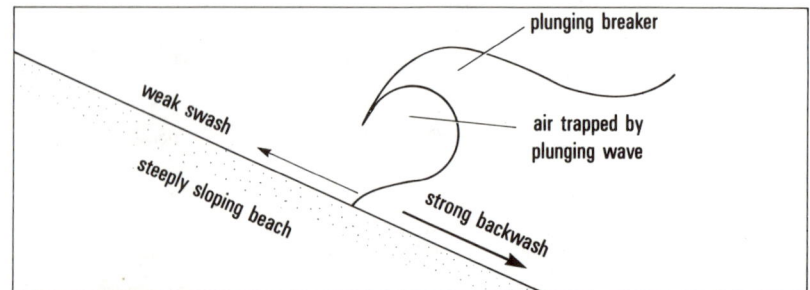

Destructive waves These are shorter, higher and therefore steeper waves which break at a rate of fifteen or more per minute. As the angle of descent is steeper than with constructive waves, the backwash is much stronger. The constructive influence of the weak swash is checked by the strong backwash from the previous waves. Consequently, there is more erosion of material dragged from the beach to the break-point bar.

EROSION

PROCESS OF EROSION

1 Corrosion Seawater chemically rots the rock.

2 Corrasion Waves hurl debris at cliff faces or slide it along the sea-bed, thereby undercutting cliffs.

3 The impact of the waves The physical weight and 'washing-out' effect of water removes softer or smaller calibre, loose material.

4 Pressure changes Air trapped in cracks, joints or caves is compressed by waves. This build-up in pressure is suddenly released as the wave retreats (as when a pressurized canister is pierced).

5 Attrition Debris is broken into smaller pieces and rounded.

LANDFORMS PRODUCED BY COASTAL EROSION

Headlands and bays as a result of differential erosion
With **discordant** coastlines alternate bands of hard and soft rock occur at right angles to the trend of the coast. The soft rock is more readily

Fig 3.39

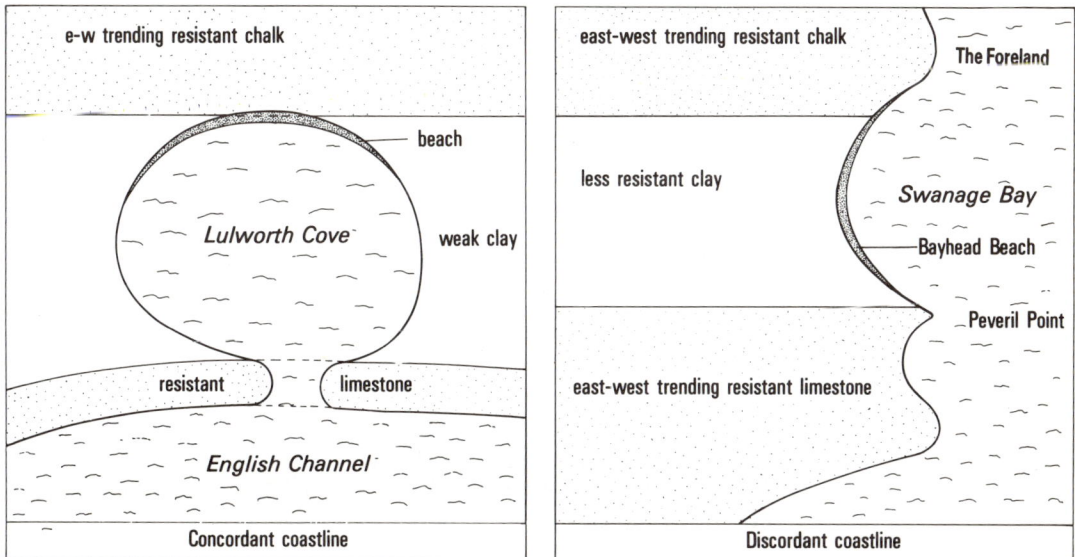

e-w trending resistant chalk

beach

Lulworth Cove

weak clay

resistant limestone

English Channel

Concordant coastline

east-west trending resistant chalk

The Foreland

less resistant clay

Swanage Bay

Bayhead Beach

Peveril Point

east-west trending resistant limestone

Discordant coastline

eroded by the sea, forming bays. The resistant rock is more slowly eroded and stands out as cliffed headlands.

With **concordant** coastlines alternate bands of hard and soft rock run parallel with the trend of the coast, the resistant band being on the seaward side. At certain places the seaward rock band has been weakened by faulting allowing the sea to break through to the soft rock behind. This softer material is easily 'scoured' away. At the same time the sea further widens the gap, in the resistant barrier. Further progress inland is slowed by the landward resistant barrier.

In each of these types of bay, **bayhead beaches** are formed from material broken away from the cliffs (and re-worked by waves), or by material brought from off shore and deposited by the swash of waves.

Cliffs and wave-cut platforms

Cliffs occur where the sea is undercutting the land, even if the land is composed of relatively soft material such as clay. Persistent erosion by waves between high tide and low tide levels results in the formation of a **wave-cut notch** in resistant rock. As this notch is widened and deepened, the overlying material becomes unstable and collapses. This collapsed material is used by the sea further to undercut the land (corrasion). Consequently, the land is driven back and steepened to form cliffs. As the cliffs retreat, a level wave cut platform is formed which is exposed at low tide. Narrow beaches may be formed from the broken-down material from the collapsing cliffs.

Fig 3.40

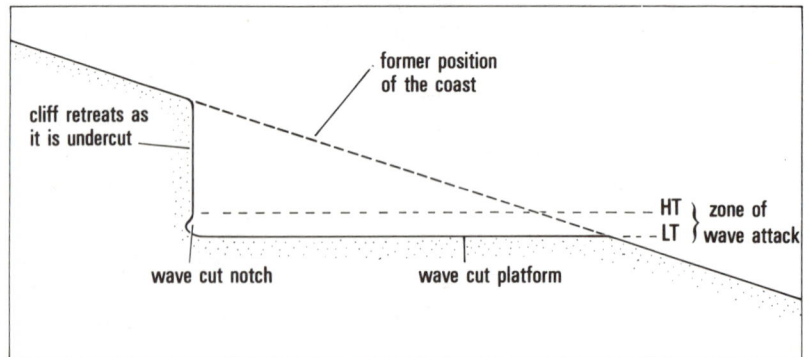

Factors influencing cliff profiles

The major factor controlling the actual **shape** of cliffs is the lithology and structure of the rocks from which they are composed. Vertical cliffs are produced where rocks are horizontally or vertically bedded (e.g. Durlsdon Head and Ballard Down near Swanage, Dorset). Where the angle of dip is towards the sea, the shape may be ragged. Where softer rock overlies more resistant rock, the profile displays a distinct break of slope, e.g. Flamborough Head, Yorkshire.

Fig 3.41 Cliff profiles

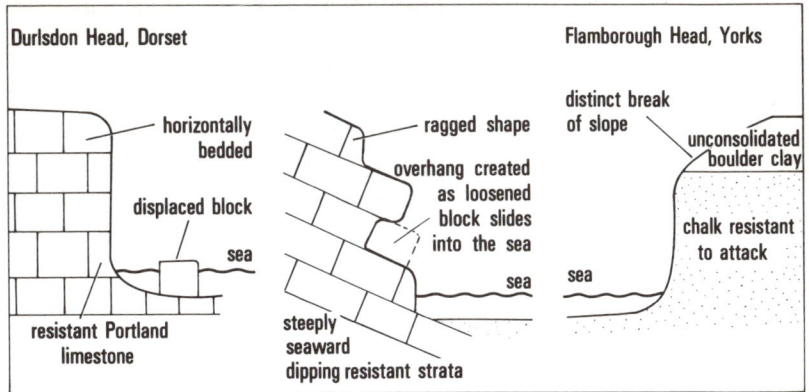

Durlsdon Head, Dorset   Flamborough Head, Yorks

horizontally bedded
ragged shape
displaced block
overhang created as loosened block slides into the sea
sea
sea
resistant Portland limestone
steeply seaward dipping resistant strata
distinct break of slope
unconsolidated boulder clay
chalk resistant to attack
sea

Numerous other factors influence cliff profiles including the length of the fetch, the effectiveness of marine erosion, the activity of sub-aerial processes, changes in sea-level and man.

Caves, arches, stacks and stumps.

Fig 3.42 Caves, arches and stacks

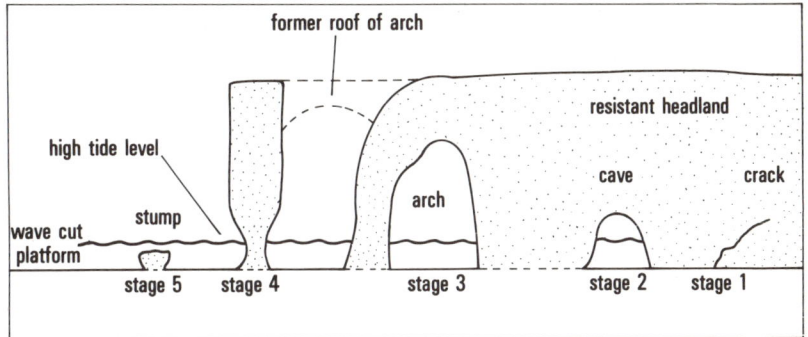

former roof of arch
high tide level
resistant headland
cave
crack
stump
arch
wave cut platform
stage 5   stage 4   stage 3   stage 2   stage 1

Where a resistant headland occurs the sea concentrates its erosion in order to remove it. Cracks, joints and any other weaknesses are widencd into caves by the processes of corrasion, corrosion, impact of the waves and pressure changes. The caves on opposite sides of a headland may meet or one cave may be drilled right through the headland to form an arch. The roof of the arch becomes unstable and collapses to form a stack. The stack is undercut and falls, leaving behind a stump. Even the stump is eventually worn away to form part of a wave-cut platform.

Examples arch – Durdle Door in Dorset
stack – The Needles, Isle of Wight
stump – the Bull in Dorset

Blow-holes and geos
The sea quickly exploits any weakness in resistant rock. Where a fault

line occurs at the base of cliffs, a cave may be created. If a joint or fault extends from the roof of the cave to the top of the cliffs above, air, compressed by waves advancing into the cave, may escape along this weakness. This will cause this fault line or joint to be enlarged forming a **blow-hole**. Eventually the roof of the cave will collapse to form a narrow sea inlet called a geo.

Fig 3.43 Geo

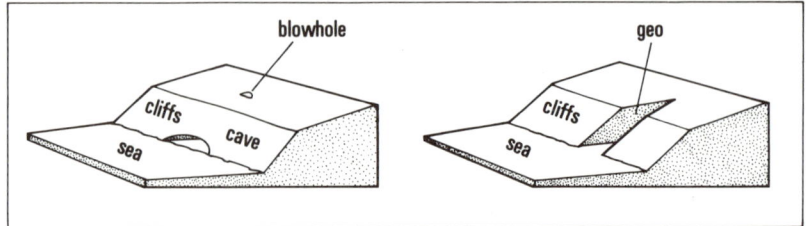

TRANSPORT AND DEPOSITION

Material eroded by waves is broken down and rounded by attrition. It may be moved off shore to form features such as breakpoint bars or it may be moved on shore to form beaches or it may be transported along the coast, especially by the process of **longshore drift**.

Fig 3.44

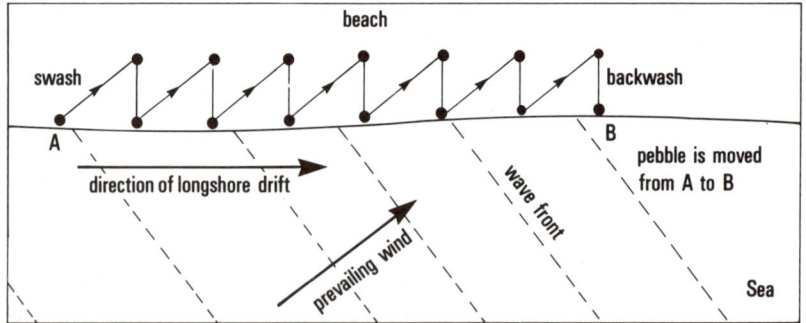

The prevailing wind causes waves to approach the beach obliquely. As the wave breaks, its forward motion (swash) moves material up the beach at an angle. When the wave loses its momentum, the backwash pulls **material** back into the sea. Consequently, material is moved along the beach in a zigzag fashion.

FEATURES PRODUCED BY DEPOSITION

Sand and shingle spits

Spits occur where longshore drift transports material along the beach. Where the coastline changes direction, some of the material is deposited in the shallow water. With continuous deposition, the height and eventually length of the spit grows, continuing the line of the coast above high tide level. The spit is not likely to extend right across an estuary as tidal scour and river action remove material as rapidly as it is deposited.

Fig 3.45

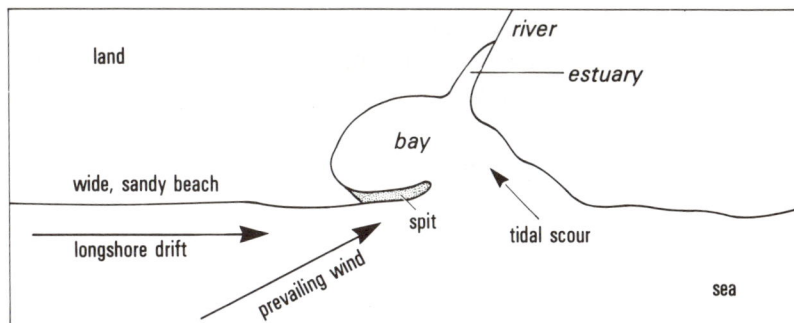

Tombolo
This is a spit or bar which has grown so that it links an island with the mainland.

Example Chesil Beach, Dorset.

Baymouth bars
This is a spit/bar which extends completely across a bay from one headland to another. The water trapped behind the bar is called a **lagoon**. They only occur where coastal deposition occurs more quickly than the sea or rivers flowing into the bay are able to remove the material.

Example Loe Bar in Cornwall.

CHANGES IN SEA-LEVEL   Over thousands or millions of years sea-levels may alter many times. These movements will produce emergent and submergent coasts.

SUBMERGENT COASTS

A rise in sea-level
This could be caused by:

1 Climatic change There is clear evidence that Britain has experienced much warmer winters (9°C or 10°C more) than during the Pleistocene Ice Age. The result has been a reduction in the volume of water locked up as ice. This water has returned to the sea (see the Hydrological Cycle).

2 Upward displacement of the sea-bed Possibly due to crustal plate movement.

A fall in coastal land levels

1 Tectonic plate movements These may produce faulting or downfolding and consequent tilting. (See tilt blocks).

2 Glaciation The additional weight of great thickness of ice during the Ice Ages forced continental plates to 'float' a little deeper on the mantle (isostatic movements).

EMERGENT COASTS

A fall in sea-level

This can be caused by:

1 Climatic change During the Pleistocene Ice Ages winter temperatures in Britain were much colder, causing heavy snowfalls and the formation of ice sheets and glaciers. As ice travels slowly, much of the water, which now rapidly returns to sea via rivers, was locked on the land (eustatic movements).

2 Downward displacement of the sea-bed Such as at destructive plate boundaries, where the oceanic plate is depressed.

A rise in coastal land levels

1 Tectonic plate movements These may cause folding and faulting, forcing land to rise (see horsts, fold mountain formation).

2 Isostatic rebound Since the Ice Ages, areas which were covered by great thicknesses of ice (such as Scandinavia) have slowly been rising. This is due to the release in pressure which was caused by the weight of the ice. The continental plate is floating a little higher on the mantle layer.

EMERGENT COASTAL LANDFORMS

Raised beaches

Fig 3.46

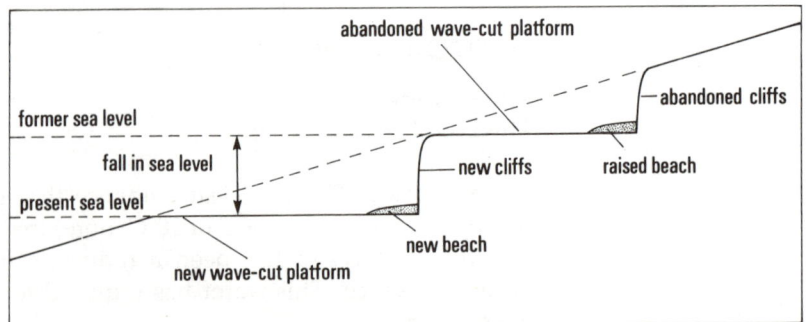

When the sea-level falls, the former beach is left high above the new sea-level. A new, lower wave-cut platform is created at the new low-tide level. New cliffs are produced as the wave-cut platform extends inland.

Example Northern sideof Morecambe Bay, near Grange-over-Sands.

SUBMERGENT COASTS

Fiords These are drowned glacial valleys. During the Ice Ages, glaciers carved deep glacial troughs to a sea-level much lower than now. At the end of this cold period, the sea-level rose flooding the glacial troughs. Consequently, fiords are steep-sided, deeper at their heads than their mouths, and display a rectangular plan form.

Example Sogne Fiord in western Norway.

Rias These are drowned river valleys. During the Ice Ages, rivers overdeepened their valleys to compensate for the fall in sea-level. At the end of this period, sea-level rose and flooded the lower parts of these river valleys. As a result, the gradient of the river flowing into the rias is steeper than necessary for a higher base level. Consequently, rivers are depositing silt in the rias resulting in the formation of marshlands.

USES OF THE COASTAL ZONE

There are many marine and land activities to be found in the coastal zone. It is the concentration of these activities that leads to conflict between them and subsequent damage to the environment.

MARINE ACTIVITIES

1 Navigation.
2 In-shore fishing.
3 Fish farming.
4 Sand and gravel extraction from off-shore areas and beaches.
5 Military zones.
6 Waste disposal.
7 Recreation.
8 Conservation zones (marine wildlife reserves).

COASTAL LAND ACTIVITIES

1 Settlement – especially ports and holiday resorts.
2 Industry – notably heavy industry occupying estuarine sites. Especially industries such as steel, petrochemicals, power.
3 Agriculture (see Book 1, Chapter 2).
　　It is clear that the increasing attraction of coastal zones is putting great pressure in some areas. During the twentieth century, seaside holidays have become the 'norm', causing increased pollution, over-

crowding of coastal resorts, increasing demands to provide extra resort amenities such as marinas, diving schools and boating pools. Heavy industry is attracted to estuarine sites because of cheap, flat land, easier disposal of waste, large quantities of fresh water, cheaper imports and exports. Each of these activities creates problems both to the land and to the marine environment.

CONFLICTS OF INTEREST

Some of the marine and coastal land activities are in direct conflict – each creating harm to the other. The development of an area for industry or recreation competes with the need for conservation. The development of industry and residence increases pollution to the detriment of the fishing industry. Oil spillage brings danger to coastal beaches. A military installation excludes recreational activities.

Fortunately, the problems are often self-solved as some of the activities are mutually repellant. The siting requirements for industries (in estuaries) are not the same as for recreation (bays and beaches) and recreation has no desire to be located near to heavy industry.

Nevertheless, problems are sufficiently acute in some areas for the need for coastal management schemes to control flood, coastal erosion and pollution problems, as well as to oversee the uses of the coastal environment to avoid excessive damage, and to make sure that people are made aware of the problems that one activity can create for another.

CHECKLIST ▶   **COASTS**

1   Waves are caused by winds. The fetch is of importance.
2   Waves may be constructive or destructive.
3   Waves erode by corrosion, corrasion, impact, pressure changes, attrition.
4   Differential erosion produces headlands and bays.
5   Many factors affect cliff profiles.
6   Erosive landforms include cliffs, wave-cut platforms, caves, arches, stacks, stumps, blow-holes and geos.
7   Longshore drift may produce spits, bars and tombolos.
8   Changes in sea-level create raised beaches, fiords and rias.
9   The coastal zone is not only an area of conflict between the land and the sea, but also of conflicting uses by mankind.

THE PHYSICAL ENVIRONMENT AND HUMAN ACTIVITY – GLOSSARY

1 The structure of the earth
block mountains mountainous area created by the uplift of land between faults.

earthquake a tremor of the earth's crust.

focus the point at which the earthquake starts.

geosyncline a large depression of the earth's crust.

geothermal heat originating from the earth's interior.

horst a mountain block created by uplift between parallel faults.

magma molten rock originating from the mantle.

oceanic ridge long, relatively narrow stretch of upland beneath the sea.

plate margins/boundaries/lines the meeting point of two plates; plates being parts of the earth's crust 'floating' on the liquid mantle.

puys a French term for a hill composed of the remnants of a cone of an extinct volcano.

Richter Scale scale used for measuring the magnitude of an earthquake.

rift valley a valley created by the sinking of land between parallel faults.

seismograph an instrument used to record earthquake shocks.

tsunamis huge ocean wave caused by an earthquake beneath the ocean bed.

2 Weathering and mass movement

carbonation as rain passes through the atmosphere it dissolves carbon dioxide to create a weak carbonic acid. This carbonic acid dissolves calcium carbonate (limestone) to form soluble calcium bicarbonate.

exfoliation the peeling off of thin layers of the surface of rocks, especially associated with hot desert areas.

fossils the remains or the mould of an animal or plant preserved for a long time in the rocks of the earth's crust.

frost shattering the break up of bare rock surfaces by the freezing and expanding of water trapped in cracks, faults, joints.

hydration the growth of crystals in rocks due to the addition of water.

igneous rocks rocks created as molten magma solidifies on or within the crust.

mass-movement the movement of weathered material down slopes.

metamorphic sedimentary or igneous rocks which have been change by heat and/or pressure.

scree a mass of angular rocks accumulating at the foot of a cliff.

sedimentary rocks rocks created from sediments laid down in layers beneath rivers, lakes or seas.

slumped masses a section of cliff which breaks away and slides down a well-lubricated surface.

soil creep slow persistent movement of soil down slopes.

3 Rivers

base level the lowest level to which a stream can erode.

catchment area/river basin area from which rain water drains into a river or stream.

coalescence the joining together of small water droplets suspended in the atmosphere.

desalinization the removal of salt from saline water.

distributaries as a river approaches a lake or sea it may split into many branches, each of which enters the sea without rejoining.

dry-ice seeding the artificial spreading of solid carbon dioxide on to clouds to induce prepicitation.

evapotranspiration the loss of moisture from vegetation, soil or bodies of open water (rivers, lakes, seas).

hydrological cycle/water cycle the circulation of water evaporated from oceans into the atmosphere, precipitated on to the land, and returned to the sea via rivers.

nick-point a break in slope of the curve of water erosion.

open system a system where there are inputs from outside the system and outputs leaving the system.

percolation the descent of water from the surface, through the pores and/or joints of rocks.

precipitation the deposition of water in the form of rain, sleet, snow from clouds. It also includes fogs, dew and frost.

regime this is a record of the run-off of a river, recorded on a daily or monthly basis over a number of years. These figures are averaged for each month to give average monthly conditions (c.f. a climate graph).

ria a river valley drowned by a rise in sea-level.

transpiration the process by which plants return moisture to the atmosphere.

tributaries a river flowing into a larger river.

water shed/river divide the higher land separating one river basin from another.

4 Ice

crevasse a deep crack in a glacier.

fluvio-glacial material material deposited by melt water originating from glaciers or ice-sheets.

glacial fans fluvio-glacial material deposited in the shape of a fan.

glacial troughs steep-sided, flat-floored valleys carved by glaciers often described as U-shaped valleys.

glaciers rivers of ice.

head-of-water the pressure created by the difference in height of water and a HEP turbine.

loess fertile soil created from the deposition of dust transported into the area by strong winds.

meltwater streams streams created from melting glaciers or ice sheets.

misfits streams occupying valleys which are too big to have been created by these streams.

moraine unsorted material eroded, transported and deposited by glaciers.

nevée compressed snow, half-way towards being changed into ice.

overflow channels valleys eroded by the overflow of water from lakes created by ice-sheets blocking the path of rivers.

piedmont glaciers an ice sheet created by the joining of several glaciers.

snouts the end of a glacier, where it melts.

truncated spurs a former interlocking spur, whose end has been chopped off by a glacier.

5 Coasts

backwash the retreating of a sea water down a beach after a wave has broken.

estuary the tidal mouth of a river.

eustatic movements large scale rise or fall of sea-level.

isostatic movements the movement up or down of the lighter continental crust floating on the mantle.

spit a narrow low tongue of shingle or sand projecting into the sea from the coast.

swash the movement of sea water up a beach caused by a breaking wave.

POPULATION

CONTENTS

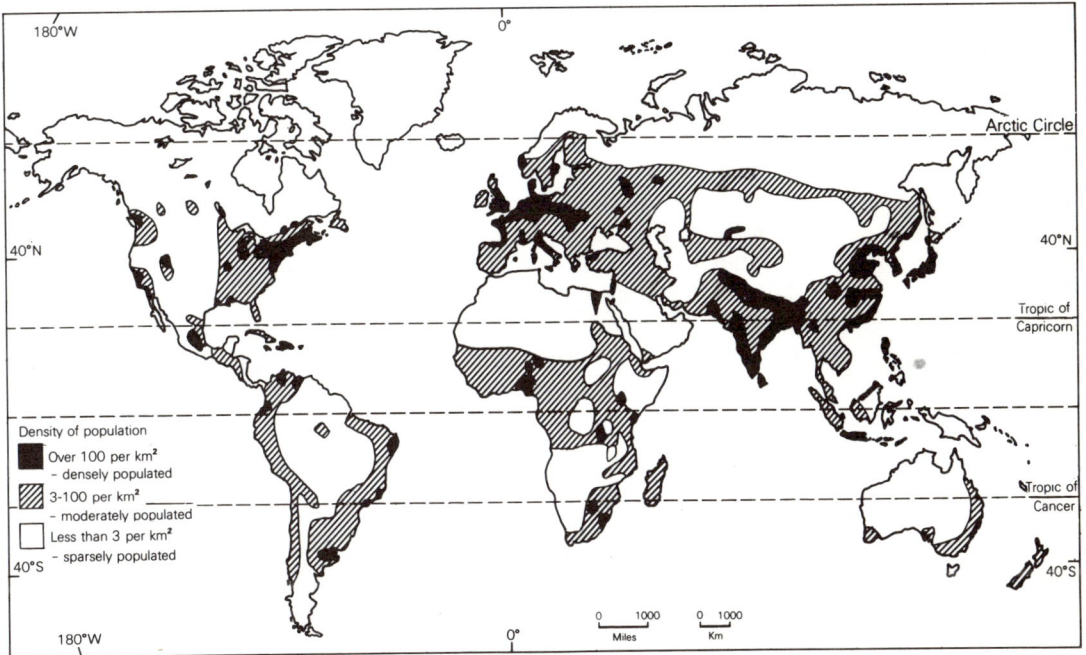

Fig 4.1 Generalized population map

The distribution of the world's population is by no means even. This is largely due to the fact that only 30 per cent of the world's surface is land, of which the majority is found in the northern hemisphere. Of this 30 per cent four-fifths is not habitable, because (a) the climate is too cold; (b) the climate is too humid; (c) the climate is too arid; (d) areas are too mountainous; (e) areas are too densely forested.

SPARSELY POPULATED AREAS

Large areas of the world are sparsely populated because **natural conditions** discourage intensive farming or industrial development.

COLD AREAS

Cold areas include the tundra lands of Eurasia and North America as well as the mountainous districts outside the tropics. These comprise approximately twenty per cent of the world's land surface. Reasons for low densities of population include:

1 Growing seasons are too short for crop growth, temperatures exceeding 0°C for only a few months of the year.
2 The permafrost results in poor drainage in lowland areas, making soils acid and waterlogged.
3 The natural tundra grassland is of poor quality and is dormant for much of the year.
4 Snow covers the pastures for much of the year.
5 Bitter arctic winds blow in winter.
6 Communications over land are difficult: land is snow covered in winter, marshy in summer.
7 Ports are frozen for much of the year.

HOT ARID AREAS

The hot deserts occupy approximately twenty per cent of the land surface and are thinly peopled. Crop growth is virtually impossible because:

1 Rainfall totals are too low to support most crops.
2 Rainfall distribution is very unreliable, with some wet years and some years with none at all.
3 The tendency for the rainfall to occur in short deluging thunderstorms causing much crop and soil damage.
4 Searing temperatures and desiccating winds which scorch and dehydrate plants so they wither and die.
   Settled pastoral farming is impossible because of:
1 The lack of natural pasture.
2 The impossibility of growing fodder crops.
3 Insufficient drinking water.
4 The inability of animals whose meat or wool is in demand to withstand such hot, dry conditions.
   Manufacturing industrial development is impossible because of:
1 Lack of communications.
2 Lack of a large-scale labour force.
3 Absence of a local market.

MOUNTAINOUS AREAS

Approximately twenty per cent of the land surface falls into the category of being too steep and soils too thin for farming. At the same time industrial development is discouraged by the difficulty of access due to the high costs of constructing roads or railways. Nevertheless, in tropical regions mountainous areas, such as Andean Peru, may attract settlement as the climate is ameliorated by height.

DENSELY FORESTED AREAS

These include the taiga belt as well as tropical and equatorial rain forests. In these areas problems include:

1   Cultivation is impossible without the removal of the natural forest, which is very expensive.
2   When the forest cover is removed in tropical forests, high persistent rainfall leaches the soil of its natural fertility.
3   Numerous tropical diseases discourage commercial animals (cattle, sheep) as well as humans.
4   High, humid temperatures discourage close settlement.
5   The lack of communications and the difficulty of constructing them discourages industry.

THE INFLUENCE OF ECONOMIC FACTORS ON SPARSELY POPULATED AREAS

Many sparsely populated areas may have dense pockets within them. This may be because of the presence of a large mineral deposit whose market price is high, making it economically viable to overcome the inherent disadvantages of the environment. Hence, the development of copper mining in the Atacama Desert of northern Chile, the oil productions of the Middle East in the Arabian desert, and oil exploitation of Alaska. Other reasons for pockets include:

1   Strategic factors. The DEW line – early warning tracking stations in Northern Canada.
2   Scientific factors. The presence of camps on Antarctica.
3   Religious factors. The Mormons in the deserts of Utah.
4   Technological factors. The development of irrigated farming such as in the Nile Valley.

DENSELY POPULATED AREAS

There are four major groupings, and many smaller pockets of densely populated areas.

1   North-east USA/South-east Canada.
2   Western Europe.
3   The Indian sub-continent.
4   South-east Asia.

It is possible to group these four areas into two:

(a)   Those areas largely dependent on industrial development.
(b)   Those areas largely dependent on intensive agriculture.

REASONS FOR THE HIGH DENSITY OF POPULATION IN WESTERN EUROPE

1   A high standard of industrial development, allowing for a larger number of people per unit area than with agriculture.
2   The presence of large coalfields, encouraging industrial development in the nineteenth and twentieth centuries.

3   The development of a dense communications network to support industry and aid in the distribution of imported food.

4   The export of manufactured goods to pay for the import of food and industrial raw materials.

5   An early start to industrial development leading to a well-skilled, educated and trained workforce.

6   Early industrial development was labour-intensive encouraging families to be large (this trend is no longer true and families are limited in size by birth control).

7   The formation of colonies provided guaranteed markets for exports and cheap food and raw materials could be imported.

REASONS FOR THE HIGH DENSITY OF POPULATION IN SOUTH-EAST ASIA

1   During the twentieth century there has been a fall in the death rate with the introduction of western medicine.
(*a*)   Preventive: inoculations, better health care.
(*b*)   Curing: drugs, operations.

2   The birth rate has remained high because of the lack of extensive application of birth control.

3   A fall in the infant mortality rate has meant more infant girls reaching child-bearing age.

4   The establishment of international charity groups, e.g. Save the Children, and more government help, more direct public appeals (Live Aid, Sport Aid) and greater United Nations involvement has reduced the number of deaths occurring at times of crisis (famine, flood).

5   Rice is the staple diet of much of the area. It is high yielding and capable of supporting a family living on a near starvation diet.

6   The monsoon climate, bringing the rain and the high temperatures needed for rice, makes it possible for multiple cropping to occur.

7   Ingenious irrigation systems and the development of terrace farming has increased food quantities.

8   The low standard of living allows for a high density of population. (See also Book 1, Chapter 2.)

Population totals – ten largest in each continent

POPULATION IN MILLIONS

Europe	764.8	Asia	2733.3	Australasia	23.5
USSR	272.5	China	1031.9	Australia	15.4
West Germany	61.4	India	732.3	New Zealand	3.2
France	58.6	Indonesia	159.4	Papua New Guinea	3.2
Italy	56.6	Japan	119.3	Fiji	0.7
UK	55.6	Bangladesh	94.7	Solomon Isles	0.3
Spain	38.2	Pakistan	89.7	Western Samoa	0.2
Poland	36.6	Vietnam	57.2	New Caledonia	0.1
Yugoslavia	22.9	Philippines	52.0	Vanuatu	0.1
Rumania	22.6	Thailand	49.5	Tonga	0.1
East Germany	16.7	Turkey	46.3	Kiribati	0.06

POPULATION IN MILLIONS

North America	386.6	South America	258.1	Africa	564.7
USA	233.7	Brazil	129.7	Nigeria	89.0
Mexico	75.1	Argentina	29.6	Egypt	44.5
Canada	24.9	Colombia	27.5	Ethiopia	38.7
Cuba	9.9	Peru	18.7	Zaire	31.2
Guatemala	7.9	Venezuela	16.4	South Africa	30.8
Dominican Republic	6.0	Chile	11.7	Morocco	22.1
El Salvador	6.0	Ecuador	9.3	Algeria	20.5
Haiti	5.2	Bolivia	6.1	Tanzania	20.4
Honduras	4.1	Paraguay	3.5	Sudan	20.4
Puerto Rico	3.4	Uruguay	3.0	Kenya	18.8

THE DISTRIBUTION OF POPULATION IN THE BRITISH ISLES

Fig 4.2 British Isles
population distribution

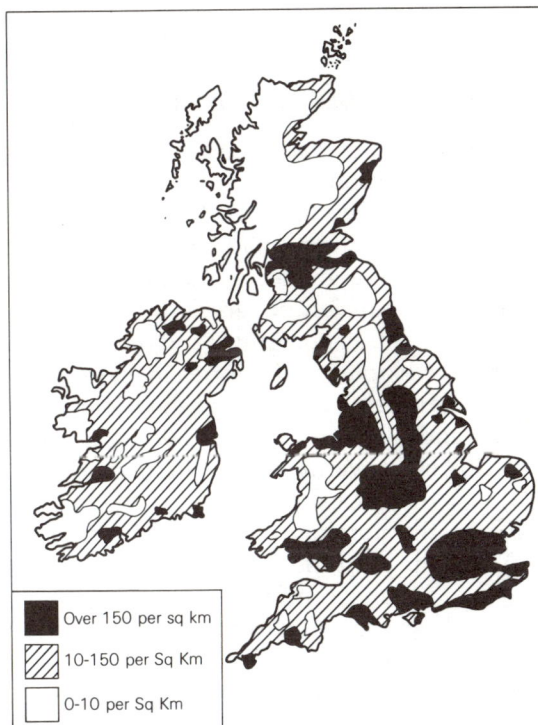

The British Isles has a population of nearly fifty-six million, and with
a very high density (about fourth highest in western Europe). Nevertheless, there are large areas which are sparsely populated. These
include the remoter areas such as the Western Isles, north-west
Scotland as well as the major upland areas. The areas containing
greatest numbers are the major conurbations and urban areas of

Greater London, south-east Lancashire, the West Midlands, west Yorkshire, Merseyside, Tyneside/Teesside, Clydeside, Belfast.

REASONS FOR SPARSE POPULATION IN THE SCOTTISH HIGHLANDS

1 Difficult environmental conditions. A short growing season, high rainfall figures, high winds, snowfall, thin infertile soils, steep relief, all discourage intensive farming methods and encourage extensive farming which supports only low population densities.
2 General difficulties of access, causing isolation, discouraging industrial development.
3 The lack of major mineral deposits.
4 The absence of coal, which was the only important power source for industry during the nineteenth and early twentieth centuries.
5 The lack of a large local market to stimulate industrial development.
6 Rural depopulation caused by the lack of job opportunities in the area and the attraction of better prospects and social facilities in urban areas of England.

ATTEMPTS TO CHECK RURAL DEPOPULATION IN THE SCOTTISH HIGHLANDS

1 THE ESTABLISHMENT OF GROWTH POINTS

The intention is that these activities will have a multiplier effect. Any industries introduced will need supplies of raw material and components. At the same time firms using the product or by-products of the initial induustry may be attracted into the area. The new work force will have greater spending power, encouraging the establishment or expansion of service industries. Hence employment multiplies, the population grows and the demand for social facilities results in the development of the area in many ways.

Governments have established four growth points in the Scottish Highlands, either by financial aid (government grants) or by the placing of a government-run industry into the area:
(*a*)   the nuclear power station at Dounreay;
(*b*)   the aluminium smelter at Invergordon;
(*c*)   the pulp and paper plant at Corpach (near Fort William);
(*d*)   a tourist centre at Aviemore.

Of these four growth points, only the Aviemore scheme could be classed as markedly successful. Invergordon aluminium smelter is at the moment 'mothballed', owing to over-capacity in aluminium smelting in the UK.

2 GOVERNMENTAL SUPPORT FOR SMALL-SCALE SCHEMES

Through the Highlands and Islands Development Board the Scottish Office has given many grants to relatively small-scale firms in order to provide employment for the young people of the area. Schemes have included the establishment of mink farms, the development of industries using natural resources of the area such as fish farms, shellfish processing, the extraction of sodium alginate from seaweed as well as the introduction of firms specializing in low weight but high value products, which can easily withstand the higher transport costs of a remote location. Products include components for computers, optical and scientific instruments.

3 FINANCIAL SUPPORT FOR CROFTING

Through the Crofters Commission, grants and loans have been advanced to crofters to improve the crofts by re-seeding pastures, the use of fertilizers and repairs to farm buildings.

4 REDUCTION IN ISOLATION OF THE AREA

The construction of more roads, the building of bridges over sea lochs to avoid long journeys, the building of small landing strips on the Islands have helped to reduce the isolation of people living in the area.

At the same time the Electricity Board has extended lines to virtually all areas. The television companies have built more transmitters. (See also Book 1, Chapter 4.)

REASONS FOR DENSE POPULATION IN SOUTH-EAST ENGLAND

1 London provides the largest market in the UK. Many industries benefit from a location near to the market especially those whose product either gains in weight (brewing), is perishable (bread), is fragile (glass), is bulky (televisions), is sold directly to the public, or is susceptible to quick changes in fashion. Consequently, many industries producing items for sale to the public plus many industries assembling small-scale products (radios, computers, etc.) benefit from a location near such a huge market.

2 London provides a massive labour supply.

3 London is the headquarters of many firms, banks, insurance companies, etc. Consequently, there are many management positions.

4 London is the country's major route centre for motorways, railways, aircraft. Therefore, access from London to most parts of the country is more direct.

5 Formerly the port of London was the foremost port of Britain providing much employment, directly, as dockers, or through port industries (sugar refining, flour milling, etc.).

6 London is the foremost shopping centre in the country.

7 London is by far the major destination for foreign and British tourists. Hence much employment is provided.

8 Because London is the centre of government, employment in administration is high.

9 Unemployment in south-east England is lower than in the north or the Midlands. Consequently, there is much migration to the area in search of jobs.

10 The south-east has more than its fair share of growth industries (manufacturing and service) and in many cases offers higher wages, salaries. It continues to act as a core region to the detriment of the declining coalfield industrial regions, which themselves have to combat the image of 'dark satanic mills'.

DISADVANTAGES OF THE DENSE POPULATION OF SOUTH-EAST ENGLAND

1 Traffic congestion, despite the develoment of many motorways including the M25. This may lead to stress, lost time, heavier fuel expenses, pollution.

2 High house prices, discouraging or preventing potential labour from the north from coming to the area in search of work.

3 Land pressure may result in very high land prices adding greatly to fixed costs, discouraging expansion or the development of new sites.

4 Sometimes the growth in number of jobs available may exceed supply of employees. Higher wages or other incentives need to be offered to supply labour requirements.

NB These disadvantages are called deglommeration economies. (See also Book 1, Chapter 4.)

THE STRUCTURE OF POPULATION

All countries need information about their inhabitants in order that (*a*) planning for future requirements can be as accurate as possible; (*b*) an indication of the size of present requirements can be ascertained. The information collected varies from one country to another, but some elements are common. These include the age and sex, home address andcountry of origin. Consequently, most countries have a census of all their inhabitants (every ten years in the UK) as well as legal obligations to register births, deaths and migrations. Much of this information can be summarized on population pyramids.

POPULATION PYRAMIDS The shape of population pyramids varies from country to country, but certain patterns can be identified. Many of the less well-developed nations (the Third World) have high birth rates, high but declining infant mortality rates, high but declining death rates and relatively low life expectancy. Hence, the pyramid will have a broad base and a rapidly tapering peak. These pyramids are called **progressive**.

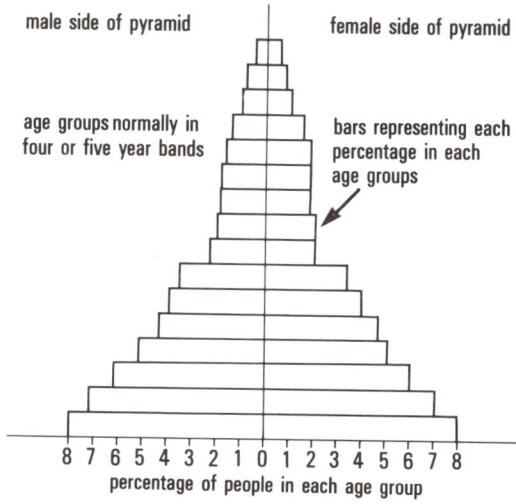

male side of pyramid   female side of pyramid

age groups normally in   bars representing each
four or five year bands   percentage in each
                                 age groups

8 7 6 5 4 3 2 1 0 1 2 3 4 5 6 7 8
percentage of people in each age group

Fig 4.3

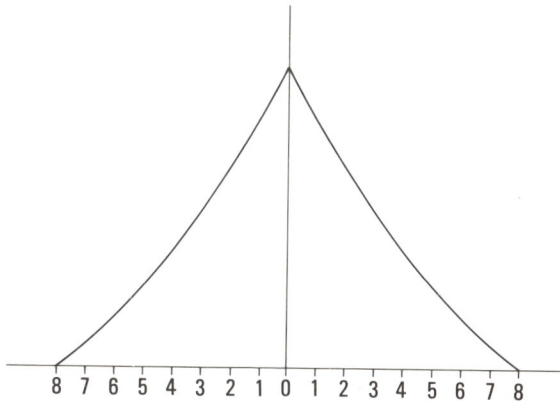

8 7 6 5 4 3 2 1 0 1 2 3 4 5 6 7 8

Fig 4.4 Progressive pyramid

Many developed nations have a declining birth rate, low death rates and long life expectancy. This pyramid will have a narrow base and a widening centre, before it begins a long taper to the peak – a **regressive** pyramid.

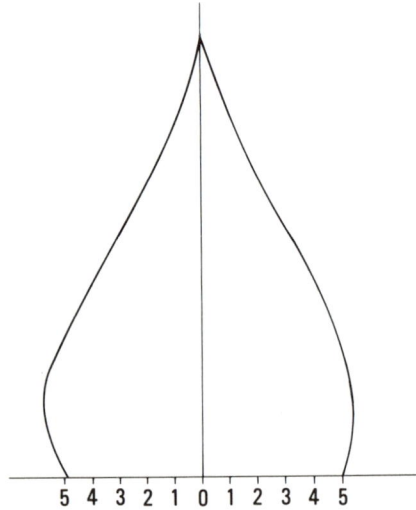

5 4 3 2 1 0 1 2 3 4 5

Fig 4.5 Regressive pyramid

There are many variations of these two pyramids.

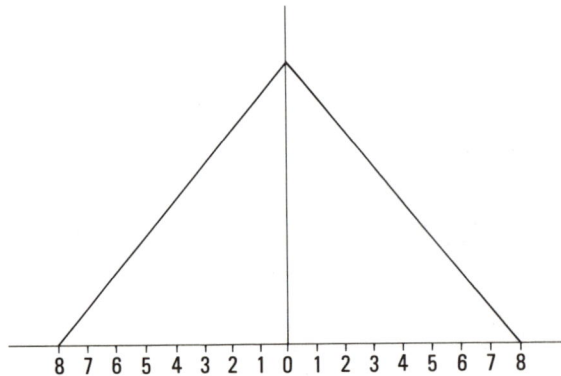

8 7 6 5 4 3 2 1 0 1 2 3 4 5 6 7 8

Fig 4.6 Birth rate remains high, high death rate

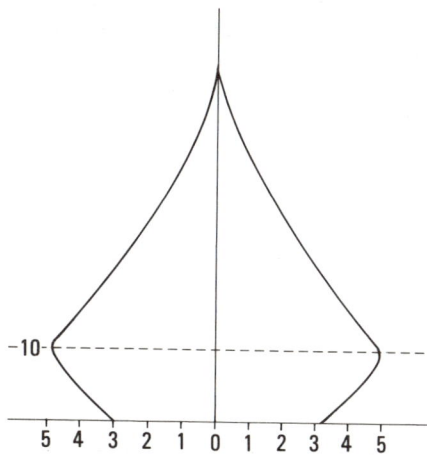

Fig 4.7 Birth rate declining dramatically for the last ten years

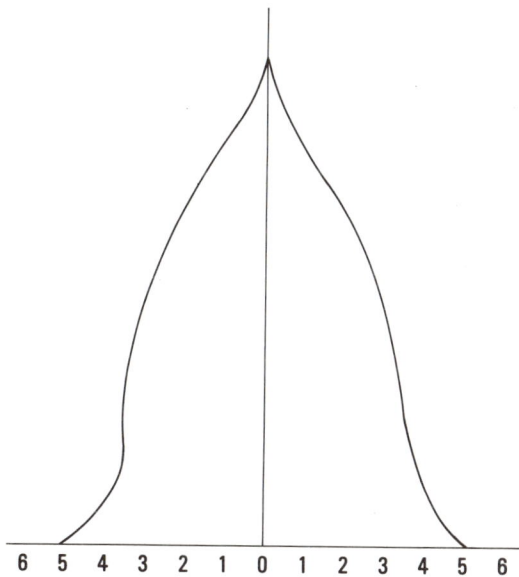

Fig 4.8 A country with formerly low birth and death rates, which is experiencing a baby boom

From the pyramids the dependency ratio may be calculated:

The dependency ratio: the number of children and retired people who have to be supported by the population of working age. In the UK children would be from 0–16 and retirement would be 65+ for males and 60+ for females. In Third World countries children are usually classified as 0–14 and the aged as 65+.

From these figures governments can estimate future educational requirements (e.g. the number of primary and secondary schools), costs of state retirement pensions, the number of retirement homes. Also an indication of future job requirements can be assessed.

Other age/sex imbalances may be revealed by the shape of the pyramid.

1 Women live longer than men, so there is an imbalance in pyramids of developed nations for the 65+ age group.

2 The effect of wars may result in fewer males in the 18–45 years age group. This may well be reflected with a reduced birth rate while men are away at war.

3 Fewer females are born, but their death rate is lower.

PATTERNS OF POPULATION GROWTH

Fig 4.9 World population growth, actual and estimated

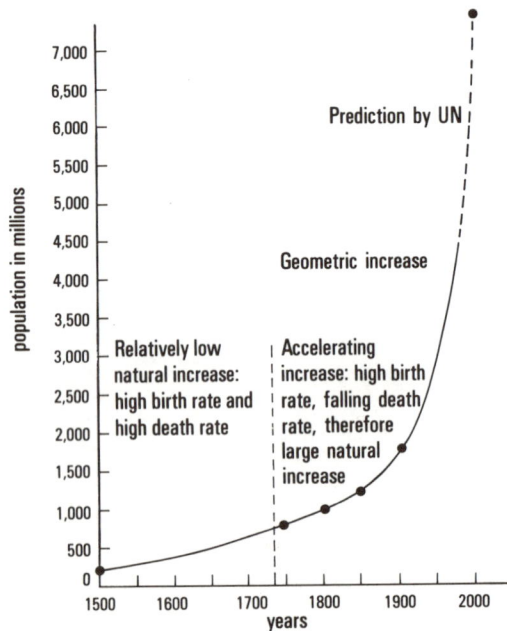

Natural increase. The simplest way of measuring world population growth is by comparing the number of births (crude birth rate) with a number of deaths (crude death rate). The difference between the two is the natural increase/decrease.

THE POPULATION EXPLOSION

From the graph it can be seen that the world's population grew slowly until the end of the eighteenth century/beginning of the nineteenth century. But since then the rate of increase has increased, especially since 1950. Between 1950 and 1980 the world's population increased from 2.5 billion to over 4 billion. United Nations estimates suggest by the year 2 000 the figure will be 7 billion. This accelerating growth is called the population explosion.

The major reason for the sudden upsurge in the world's population lies with the massive rise in the natural increase of Third World nations since the 1950s (a rise which had already occurred in the eighteenth and nineteenth centuries in Europe!) This rise is due to:

1   A fall in the death rate owing to:
    (a)   inoculation against major diseases, e.g. smallpox;
    (b)   drugs such as penicillin which have been widely introduced;
    (c)   overseas aid in times of crises;
    (d)   improved diet;
    (e)   better health care, such as purified water.
2   The birth rate remaining high owing to:
    (a)   lack of contraception, possibly due to religious objection, such as in Catholic South America;
    (b)   worship of ancestors in China;
    (c)   the continuing need for child labour in the fields;
    (d)   the lack of education in contraceptive methods;
    (e)   the lack of finance to afford contraceptive devices;
    (f)   the sheer scale of the problem.
3   A major reduction in the infant mortality rate with, therefore, more girls reaching child-bearing age, so that the population increases at a geometric rate.
4   Life expectancy increasing, especially in the developed nations.

DISTRIBUTION OF POPULATION GROWTH

Natural increases are usually expressed as percentages of each country's population. At present the world average is approximately two per cent. By study of the above diagram it is clear that there are great variations in natural increase growth rates (from nought to four per cent). Highest figures occur in tropical latitudes, in the developing nations, especially in Central and South America. These are the countries of the world which are less capable of handling such massive increases. For instance, India's population in 1981 was 800 million and the natural increase rate was 2.3 per cent. Without emigration this is an annual increase of over 18 million people. Yet India's natural increase rate is only just above the world average! In the developed countries of the world natural increases are negligible (Sweden is 0 per cent, UK is 0.1 per cent) and in some cases a net decrease has occurred in some years (France). These countries are generally much richer than the developed nations and yet unemployment may still be quite high; but the problems are minute compared with those in the Third World!

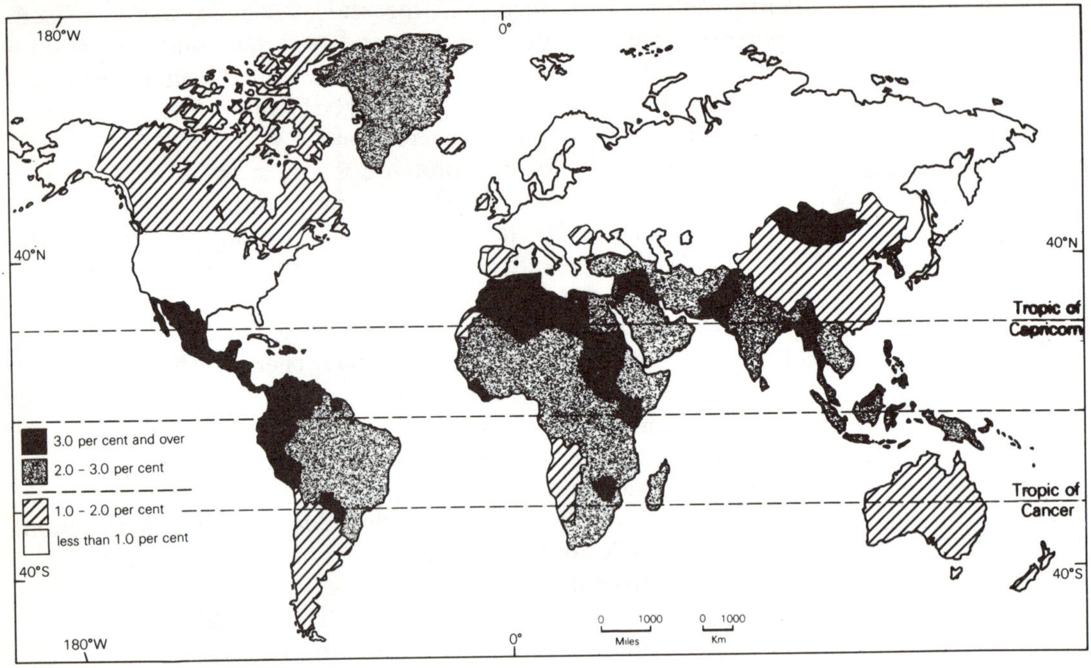

Fig 4.10 Natural increase rates of countries

THE RESULTS OF THE POPULATION EXPLOSION

1 Lack of food for two-thirds of the world's population. Therefore:
   (a)   many are below starvation level;
   (b)   poor diets lead to malnutrition.

2 The land occupied by poor native families is incapable of supporting the whole family. Therefore:
   (a)   some leave to seek work in towns;
   (b)   rapid urbanization occurs in Third World countries;
   (c)   shanty towns develop because towns are incapable of absorbing such high levels of rural-urban migration.

3 The growth rate of industries is insufficient to keep pace with the growing demand for jobs. Therefore:
   (a)   unemployment rates are very high;
   (b)   high unemployment may lead to a return of migrants to the country areas, increasing rural population pressure;
   (c)   in some areas, discontentment grows, leading to the breakdown of civil order.
   (d)   it is these pressures that are the major cause of wars within the developing world.

4 The world's resources are not equally shared – the developing world, with a smaller share of the world's food has to cope with a faster-growing population.

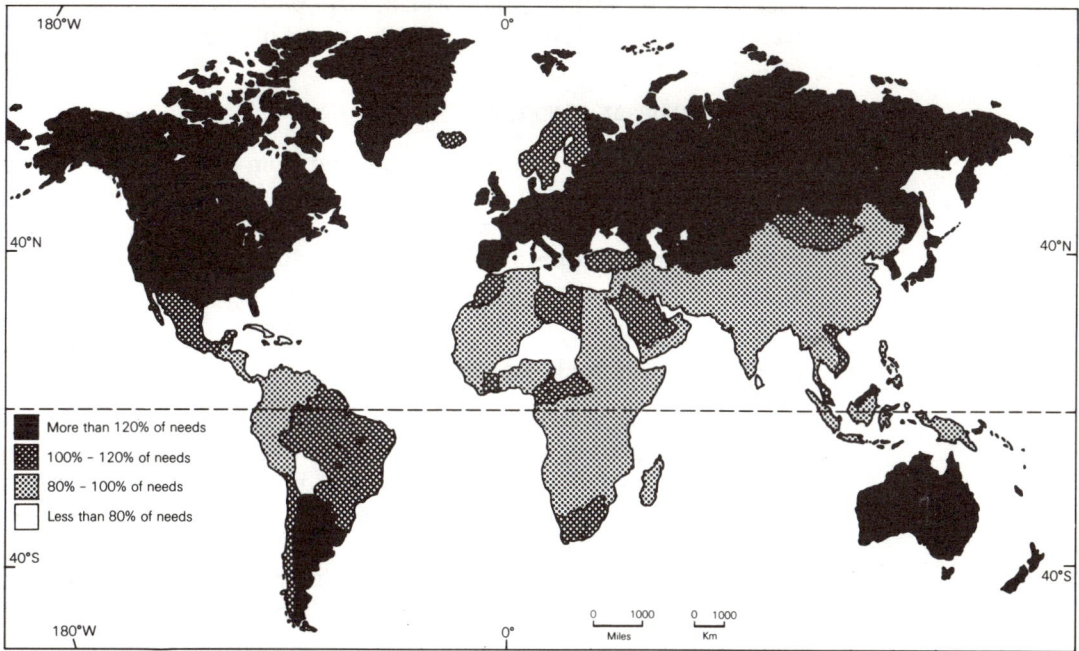

Fig 4.11 Food intake as percentage of needs

Legend:
- More than 120% of needs
- 100% – 120% of needs
- 80% – 100% of needs
- Less than 80% of needs

SOLVING THE PROBLEM

1 CONTROLLING POPULATION GROWTH

Modern methods of birth control have been used in the developed world and have successfully reduced the rate of population growth, but in Third World countries their application is limited because:

1 The people are too poor to pay for them; governments are too poor to provide devices free.
2 There are some religious objections, especially in South America where population growth rate is especially high.
3 It is traditional to have large families for support in old age.
4 The need in agricultural communities for child labour.
5 The standard of education is low.

2 REDISTRIBUTION OF POPULATION

Emigration from overpopulated areas to less densely populated areas has happened in the past (from Europe to the New World during the European population explosion in the nineteenth century). This solution is unlikely to have a major influence on reducing the problem in overpopulated areas now because of:

1 The huge scale of emigration that would be required (between 1980 and 2000 AD it is estimated that the population in the less-developed nations will increase by nearly 1,400 million).
2 Most, if not all developed nations, who would expect to receive these

migrants from the developing world, have passed laws against immigration or set significant limitations by means of quotas.

3 IMPROVING URBAN CONDITIONS

Various attempts are being made, ranging from the provision of low cost housing, the installation of basic services (fresh water, electricity, drainage) to slums and shanty towns to building new and satellite towns. But these efforts are limited largely due to the lack of available finance and the escalating size of the problem.

4 PROVIDING MORE INDUSTRIAL EMPLOYMENT

This is being achieved in some areas by the introduction of labour-intensive industries such as textiles or assembly industries. The cheapness of the labour helps produce products whose selling price is able to compete with goods produced in the developed world by means of greater mechanization.

Although it is often suggested that industrialization is the panacea to the problems of the Third World it should be remembered that:

1   much initial capital is required in first establishing large scale factories;
2   many industrial developments are by multinational forms and although they do provide jobs and provide essential industrial training, profits largely return to developed nations;
3   for industrial development, a great expansion of developed power resources and the expansion of communication networks is essential;
4   standards of training and education greatly need improving;
5   the standard of living of the developing nation needs improving to provide a home market (an essential initial firm industrial base).

5 INCREASING FOOD SUPPLIES

1   Increasing the area of farmland by farming areas at present not used.
2   Increasing yields from existing cropland by:
    (a)   the greater use of chemical fertilizers;
    (b)   crop selection, leading to better yielding plants;
    (c)   irrigation;
    (d)   the use of pesticides and fungicides;
    (e)   education in modern farming techniques;
    (f)   in some areas, the introduction of mechanization or the provision of simple agricultural tools such as hoes;
    (g)   rotation system.
3   Increasing yields from animals by:
    (a)   the use of hormone injections;
    (b)   an extension of factory farming methods;
    (c)   cross-breeding;
    (d)   the growth of irrigated fodder crops;
    (e)   controlled grazing;

(f)   the improvement of pasture with fertilizers and seed selection.

4   More efficient methods of fishing:
(a)   fish farms;
(b)   the stocking of reservoirs.

Over the last twenty years the increase in total world food production has more than outpaced total world population growth, but it is not the developing nations which have been the prime beneficiaries. Much of the extra food produced in these countries has been exported to the developed nations to pay for the increased import of manufactured goods and power supplies (such as mineral oil). Consequently, food supply conditions in these poor countries has not improved to any great extent. In fact, schemes to increase food supply may partly lead to desertification and greater famine. In areas of war and revolution, the poor distribution of food supplies and the destruction of farmers' fields further increases the problems of malnutrition and starvation. (See Book 1, Chapter 2.)

6 INTERNATIONAL AID

Most of the solutions to the problems created by the population explosion are dependent on considerable foreign aid from the developed rich world. Despite efforts by the United Nations to encourage these countries to give up to one per cent of their GNP to overseas aid, too little money or other forms of aid is going to Third World nations to alter significantly the present situation.

Consequently, the future looks bleak unless significant changes take place. Change in:

1   population control;
2   government/bureaucratic attitudes towards food mountains;
3   people's attitudes to food prices;
4   financial support for developing nations.

THEORIES OF POPULATION GROWTH

THE THEORY OF THOMAS MALTHUS

At the end of the eighteenth century Thomas Malthus produced a theory in which he declared that the population of a country grows at a geometric rate (2, 4, 8, 16, 32, 64, etc.), but food supply only grows at an arithmetic rate (2, 4, 6, 8, 10, 12, 14, etc.). Therefore the growth in food supply will not keep up with the food supply requirements. The result would be a 'crash' with a great increase in the death rate by means of the natural controls of famine, disease and war. This crash occurs when the country has fully developed its resources for producing food – the resource limit.

As Malthus was living at the time of the 'population explosion' in Britain, he predicted great devastation would occur when Britain reached its resource limit. The only way to avoid this cataclysmatic event was to practise birth control ('restraint!').

This devastation never arrived in Britain due to:

1 The importation of extra food supplies from abroad, paid for by the export of manufactured goods.
2 Contraceptive methods were developed, thereby slowing the rate of population growth.
3 Extra food was produced in the UK with the assistance of an agricultural revolution: fertilizers, rotation systems and mechanization.

Nevertheless, it could be argued that Malthus's dire prediction may be being fulfilled in some twentieth century developing nations, as present trends clearly indicate that population increase is occurring at an increasing rate and although extra food is being produced, it is not for consumption internally but for export. Famine, war and disease certainly occur extensively in much of Africa and Central America. (Are these the natural checks that Malthus meant?)

THE S CURVE

An adaptation of Malthus's theory is that as the population begins to approach the resource limit, then the rate of population growth slows so that the increase in population matches any increase in food supply. Therefore food supply and population growth remain in balance, neither outgrowing the other.

Fig 4.12

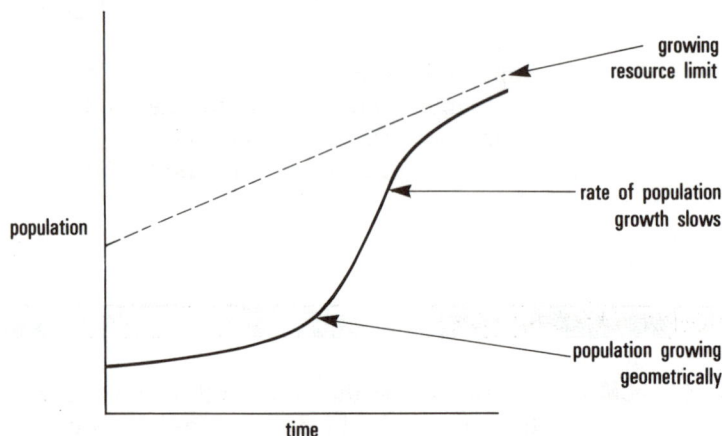

Certainly, many west European countries reveal an S-shaped population growth pattern. At present many have populations which are static or growing extremely slowly, (UK 0.1 per cent, Sweden 0 per cent, Norway 0.3 per cent), having undergone massive increases in the eighteenth and nineteenth centuries.

It can only be hoped that this theory will prove to be correct in other parts of the world, as there is little doubt that many developing countries appear to be near or have crossed their present food-resource limits. Either the limits will have to grow or the population growth rate be reduced greatly.

On a world scale, the total population is increasing at a geometric rate, but it is doubtful that the world has reached its food resource limit. The problem is more one of maldistribution of resources in relation to population growth, than a case of the world being over-populated.

THE DEMOGRAPHIC CYCLE

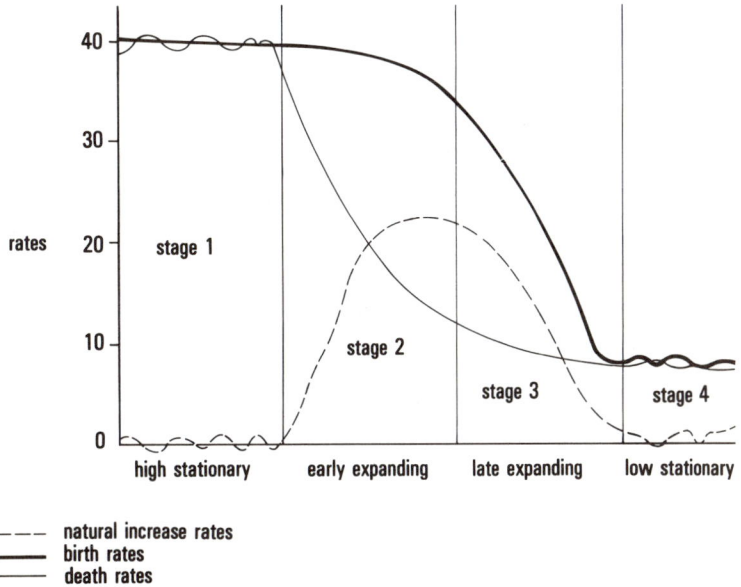

Fig 4.13 The demographic cycle

- - - - - - natural increase rates
———— birth rates
———— death rates

This theory is based on the pattern of population growth occurring in the UK from 1750 to the present day. From the observations four stages are identified.

Stage 1
High but fluctuating death rates and high birth rates lead to very little population change.

Stage 2
A rapidly falling death rate (due to improved diet, health care and medicines) accompanied by a continuing high birth rate, leads to a massive population growth.

Stage 3
The death rate begins to flatten out and the birth rate starts to fall. The result is a declining rate of natural increase, large at the beginning of Stage 3 but small by the end of it.

Stage 4

Birth and death rates remain low. Therefore the population is fairly static showing slight natural increases at times of 'baby booms'.

Attempts have been made to apply these stages to present-day countries.

Stage 1

It is doubtful whether any whole country is still in this stage, but isolated tribal groups such as in the Amazon basin do display high birth and death rates.

Stage 2

Many African developing nations are at this stage, Nigeria, Ethiopia, Malawi. Many of these countries are at the end of Stage 2 and therefore show massive natural increases, e.g. Nigeria 3.3 per cent, while others are at an early stage, e.g. Malawi 2.4 per cent, indicating that their natural increases have yet to reach their peaks.

Stage 3

The majority of Third World countries are in this stage.

Brazil	2.2%
Mexico	2.9%
India	2.2%
Peru	2.5%

Stage 4

The developed nations of western Europe, North America and Japan are in this stage where natural increase rates are below 1 per cent.

UK	0.1%
USA	0.7%
Japan	0.7%

THE DEMOGRAPHIC TRANSITION MODEL AND FUTURE

Population growth

If countries in Stages 2 and 3 follow the pattern of the world, then eventually the world population total will settle at a high stationary figure. In the meantime massive population increases are to take place especially in Third World nations. If the world is not to be overpopulated, then countries must pass through the demographic stages much more quickly than did Britain (Britain took over 200 years to pass through from Stage 1 to Stage 4!)

It is assumed that countries will follow the pattern set by Britain and start to lower their birth rates at the start of Stage 3. This pattern may not be followed:

1 contraceptive methods may not be so widely available;
2 the desire for consumer goods in place of a large family may not become the pattern of other nations.

OVERPOPULATION

This means that the population of an area has grown too large for the resources of the area. The population is bigger than required for the efficient use of these resources and therefore the standard of living of the area is being depressed.

In simple economies, it is easy to identify overpopulation. For instance, in a subsistence economy, if a rise in population size leads to food shortages which did not previously exist and this cannot be overcome by increasing available food supplies, then the area is overpopulated. In advanced economies it is not so easy to identify whether a country is overpopulated. The standard of living is not so closely related to the land, but is based on industrial development and food may be imported from abroad. Therefore, developed industrial nations may have very high densities of population and still not be overpopulated: the Netherlands is one of the most densely populated countries in the world and yet has a high standard of living – a standard of living which has grown and not been depressed as the population has grown.

Overpopulation also varies with time. Initially, an increase in population may cause a depressing of the standard of living (overpopulation), but technological advancement may enable better use of resources (for instance, irrigation to increase crop yields). Therefore, the area may no longer be overpopulated even though its population is the same size as when it was overpopulated!

CHECKLIST ▶   **POPULATION**

1 The world's distribution of population is very uneven.
2 High population densities occur in developed industrial countries and in Third World agricultural countries.
3 A country's population can be summarized on a population pyramid, the shape of which indicates both past and future trends.
4 Third World countries have wide-based pyramids.
5 The 'population explosion' has largely been due to a fall in the death rate, while the birth rate remains high.
6 The 'population explosion' displays a geometric rate of population increase.
7 The 'population explosion' is at present occurring in the poor countries of the world, resulting in a lowering of the people's living standards, starvation, malnutrition, unemployment, urbanization.
8 Overcoming the problems created by the population explosion include: (a) population

control; (*b*) population redistribution; (*c*) improvements in urban conditions; (*d*) increase in industrial employment; (*e*) increase in food supplies; (*f*) international aid.

9   Theories of population growth include: (*a*) Thomas Malthus; (*b*) the S curve; (*c*) the demographic cycle.

10 Overpopulation can occur in developed and developing countries.

POPULATION – GLOSSARY

'baby booms' a sudden increase in the birth rate.

consumer goods articles produced for general public use, especially in the home. These include 'white goods' (cookers, washers, refrigerators) as well as electrical, electronic equipment (radios, televisions).

crude birth rate the number of live births in one year.

crude death rate the number of deaths in one year.

deglommeration economies the disadvantages created by too many industries being located on the same/nearby site. These include congestion, excessive competition for labour and land.

growth industries industries which are expanding due to increasing demand for their products. At present, this would include industries such as electronics.

infant mortality the death of children at birth or before reaching the age of one year.

labour intensive activities which employ many people to make a good/ farm the land, rather than using machines with little labour required.

life expectancy the number of years which the 'average' person is expected to live.

'mothballed' industries which have ceased production, but whose buildings and machines are kept in working order.

natural increase rate the rate at which the size of the population is increasing due to the number of births exceeding the number of deaths in one year. Migration numbers are not included in the natural increase rate.

overpopulation where the standard of living of an area is decreased by an increase in population, i.e. the population of the area has grown too large for the area's resources.

population density the number of people per unit area. This is usually measured per square kilometre or mile.

rural depopulation the excessive out-migration from rural areas leaving an imbalanced population structure.

POPULATION MOVEMENTS

CONTENTS

TYPES OF MIGRATION

The permanent or semi-permanent movement of people from one place of residence to another is called migration. This can take place at a great number of scales – short-distance movements of only a few miles, large-scale movements but remaining within the same country (internal migration) or movements which cross country borders (international migration). It may involve the movement of only a few people or may involve the movement of millions. It may be voluntary or it may be enforced (refugees). It may be government planned or it may be the result of the decision(s) of individuals. It may be the movement of people from town to countryside (urban–rural migration) or from countryside to town (rural–urban migration). it may involve the movement of whole families or it may be the movement of young men in search of work. It occurs in developed as well as developing nations.

INTERNATIONAL MIGRATION

Large-scale international migration has occurred since the earliest times (the exodus of the Jews from Egypt to Palestine), and is still happening now (the Vietnamese boat people).

MAJOR MIGRATIONS OF THE EIGHTEENTH, NINETEENTH AND TWENTIETH CENTURIES

Dates	From	To	Causes
1700–1860	West Africa	Caribbean Southern USA Brazil	Need for slave labour for plantation farming
1840–1910	Ireland	North America	Famine caused by potato blight and British religious persecution of Irish Catholics in search of a new future
1947	Pakistan/India	India/Pakistan	Partition of India. Muslims to avoid persecution to Pakistan. Hindus to India
1950–1965	W Indies	UK	Invited by UK to fill job vacancies
1978	Vietnam	Anywhere they could go	To escape communist regime, in search of new future

CAUSES OF INTERNATIONAL MIGRATION

Causes are numerous and vary according to each migration, but invariably both push and pull factors contribute to the final decision.

Push factors	Pull factors
War, insurrection, religious persecution	Religious tolerance
High unemployment	The chance of a brighter future
Unacceptable political regimes	Political freedom
Overpopulation/low standard of living	Higher standard of living
Limited career opportunities	To join relatives
Natural disaster (floods, earthquakes)	

THE EFFECTS OF INTERNATIONAL MIGRATIONS

Migrations affect not only the country in which they arrive but also the area which they have left.

EFFECTS ON COUNTRY OF LARGE-SCALE INTERNATIONAL EMIGRATION

1 If emigrants consist of mainly young males, then the population pyramid will show a marked indentation of the age range sixteen to thirty. This will have the effect of depressing the birthrate, thereby checking the rate of natural increase. Older people will form a higher proportion of the total population.

   If substantial numbers leave, this could have a detrimental effect on the size of the work-force. Older people may have to work to a greater age before retirement. But if the natural increase rate is already high, the departure of many young people could be advantageous by reducing population pressure, helping to lower the birth rate and ensuring that the unemployment rate is lowered.

2 If emigration consists of young families, then the birth rate and natural increase rate will be lowered. The population will become an ageing one, with possible problems about providing work-forces for agriculture and/or industry.

3 It is often argued that the young are less conservative and have more drive. They are therefore more willing and able to introduce and/or accept change. If these people emigrate, then it is more difficult for an area to adapt to new methods, such as new agricultural methods or the introduction of industry.

EFFECTS ON A COUNTRY OF LARGE-SCALE IMMIGRATION

As with emigration, the effects vary according to the age and sex of those people who migrate, as well as with other factors such as their skills, values and attitudes. Much also depends on the attitude of the people in the receiving country.

1 The majority of migrants have been/are young. Consequently, immigrant groups tend to have high birth rates and if the migrants are mainly male, there is much intermarriage with the host population.

2 Immigrants will form part of the working population. When and where jobs are plentiful migrants are welcomed by host countries. (In the 1950–65 period they were many job shortages in the UK, especially of the manual or low-skilled variety; consequently many West Indians were encouraged to fill jobs as hospital porters or to work for London Transport, etc.) If jobs are scarce, then there is likely to be friction between immigrants and the host peoples. If there are racial differences, then problems may be shown through racism rather than as an economic problem!

3 As migrants to the New World in the eighteenth and nineteenth century tended to be young, it is suggested that this is the reason for the great development of the USA: a vigorous go-ahead population.

4 Migrant numbers may be so large as to dominate totally the host nation, leading to a total transformation by the introduction of an alien culture (the destruction of the Indian way of life in the USA).

5 If migrant numbers form a large minority of the population, then civil strife might result (witness problems between Tamil separatists and the Ceylonese in Sri Lanka).

6 Many migrants are refugees. These people may not be welcome in the country of refuge and may not themselves wish to remain, but have little choice. They may be kept in refugee camps and be stateless, often becoming a source of embarrassment for host governments (the Vietnamese boat people kept in camps on offshore islands in Hong Kong as no foreign government is willing to take such numbers) or may result in virtual civil war or outright hostility (Palestinians in refugee camps in Lebanon).

7 Migrants take skills with them which may be of great benefit to the host country, but of great loss to the country from which they have come. Many of the early farming and industrial skills of the USA initially came from Europe brought by the immigrants.

8 Migrants often bring their own culture, customs and values which enrich the host nation by adding diversity and help break down stereotyped ideas about 'foreigners'. At the same time if migrants cluster in large enclaves in cities, ghettos are created. These may become ports of 'foreign territory' and bring racist reactions from the host peoples.

**CHANGES IN
INTERNATIONAL
MIGRATION PATTERNS**

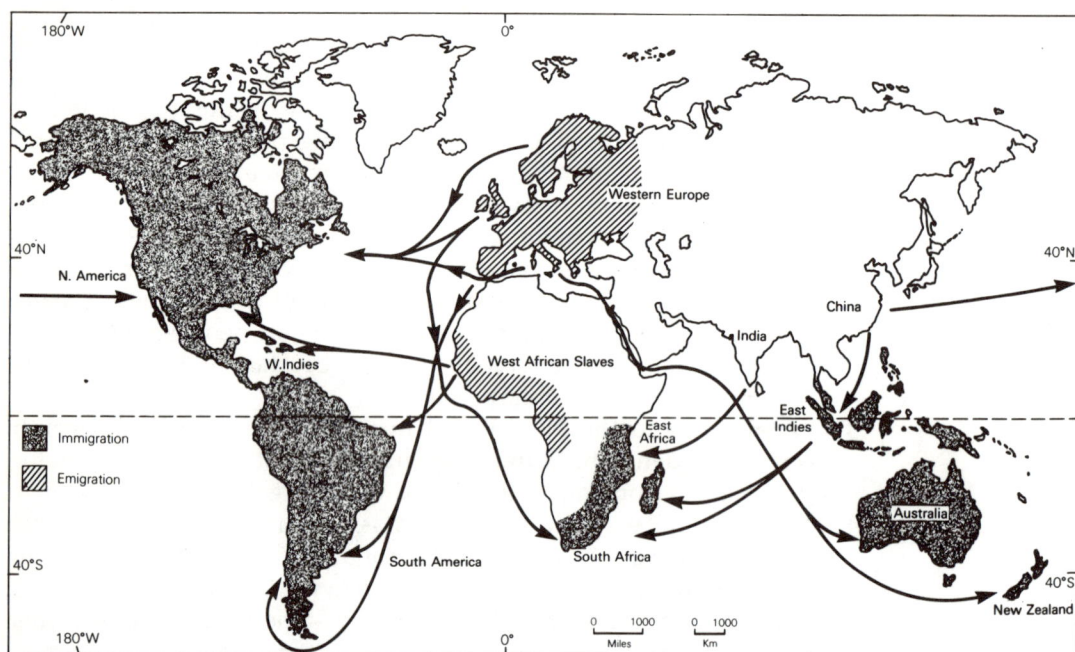

Fig 5.1 Permanent international migration from 1850 until the early twentieth century

1 Origin of migrants 1850–1920 The major population boom in the nine-teenth century was in western Europe and it was from here that the majority of the voluntary migrants originated. Significant numbers also left China and India. Forced migrants included West Africans as slaves.

2 Origin of migrants since 1945 At the end of the Second World War, many refugees from western Europe left for Canada, USA, Australia and Israel, but apart from movement to the latter this migration has now largely ceased. Many West Indians and Algerians moved to Britain in the 1950s and 1960s. Many French-Algerians returned to France on Independence. In the late 1940s and early 1950s many Palestinians left the new state of Israel. Nowadays the major movements are in Africa and of the Vietnamese boat people. These consist of move-ments, voluntary or compulsory, out of developing nations.

3 Destinations of migrants 1850–1920 Migration was to the relatively sparse-ly populated areas of the Americas, South Africa and Australia where development was less advanced than in Europe. Chinese and Indian migration followed a similar pattern but with greater concentration on East and South Africa and the islands of the East Indies.

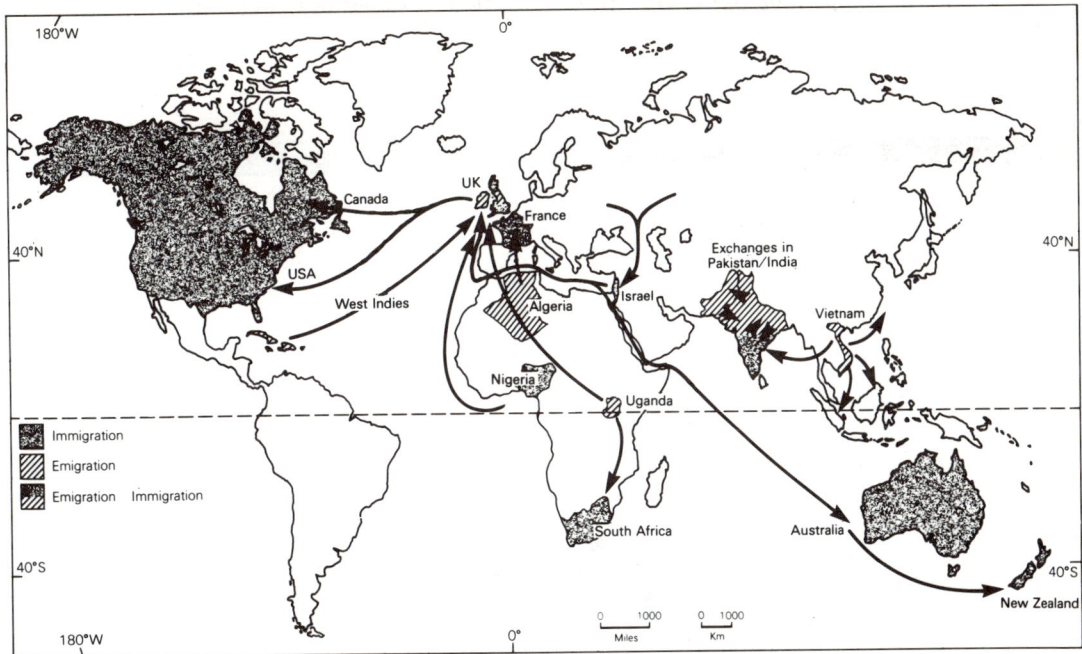

Fig 5.2 Permanent international migration since the Second World War

4 Destinations of migrants since 1945 Migration to USA, Canada and Australia was quite large immediately after the Second World War but with the introduction of immigration control numbers have been greatly reduced. Migrants include those from developed nations as well as from developing countries. Also during the 1950s and 1960s there was significant migration into western Europe especially to countries which had colonies (UK, France). Israel has also received many migrants: Jews from Europe, Asia and America. Significant migration occurs in Africa from poorer countries to the wealthier such as South Africa and Nigeria.

5 Causes of migration 1850–1920 Apart from the transfer of slaves, largely from West Africa, movement was mainly voluntary. People left due to poor living standards in search of new opportunities.

6 Causes of migration since 1945 At the end of the Second World War, there were many European refugees, some due to the war, others fleeing communism. Many left in search of new opportunities and away from the restrictions of war-devastated Europe. Jews left to return to their 'homeland'. The movement of people from colonies to their mother country was a forerunner of the present trend of people leaving developing nations with low standards of living and employment opportunities to settle in developed nations where there were jobs and the standard of living was higher. This trend still continues but is greatly curtailed by immigration controls. Consequently, the trend now is the semi-permanent migration of workers from developing countries to more developed or richer nations in search of jobs.

SEMI-PERMANENT INTERNATIONAL MIGRATION

Fig 5.3 Origin of migrant workers in France (1974)

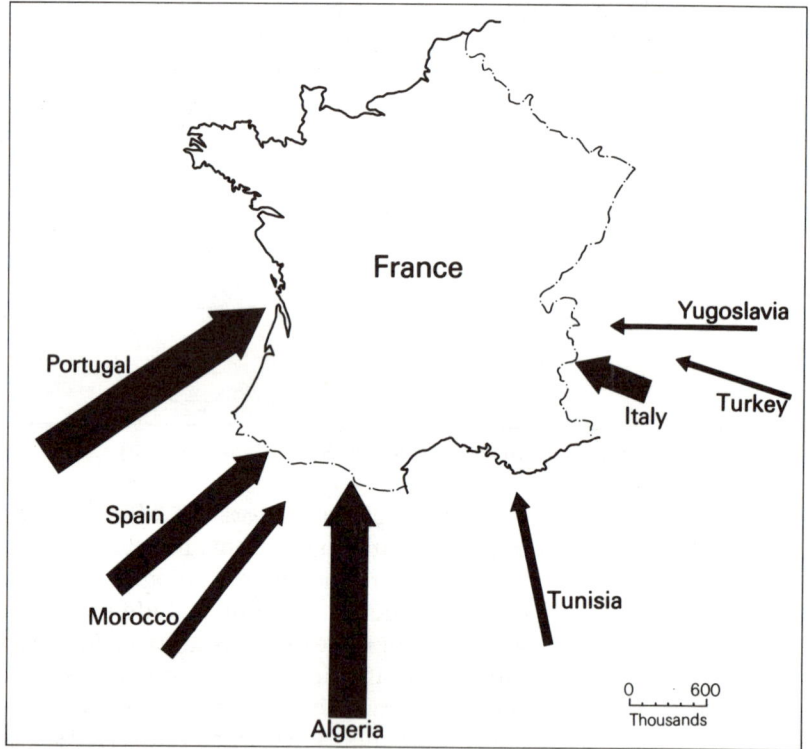

FACTORS INFLUENCING CHOICE OF DESTINATION

1 **The standard of living** Countries with higher standards of living mean greater job opportunities and higher wages (Switzerland, Germany).

2 **Distance** Temporary migrants are more likely to seek jobs in bordering countries, rather than distant ones (Italians to Switzerland, Spaniards to France, Irish to UK).

3 **Colonies** Colonial connections often make entry into the mother country much easier (West Indians to UK, Algerians to France).

4 **Family** It is much easier to arrive in a foreign country if relatives are already there.

5 **Immigration controls** Some controls definitely favour certain peoples.

INTERNAL MIGRATION

This involves the permanent or semi-permanent movement from one abode to another without crossing international boundaries. This type of migration is occurring in all countries, whether they be developed or developing.

INTERNAL MIGRATION IN DEVELOPED NATIONS

There are many reasons for the movement of peoples within their own country: of these, four major patterns can be identified.

1 Movement for retirement.
2 Rural depopulation.
3 Movement from urban areas into suburbs and outlying villages.
4 Movement from urban areas of high unemployment to urban growth areas.

1 MOVEMENT FOR RETIREMENT

In the UK large numbers of people 'retire' and move. Reasons for this growing trend include:

1 Earlier retirement More people retire before 60/65 years, accepting the early retirement schemes introduced to reduce the unemployment rates of the young, or to cut labour costs.

2 People are living longer As life expectancy has increased to 71–73 years, and with earlier retirement, it is worth starting a new life in a new area.

3 Pensions With the advent of state pensions and the increase of work pensions (contributory or non-contributory), pensioners have been able to afford to move areas and maintain a relatively high standard of living.

4 Health Many move for health reasons, especially to areas of milder climates or cleaner air. As developed nations become more health conscious this trend is likely to expand.

5 Attitudes towards the old As the twentieth century has progressed, there has been less tendency for the old to live with their children. Reasons for this include the reduction in family size, the greater likelihood that the children themselves will have left the area of the family home, as well as the improved health of the old and a changing attitude towards age.

The effects of movement for retirement

1 Some counties of the UK have a disproportionate number of older people. This may lead to an intolerable burden on the local national

health authority, with extra long waiting lists for hospital beds, operations and an overconcentration on geriatric care.

2   House prices may be pushed up by demand, resulting in the departure of the young to other areas.

3   An imbalance in the community often leads to a general 'conservatism' developing, where the large number of old people use their political influence to resist change. Seaside towns become 'sleepy', not attracting young tourists.

2 RURAL DEPOPULATION

(See pages 192–3 above).

3 URBAN – RURAL MIGRATION

As communication systems have been becoming quicker and more efficient, and with the rise in car ownership giving greater mobility to the majority of the population in the UK, there has been a move out of towns into the more pleasant environment of the countryside. here, people can enjoy the advantages of less pollution, less congestion, gardens, the open countryside and a village community atmosphere; but at the same time have easy access to the city or town for shopping, social activities and employment.

This movement has brought great changes both to the towns and the countryside.

Effect on towns

1   Very little residence in city centres creating a 'dead heart'.

2   Outward growth of towns as suburbs grow along main arterial roads. This is called 'urban sprawl'. In extreme cases towns may join up and huge built-up areas (conurbations) are created.

2   If people move beyond the authority boundary it may lead to a reduction in money collected by the local authority in rates. Less money will be available to combat the problem of inner city deprivation.

4   Traffic congestion and parking difficulties at peak times.

5   The development of suburban business districts.

Effect on the countryside.

1   Rise in land and house prices. Therefore a temptation for farmers to sell their land as building land (once the status of the land has been changed by planning regulations).

2   Local young residents may find difficulty in affording house prices.

3   Villages change – housing estates greatly expand the village population leading to an increase of local shops and services. Many would suggest that the village atmosphere is destroyed.

4   The village becomes a 'dormitory' settlement with commuting to neighbouring large towns for work, shopping and social activities.

5 The Green Belt is invaded, as population pressure forces changes in planning regulations. (See also Book 1, Chapter 4.)

INTERNAL MIGRATION IN DEVELOPING NATIONS

Two major patterns can be identified:

1 Rural – urban migration.
2 Movement from periphery areas to core regions.

RURAL-URBAN MIGRATION

This is the movement from farms to the towns. Reasons include both push and pull factors.

Rural–urban migration causes

Push factors	Pull factors
Population pressure due to high natural increase rates.	Greater opportunity of a higher standard of living.
Agricultural reform leading to less demand for labour.	To join relatives in cities.
Inheritance schemes: (a) only the eldest son receives the land; others leave; (b) land is sub-divided between all sons and plots become incapable of supporting families.	Poverty is lower, as wages are higher for those who find work. Better medical and educational facilities. Some pure water and sewerage disposal in operation, but standards still very low.
Poor living conditions: no sewerage, pure water, electricity.	Possibility of industrial employment.
Lock of alternative forms of employment.	Greater prospects for some.
lack of opportunities.	Greater assistance in times of natural disasters.
Natural disasters: drought, flood, etc.	

(For other information see pp. 192–3 above.)

MOVEMENT FROM PERIPHERY AREAS TO CORE REGIONS

As certain areas develop, perhaps due to the exploitation of mineral resources or industrial development or the building of a new port, people from other areas with slow growth migrate to these growth points. The initial movement is in search of work, but a number of the push and pull factors in the table above can be contributory causes.

Invariably the result of such migration results in escalating growth at the growth points, but a decline in the periphery regions. Study of Fig 5.4 will explain why.

Fig 5.4 Causes of
migration from periphery
areas to core regions

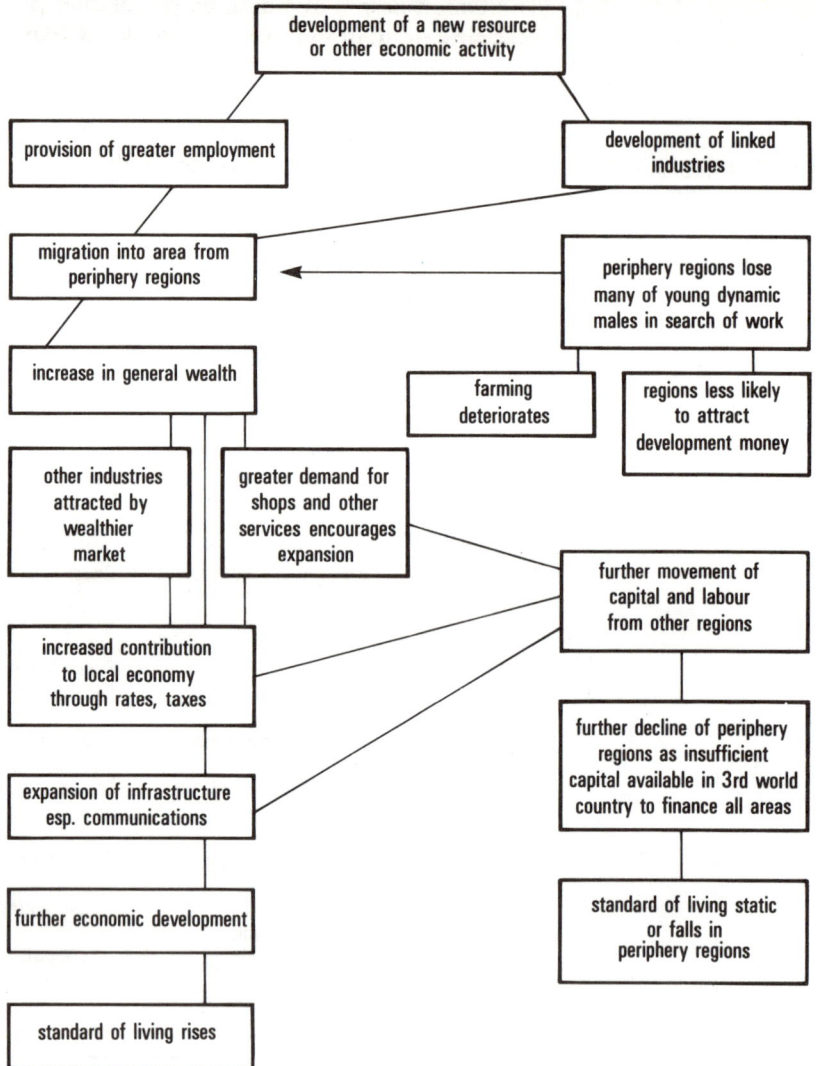

```
                        ┌─────────────────────────┐
                        │ development of a new     │
                        │ resource or other        │
                        │ economic activity        │
                        └─────────────────────────┘
                          ↙                    ↘
┌──────────────────────────┐          ┌─────────────────────┐
│ provision of greater     │          │ development of      │
│ employment               │          │ linked industries   │
└──────────────────────────┘          └─────────────────────┘

┌──────────────────────┐          ┌──────────────────────────┐
│ migration into area  │ ◄─────── │ periphery regions lose   │
│ from periphery       │          │ many of young dynamic    │
│ regions              │          │ males in search of work  │
└──────────────────────┘          └──────────────────────────┘

┌──────────────────────┐    ┌────────────┐  ┌──────────────────┐
│ increase in general  │    │ farming    │  │ regions less     │
│ wealth               │    │ deteriorates│  │ likely to attract│
└──────────────────────┘    └────────────┘  │ development money│
                                             └──────────────────┘

┌────────────────┐  ┌──────────────────┐
│ other          │  │ greater demand   │
│ industries     │  │ for shops and    │
│ attracted by   │  │ other services   │
│ wealthier      │  │ encourages       │
│ market         │  │ expansion        │   ┌──────────────────┐
└────────────────┘  └──────────────────┘   │ further movement │
                                            │ of capital and   │
                                            │ labour from      │
┌──────────────────────┐                    │ other regions    │
│ increased            │                    └──────────────────┘
│ contribution to      │
│ local economy        │                    ┌──────────────────────┐
│ through rates, taxes │                    │ further decline of   │
└──────────────────────┘                    │ periphery regions as │
                                            │ insufficient capital │
┌──────────────────────┐                    │ available in 3rd     │
│ expansion of         │                    │ world country to     │
│ infrastructure       │                    │ finance all areas    │
│ esp. communications  │                    └──────────────────────┘
└──────────────────────┘
                                            ┌──────────────────────┐
┌──────────────────────┐                    │ standard of living   │
│ further economic     │                    │ static or falls in   │
│ development          │                    │ periphery regions    │
└──────────────────────┘                    └──────────────────────┘

┌──────────────────────┐
│ standard of living   │
│ rises                │
└──────────────────────┘
```

This type of migration is frequently only semi-permanent in Africa with migrant workers living for many months in dormitories provided for young males. At the end of a period of employment, these migrant workers return home to their village or family before returning for another working session. The villages from which the migrants have come, may have half or more of the male members of the family working hundreds of miles away; so agricultural activities have to be performed by old men, young children and women.

TEMPORARY MOVEMENTS OF PEOPLE

This involves the movement of people from their permanent home to a temporary base before returning. This may involve movements of limited distance and of short time scale (such as shopping trips) or more extended periods and distances (holidays). These types of movement are largely restricted to the developed countries of the world, but there are many examples in Africa of people trekking hundreds of miles to feeding and medical centres established by relief workers with the intention of returning with food.

1 COMMUTING

The strict definition of commuting is the daily travel to and from work, but it can be extended to include other regular trips such as for shopping or entertainment.

Commuting for work In the UK millions of people live in dormitory villages, travelling each day to the nearby town for work and return at night. This causes great problems:

(*a*)   traffic congestion as arterial roads become choked at peak times;

(*b*)   parking problems, as most towns were not constructed for motor traffic and space is at a premium;

(*c*)   pollution from vehicle fumes and noise levels;

(*d*)   excessive requirements from public transport systems for two short periods in the day, and little demand for the rest of the time;

(*e*)   stress levels are high, as are road accidents;

(*f*)   inefficient use of time spent on the journey to work, and often adding a few hours to the working day;

(*g*)   damage to roads, sewerage systems and buildings through excessive road usage.

In south-east England and in many areas of the USA people may travel great distances to work (e.g. from Southampton, Birmingham and Dover to London). For many, distances are so great that people commute on a weekly basis: travelling to work on Monday morning, returning home on Friday night.

2 SHOPPING TRIPS

This may involve regular trips to town, to take advantage of cheaper prices and greater ranges of goods than those found in the dormitory villages. It might involve the weekly visit to the hypermarket for bulk purchase of groceries. It may be a specific visit to a large town to buy a specific item. In the UK there has been a growth of shopping trips to London organized by local coach companies. Cross-border trips may be organized to take advantage of cheaper prices (e.g. from Eire to Northern Ireland) or cross-channel trips to take advantage of the 'duty-free'.

3 SECOND HOMES

This is the purchase of another home, which is visited during leisure time (weekends, holidays). As there has been a rise in the general standard of living in the UK, and as the length of leisure time has increased, plus the greater mobility brought about by the universal ownership of motor vehicles, then some people have purchased second homes. Many of these homes are in rural areas, such as North Wales, the Lake District, Scottish Uplands, the Cotswolds or in south-west England. Their development can bring advantages and disadvantages to the areas in which they are sited.

(a)   They bring finance to the rural communities, increasing the demand for local tradesmen and provide custom for shops, cafés and public houses.

(b)   They restore neglected buildings, improving the general environment.

(c)   They compete with locals for houses, leading to a rise in house prices, making it very difficult for the young of the village to buy their first home. This may encourage rural depopulation.

(d)   Many houses may be empty during much of the year.

(e)   In North Wales, some of the second homes owned by English people have been destroyed by fire-bombs.

4 MOVEMENTS FOR HOLIDAYS

(See pages 112–120 above).

CHECKLIST ▶

POPULATION MOVEMENTS

1   There are many forms of population movement.
2   Movement can be classified into: permanent, temporary, daily movement; international or internal movement.

International migration

1   Push and pull factors cause people to migrate.
2   Migrations have effects on both the country receiving immigrants and the country exporting people.
3   International migrations have a distinct age and sex bias.
4   Major migrations before 1920 were from western Europe to the relatively sparsely populated New World.
5   Modern migrations are on a smaller scale involving movements from developing to developed nations.
6   Immigrations controls in developed nations greatly limit international migration.
7   Factors influencing the choice of destination for emigrants include:
    (a)   standards of living;
    (b)   distance;
    (c)   colonial ties;
    (d)   family connections;
    (e)   immigration controls.

Internal migration

1 An increasing number of people in developed nations move house when they retire.
2 Highland areas often suffer rural depopulation.
3 Urban-rural migration is a feature of developed industrial nations.
4 'Dead-hearts', urban vandalism, 'urban sprawl' are three of the results of urban-rural migration in the developed world.
5 Rural-urban migration (urbanization) is very active, in developing nations.
6 In developing nations there is considerable regional migration from 'periphery' areas to 'core' regions.

Temporary movements

1 Commuting is a common feature of developed nations.
2 Commuting takes a number of forms:
  (*a*)   commuting for work;
  (*b*)   shopping;
  (*c*)   second homes.
3 Holidays – residential or non-residential – are another common feature found in the Developed World.

ORDNANCE SURVEY MAPWORK

Contents

CONVENTIONAL SIGNS

It is vital that all map readers should have a thorough knowledge of the 1:50,000 and 1:25,000 OS conventional signs as this is the basic language of maps. Many examination boards provide OS maps with accompanying keys, but some may not. Also it is quicker and easier to read a map without constant reference to conventional signs.

COMPASS DIRECTIONS

Fig 6.1 Compass directions – 16 points

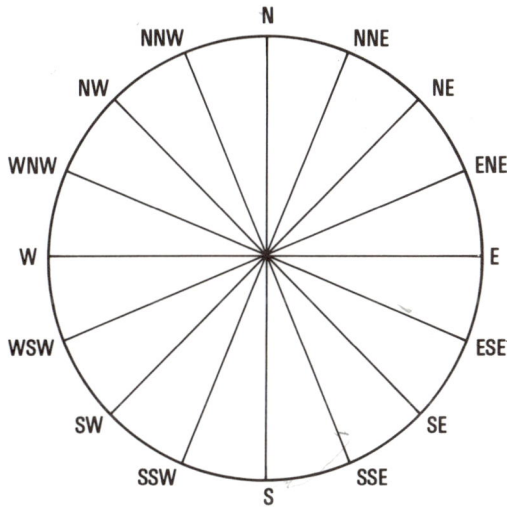

CONTOUR PATTERNS

Contours are lines joining places of equal height above sea-level. Therefore they are continuous (like circles) and do not cross each other. The vertical interval (the difference in height between each contour line) is usually regular, but varies according to the scale of the map, i.e. 10 m intervals on the 1:50,000 2nd series maps, but 5 m intervals on the 1:25,000 scale maps.

Contours indicate not only the height of the land but also its steepness. Where contours are closely spaced, the land is steep;

where they are widely spaced the land is gently sloping; absence of contours indicates flat land.

Contours also reveal the shape of the land surface by indicating convex, concave, uniform or stepped slopes.

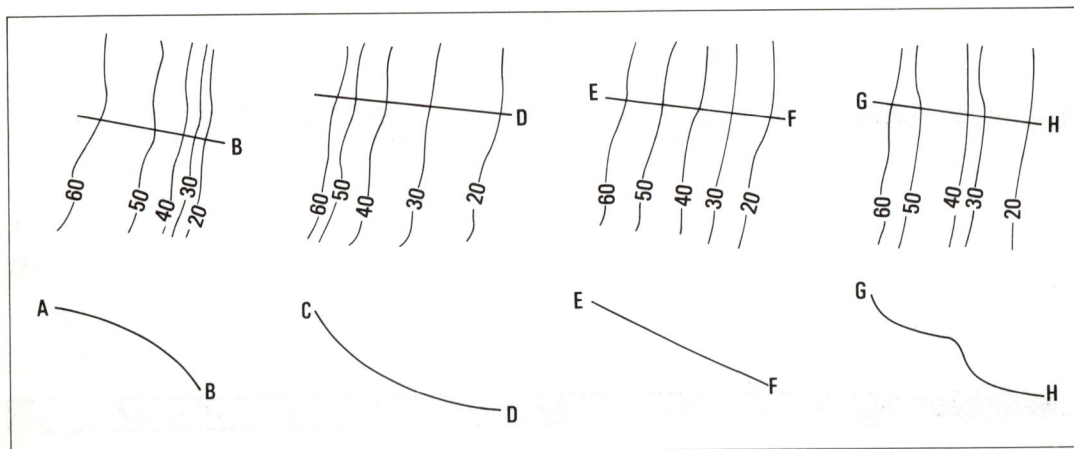

Fig 6.2 Contour patterns and sketch sections to show different slopes

Certain landforms have distinct contour patterns. It is important to be able to recognize these patterns in order to transform a two-dimensional map into a three-dimensional landscape. Once this is achieved, reasons for settlement patterns, farming activities, patterns of communications become much clearer.

Fig 6.3 (a) A cuesta, (b) ridge and (c) flat-topped ridge

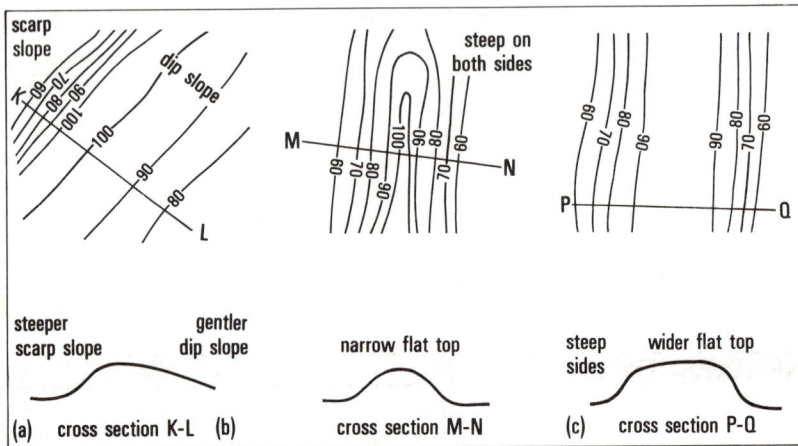

Fig 6.4 (a) A plateau and (b) a dissected plateau

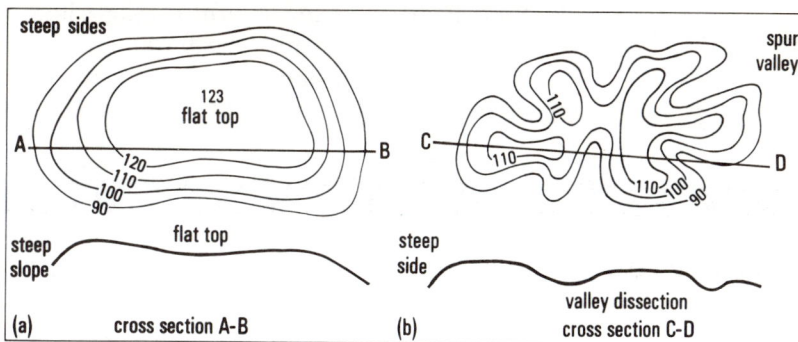

Fig 6.5 (a) A valley, (b) spur and (c) knoll

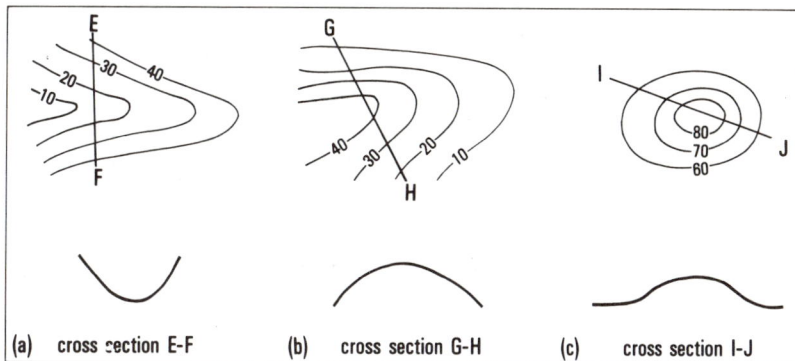

GRID REFERENCES

Grid references are used to aid location on a map.
1 Numbers at the bottom of the map (Eastings) should be given before those at the side (Northings).
2 Four-figure references refer to a square.
3 Six-figure references refer to a point within a square.

MEASURING DISTANCES

A STRAIGHT-LINE DISTANCES
1 Lay a straight edge between the two points.
2 Mark on to the straight edge the position of the two points.
3 Lay the straight edge against the relevant linear scale on the margin of the map.
4 Read off the distance using the correct units.

B TWISTING ROUTES
1 Lay a length of string along the route between the two points, following each curve and corner.

2   Stretch out the string to form a straight line.
3   Lay the string against the linear scale in the margin of the map, reading off the distance.

SECTIONS

A CROSS-SECTIONS

1   Lay a sheet of paper with a straight edge between the two points on the map.
2   Mark on to the paper the height of each contour crossed. If too many contours are crossed, just mark on every thicker one.
3   On to a separate sheet of paper draw a horizontal line the same width as the distance between the two points.
4   Parallel to this line, at 2 mm intervals, draw a series of parallel lines, each one representing a contour.
5   Put on the height of each contour.
6   Beneath the grid you have constructed, lay your initial sheet of paper.
7   Transfer the information from your initial sheet of paper on to the grid.
8   Join up freehand to construct a cross-section.
9   On to this cross-section label the major features of relief and drainage.

B SKETCH SECTIONS

For this skill a free-hand (not measured) section must be drawn.
1   Note the highest and lowest points.
2   Where contours are close together a steep gradient should be drawn.
3   Where contours are well spaced a gentle gradient should be drawn.
4   Where contours are very widely spaced or absent the gradient should be nearly flat.
5   Look out for concave, convex or regular slopes.
6   Note whether the slope is uphill or downhill.
NB Numbers on contours are written so that they read as if you are looking uphill.

Fig 6.6 Contours are written as if you are looking uphill

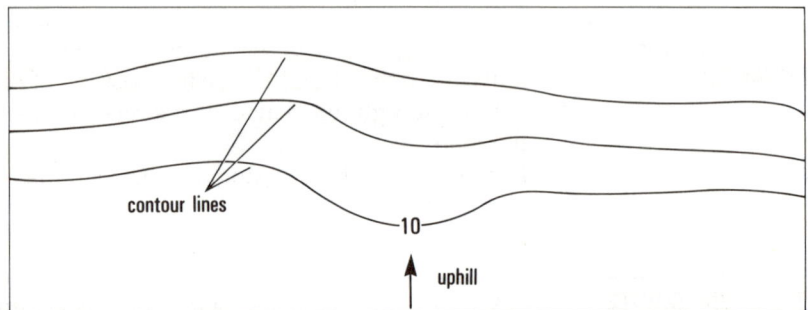

INTERVISIBILITY

To see if it is possible to see one point from another

either:

1 Note the heights of the two points.
2 Look at the height of the land between the two points – would this land obscure the view?
3 Note the shape of the land between the two points – if the slope between the two points is convex, then it probably will *not* be possible to see one point from the other.

or

4 If sufficient time is available, construct a cross-section, draw a straight line between the two points. If this straight line crosses the line of the cross-section, the view will be obscured.

AERIAL PHOTOGRAPHS

ORIENTATION

When it is necessary to orientate a photograph to a map, look for major landmarks on the photograph which will be also shown on the OS map, e.g. church with tower, a crossroads, a river bend, a bridge and so on. Twist the photograph round so that a straight line between the two identified major landmarks on the photograph fits a straight line between the same two points on the OS map.

NB Maps are constructed so that grid north is at the top of the map.

What a photograph may reveal that a map does not

1 The time of the day may be revealed by the length of the shadows.
2 The volume of traffic.
3 Types and styles of buildings, and therefore an indication of the age structure of a town, which may be used to indicate directions of growth.
4 Types of farming, including field sizes, field boundaries and farm buildings.
5 The weather.

GRADIENTS

1 Measure the horizontal distance (in metres) between the two points.
2 Calculate the difference in height (in metres) between the two points.
3 Use the formula:
3 Use the formula:

$$\text{gradient} = \frac{\text{difference in height}}{\text{distance apart}}$$

4 **Either** multiply the answer by 100 to make a percentage **or** reduce your answer to its lowest fraction, e.g.:

$$\frac{90}{1500} = \frac{1}{16.7} = 1:16.7 = 1:17$$

With all descriptions, describe the **general pattern** first and then name and give grid references of the **exceptions**.

COASTAL DESCRIPTIONS

1 Identify the general **trend** of the coastline (i.e. the direction the coastline runs in).
2 Name the general **type** of coastline – a smooth (gently curving) lowland coastline, an indented (many 'ins and outs') coastline, or headlands and bays.
3 Describe the coastal landforms in some detail, e.g. the size and composition of the beach(es), the height, steepness and shape of the cliffs.
4 Identify and locate with grid references coastal features such as stacks, spits, islands, caves, estuaries, rias, fiords and so on.

A COASTAL DESCRIPTION EXAMPLE

Fig 6.7 Coastal description example

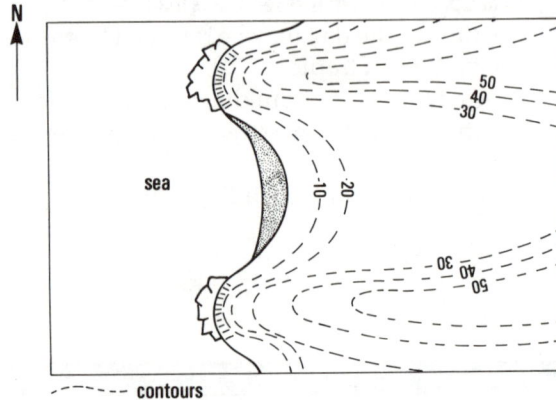

Trend N → S.

Type Headlands and bays.

Coastal landforms
(a)   Long wide sandy beach in the bay.
(b)   Cliffed headlands, 10–20 m high, very steeply sloping.

Coastal features

(*a*)   Wide wave-cut platforms off both headlands.

(*b*)   Stacks at GR 002513.

DESCRIPTIONS OF AREAS OF UPLAND RELIEF

1   Study the map by carefully observing the contour patterns. From your observation try to identify the **major landform(s)** in the area you are describing.

2   If relevant to the landform(s) you have identified give its **trend**.

3   State its **general height** giving grid references for the highest and lowest points.

4   Describe the **nature** of the surface of the landform(s) – flat or undulating.

5   Describe the **sides/slopes** of the landform(s), mentioning **steepness** and **shape** (concave, convex, regular).

6   Comment on the degree of **dissection** of the landform and what has caused this dissection, e.g. deeply dissected by steeply sloping river valleys.

7   If obvious, state whether the rock is impervious or porous.

AN EXAMPLE OF UPLANDS DESCRIPTION

Fig 6.8 An example of uplands description

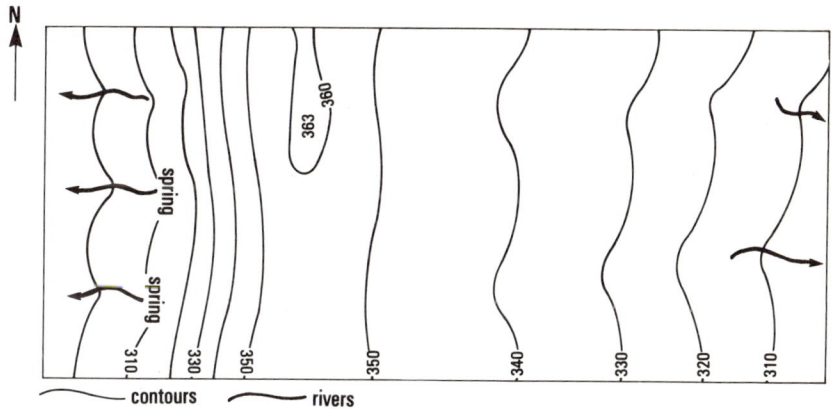

Major landforms Cuesta trending north to south, escarpment facing west, dip slope to the east.

Heights Top of scarp approx 350 m max. height at trig. point 363 m foot of scarp disappears off map at 300 m, dip slope 310 m.

Slopes

(*a*)   Scarp very steep, concave.

(*b*)   Dip moderately steep, fairly regular.

Dissection

(*a*)   Scarp little dissection above 310 m.

(*b*)   Dip dry valley above 310 m.

Porosity of rock Lack of surface drainage above 310 m, evidence of spring line on dip and scarp slopes at 310 m.

DESCRIPTIONS OF AREAS OF LOWLANDS RELIEF

1   By careful observation of the contour patterns name the **type** of landform, e.g. flood plain, clay vale, coastal plain.
2   Describe the general **slope** of the land: give an idea of the degree of slope, the general direction of slope and the nature of the surface, e.g. gently sloping to the north, land undulates gently towards the south-east.
3   Give the general **height** of the land, noting the maximum and minimum heights.
4   Give grid references of **specific features**, e.g. marshland, a knoll.

AN EXAMPLE OF A LOWLANDS DESCRIPTION

Fig 6.9 An example of lowlands description

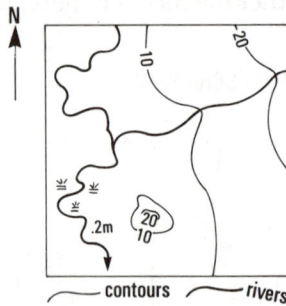

Type Flood plain and valley side.

Slope
(*a*)   Very gentle valley side.
(*b*)   Flat valley floor.
(*c*)   West towards main river.

Height
(*a*)   Valley floor < 10 m.
(*b*)   Valley side 20 m > 10 m.
(*c*)   2 m on southern edge.
(*d*)   20 m+ knoll, valley side.

Features
(*a*)   Knoll on flood plain.
(*b*)   Marshland by main river.

DRAINAGE PATTERN DESCRIPTIONS

1 Comment on the **quantity of surface drainage**.
2 Comment on the general direction of drainage.
3 Note any **watersheds**.
4 Comment on the **form** of drainage, e.g. mainly artificial drainage ditches, many tributaries, many lakes.
5 If there is a lack of surface drainage, it is **not** correct to say there is no drainage, but it is correct to say that drainage is **subsurface**.

AN EXAMPLE OF A DRAINAGE PATTERN DESCRIPTION

Fig 6.10 An example of drainage pattern description

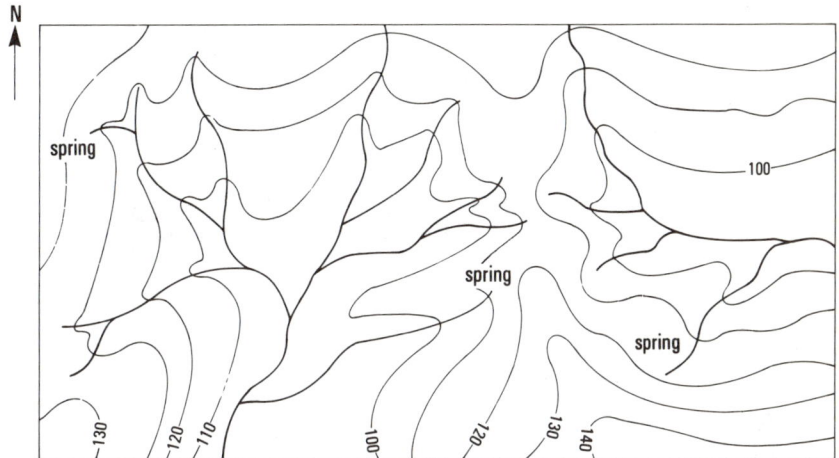

Quantity There is abundant surface drainage.

Direction Tributaries flow into two main rivers, one of which flows in a generally southerly direction, the other in an easterly one.

Watershed There is a major watershed separating the two river basins. This watershed runs approximately north to south down the centre of the map.

Form Drainage is natural, consisting of two rivers receiving many fast-flowing tributaries.

Subsurface There appears to be little surface drainage above 120 m. This, plus the presence of springs at this height could indicate subsurface drainage within porous/permeable rock. The reappearance of water at 120 m indicates a spring due to the junction with an impervious rock.

DESCRIPTIONS OF THE RELIEF AND DRAINAGE OF AREAS OF MIXED RELIEF

It is quite likely that you may have to describe an area containing both upland and lowland. Under these circumstances, it is invariably easier, clearer and quicker to draw a simple sketch map and annotate it.

Fig 6.11 Sketch map showing an imaginary area of mixed relief

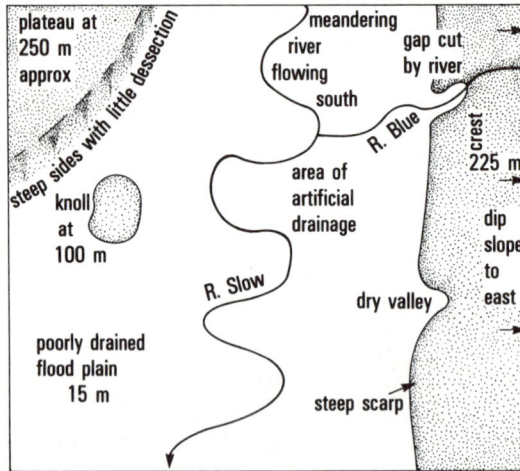

DESCRIPTIONS OF RIVERS AND VALLEYS

DESCRIPTION OF RIVERS

1 Describe the **direction of flow.** This may be indicated as shown in Fig 6.11.

Fig 6.12 Recognizing flow directions of rivers

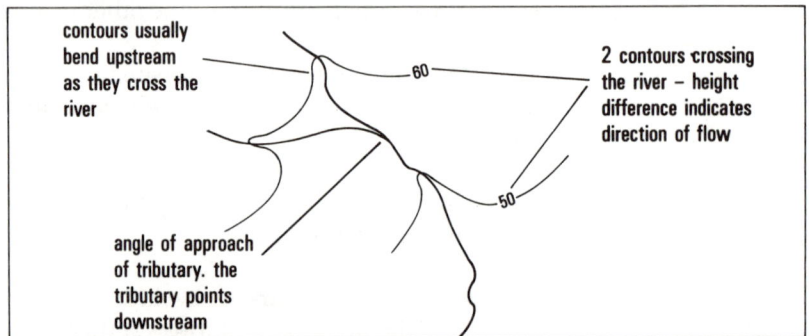

2 Describe the **width** of the river. If it varies state extremes as well as a general width.
3 Describe the **speed** of flow. This may be indicated by the gradient of the valley floor (the number of contours crossed by the river in comparison with the distance the river flows) *or* if the river is meandering, it will be slow flowing.
4 Describe the **shape** of the river, e.g. winding, meandering, straight.

5 Count the number and comment on the size of *tributaries*.
6 Look for **river features**, e.g. cut-offs, islands, estuaries.
7 Look for **artificial features**, embanking, straightening, drainage ditches.
NB Remember to make a generalized description and then give grid references of individual features or comment on the exceptions to your generalizations.

AN EXAMPLE OF A RIVER DESCRIPTION

Fig 6.13 An example of a river description

Direction of flow To the south-west (angle of approach of tributaries, contour crossing the river points upstream).

Width River generally narrow but becomes progressively wider, until it could be called very wide on the western edge of the map.

Speed of flow Slow flowing (only one contour crossed by the main river as it crosses the map).

Shape River meanders, but meanders become *less* accentuated downstream.

Tributaries The river receives four tributaries, most of which are on the north (right) bank.

River and artificial features There is an ox-bow lake at GR and the river is embanked on the western edge of the map.

DESCRIPTION OF VALLEYS

Study the long profile, the cross profile and the plan of the valley.

1 Long profile Comment on the steepness of the valley floor, by comparing the number of contours crossing the valley floor with the length of the valley being studied.

2 Cross profile

(*a*)   Comment on the **width of the valley** – wide or narrow?

(*b*)   Comment on and measure the **width of the valley floor.**

(*c*)   Comment on the **steepness** and **shape** of the **valley sides** – steep or gentle, convex, concave, uniform or stepped?

(*d*)   Comment on the **depth** of the valley – deep or shallow?

3 Plan

(*a*)   State the general **trend** of the valley.

(*b*)   Comment on the straightness of the valley.

4 What *type* of valley is it? Glacial trough, river valley, fault guided valley or dry valley.

AN EXAMPLE OF A VALLEY DESCRIPTION

Fig 6.14 An example of a valley description

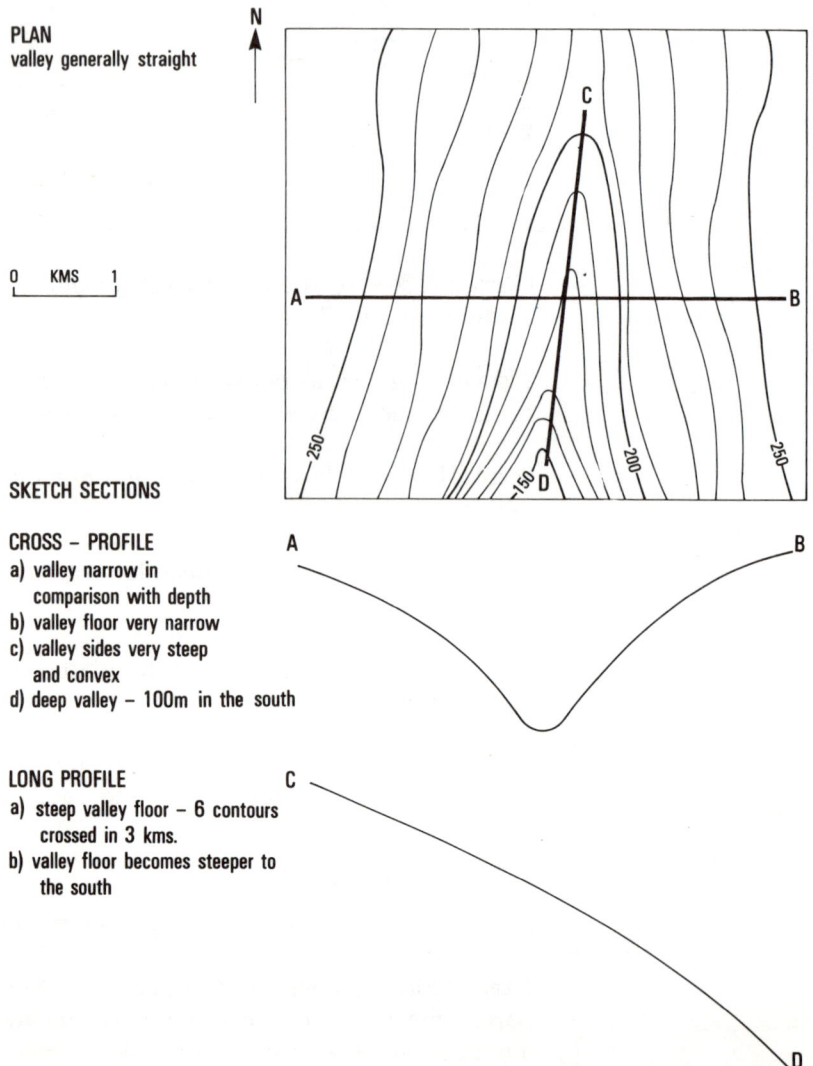

PLAN
valley generally straight

0   KMS   1

SKETCH SECTIONS

CROSS – PROFILE

a) valley narrow in comparison with depth
b) valley floor very narrow
c) valley sides very steep and convex
d) deep valley – 100m in the south

LONG PROFILE

a) steep valley floor – 6 contours crossed in 3 kms.
b) valley floor becomes steeper to the south

DESCRIPTIONS OF ROUTES

1 Give the overall **trend** of the route, noting any significant changes away from this direction. Do **not** mention all the minor changes of direction!

2 Give any significant **heights**, such as starting and finishing heights, maximum and minimum heights, the height of a bridge, a pass, a flood plain, a col.

3 Study the relief of the land and note whether the road/railway/canal **follows certain landforms**, e.g. valleys, passes, ridge tops, cols.

4 Note whether the route **avoids certain landforms**, e.g. escarpments, flood plains, steep valley sides.

5 Have there been any attempts to reduce gradients, adapt the natural route or to **overcome natural obstacles** by means of bridges, hairpin bends, tunnels, cuttings, embankments. If so, give grid references.

6 How has the location of settlements affected the route? Are there obvious detours to link up various forms of settlement?
   (a)   minor roads link farms to villages;
   (b)   secondary roads link villages to towns;
   (c)   major roads link towns;
   (d)   motorways link major areas (industrial, tourist, port), generally avoiding towns.

7 As a general rule routes are not straight, even though this would be cheaper, so ask yourself why is this route not straight? Is it to follow landforms to make the route easier? Is it to avoid landforms to stop flooding or keep down construction costs? Is it so as to link up other settlements?

AN EXAMPLE OF A ROUTE DESCRIPTION

Fig 6.15 An example of a route description

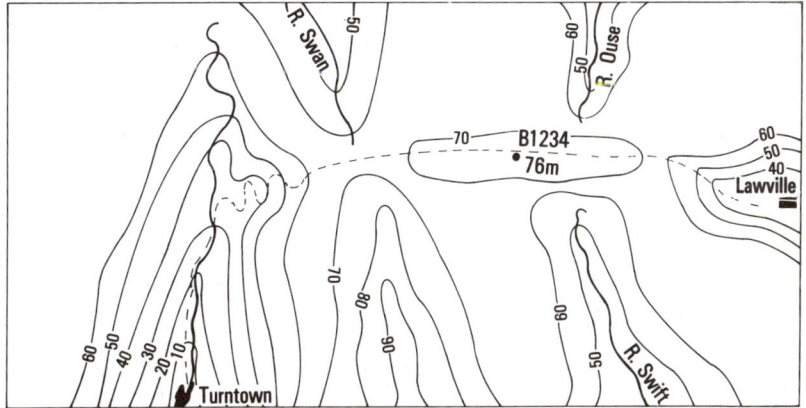

Describe the routes of the B1234 from Turntown to Lawville

Trend From Turntown to Lawville is ENE, but at first road heads north, then generally east, finishing in a south-easterly direction.

Heights Starting height < 10 m, max height 76 m in col finishing height 30–40 m.

Landforms followed
(a)   Valley of river Turn.
(b)   Dry tributary valley of the river Turn.
(c)   East-west trending flat-topped ridge including col.
(d)   Dry valley leading into Lawville.

Landforms avoided
(a)   Steep-sided narrow valleys of river Swift, River Ouse and river Swan.
(b)   Steep-sided ridge trending NNW to SSE.

Measures taken to overcome natural obstacles
(a)   Bridge over the river Turn.
(b)   Hairpin bends out of Turn valley.

Influence of settlement None revealed.

Starting at a height of less than 10 m, the B1234 initially heads due north along the floor of the Turn valley. After approximately 3 k the road swings to the north-east crossing the river Turn by a bridge before climbing out of the steep-sided valley, easing the ascent by using a dry tributary valley. This steep climb is made even easier by the construction of hairpin bends. The road passes around the northern edge of a ridge and to the south of the head valley of the river Swan.

The B1234 now heads generally east taking advantage of the flat top of an east-west trending ridge. At its maximum height of 76 m at GR   it passes through a col, thereby avoiding the steep sided valleys of the rivers Ouse and Swift. From this point, the road heads south-east descending into Lawville by means of a dry valley, finishing at a height of between 30 m and 40m.

DESCRIPTIONS OF LAND USE

Land use is all the uses made of the land by mankind, both past and present. Comment on the general patterns of all the following:

1 Types of settlement Farms, hamlets, villages, towns. If relevant consider the reasons for the patterns you have found (such as nucleated, dispersed, linear, regular or irregular). To what extent are these patterns a reaction to natural factors such as relief, drainage, coastline? To what extent are these factors a result of exploitation of mineral resources, communication patterns? To what extent do models such as central place apply?

2 The modes of transport Road, rail, canal. What factors, natural or artificial, influence these patterns?

3 Farming Note the sizes and numbers of farms, the sizes of fields. Is there any evidence of types of farm?

4 Areas of artificial woodland What is the size of these patches? What types of tree are they composed of? What factors influence their distribution (e.g. relief, aspect)? What is their purpose? (lumbering, shelter belts, landscaping, checking soil erosion).

5 Areas of mining or quarrying Note the frequency and distribution. Is there any evidence of what is being mined or quarried?

6 Areas of industry Is there any indication of the types of industry? Is it heavy or light? Old or modern? Small- or large-scale? What factors have encouraged its establishment/growth? (communications, relief, water supply, labour supply, market, raw materials?).

7 Others e.g. water supply, tourism.

Does it seem that there could be conflicts of interest or environmental problems, e.g. industry, mining versus tourism, pollution, spoiling of scenic beauty?

DESCRIPTIONS OF INDIVIDUAL SETTLEMENTS

A good description of a settlement should include reference to its site, situation, form and functions.

SITE

This is the area covered by the buildings comprising the settlement. Reference should be made to:

1 Height If the place is on sloping land give maximum and minimum and if possible the height of the original centre (the major church, main crossroads?)

2 Aspect State the general direction the settlement faces e.g. south-facing for more hours of sunshine.

3 Landform Name the landform on which the place stands.

4 Slope of the land Describe the slope – steep or gentle.

SITUATION

This is the area surrounding the settlement, i.e. much of the rest of the map. Briefly describe the general relief and drainage of the area, indicating where the place being described fits into this description.

FORM

This is the shape of the settlement.

1 Describe the overall **outline shape** of the settlement, e.g. compact, loose-knit, linear, star shaped.
2 Comment on the **street patterns**: rectangular, crescents (curves), haphazard; give located example of patterns identified.
3 Note evidence of change of form due to *growth*, e.g. the building of estates on the outskirts, spread of settlements down on to a flood plain and so on.

FUNCTIONS

These are the 'jobs' a settlement does for itself and the surrounding area. Give past and present functions, quoting map evidence.
    Look for the following:

1 defence – a castle, an ancient tower;
2 communications centre – main roads meeting, a bridging point;
3 industry – factory, mill, works;
4 mining – mine, quarry;
5 service centre – hospital, bus station, college;
6 administrative centre – county hall, town hall;
7 tourist centre – marina, pier, youth hostel, tourist information centre;
8 market town – a minor route centre set in a farming region;
9 religious centre – cathedral, bishop's palace; do *not* count numbers of churches or chapels;
10 port – harbour, ferry routes.
    It may be easiest to draw a simple sketch map and annotate it.

CHECKLIST ♦

ORDNANCE SURVEY MAPWORK

1 Contours indicate the shape, height and steepness of the land.
2 Sketch sections are quicker but less accurate than cross-sections.
3 Aerial photographs reveal information not shown on OS maps.
4 Checklists aid map descriptions:
    (a)   coasts: trend, type, landforms, features;
    (b)   uplands: landforms, general height, nature of surface, slopes, degree of dissection;
    (c)   lowlands: landform, slopes, height, features;
    (d)   drainage: quantity, direction, watersheds, form;

Fig 6.16 An imaginary sketch map describing site and situation (*see function 10 opposite*)

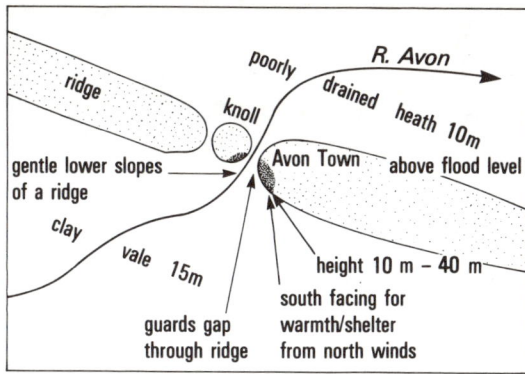

(e) rivers: direction, width, speed, shape, tributaries, natural features, artificial features;

(f) valleys: long profile, cross-profile, plan, type;

(g) routes: trend, heights, landforms followed, landforms avoided, overcoming obstacles, settlement;

(h) land use: settlement types, transport modes, farming, woods, mining, industry.

5 Individual settlements can best be described by referring to site, situation, form, function, growth.

GLOSSARY

col a high pass often formed by two rivers on opposite sides of a ridge cutting back towards each other.

compact an individual settlement where buildings are closely spaced.

contours lines joining places of equal height above sea-level.

dissection the process by which an upland area is carved up into separate units each of which is separated by valleys.

form the shape of a settlement.

linear a settlement where individual buildings are largely strung out in a relatively straight line. This may occur along a road or in a narrow steep-sided valley.

loose-knit a settlement which contain a number of clusters of buildings, each of which is separated by open ground.

sketch section a 'free-hand', side view of the steepness, shape and height of the land betwen two points.

SPECIMEN QUESTIONS

Answer **one** *question on this theme.*
Study the model of economic growth below which shows how industry can develop.

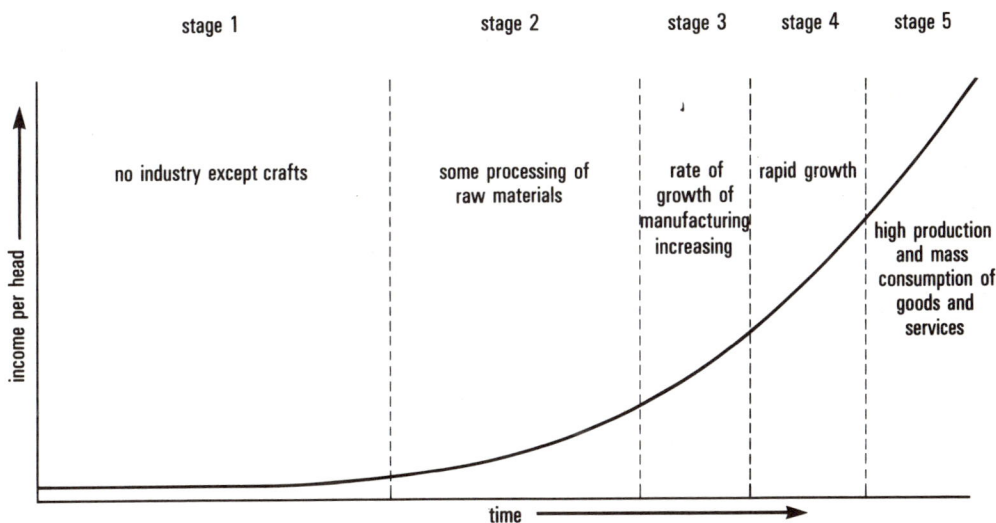

(a)   Developing countries have only reached stage 2 or 3 on the model. With reference to West Africa use the model to help you to explain why they have been slow to industrialize.
(b)   Developed countries have reached stage 4 or 5 on the model of economic growth. Using example from countries other than Great Britain:
(i) describe the conditions that have led to a high level of industrial development;
(ii) suggest how industrial development might change in the future.
(c)   Study the map below which shows losses in industrial jobs in Great Britain between 1978 and 1983.
   On your answer paper name **one** region (1–10) which has suffered industrial job losses of:
(i) 28% or more,
(ii) less than 18%.

(*d*)   Describe the general pattern of industrial job losses shown on the map.

(*e*)   Explain why jobs have been lost in one named region.

(*MEG*)

Fig A

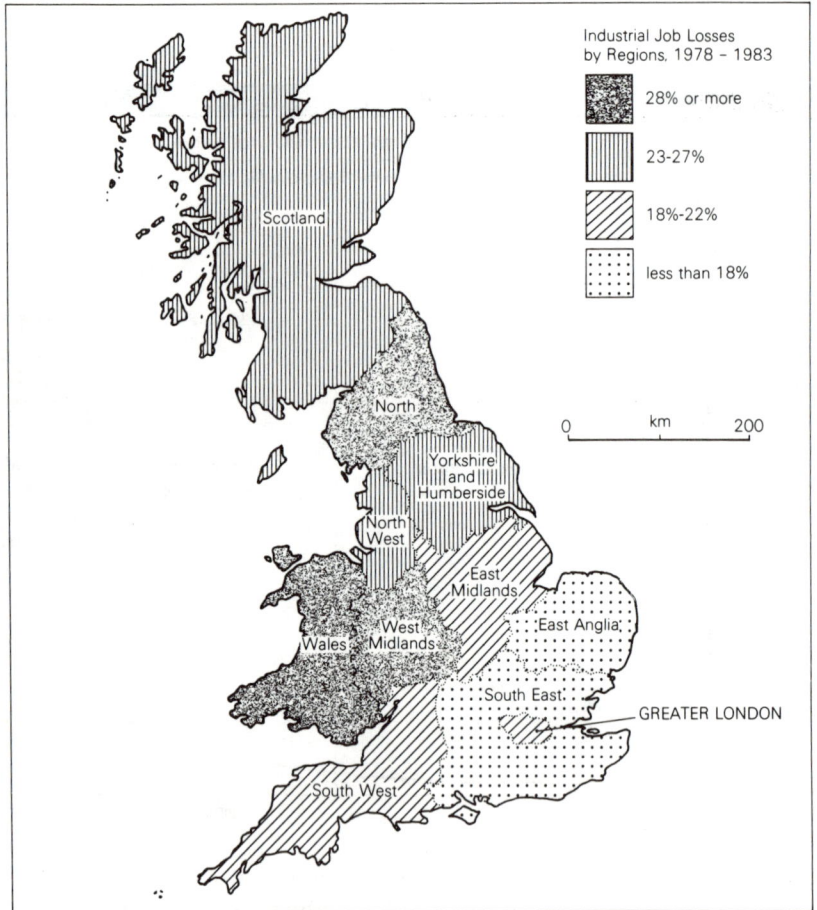

Industrial Job Losses
by Regions, 1978 – 1983

28% or more

23-27%

18%-22%

less than 18%

0   km   200

2 MIGRATION

Fig B

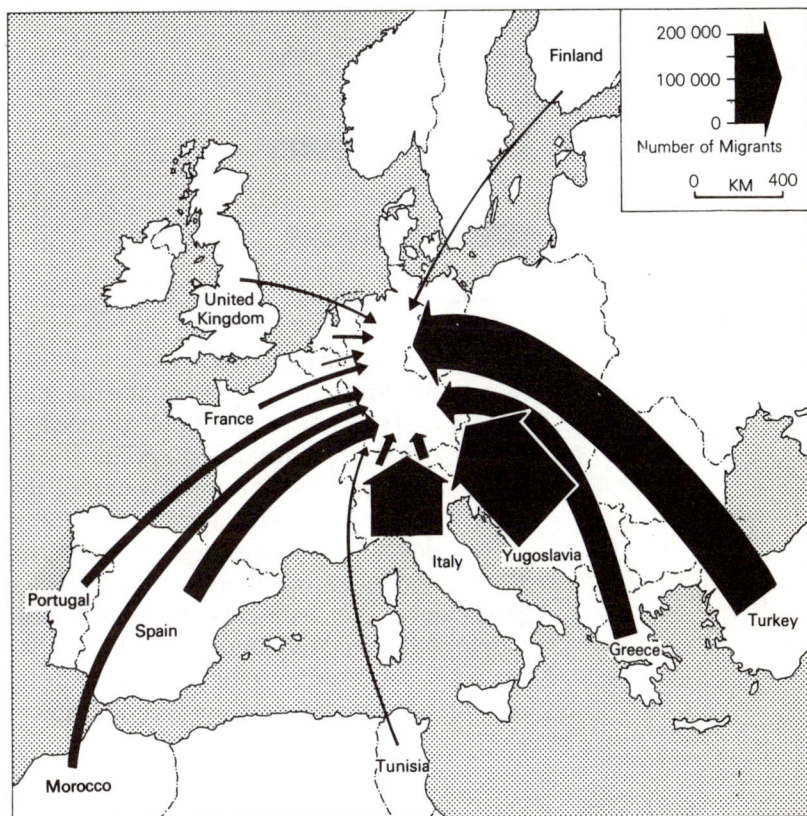

(a)   (i) In *rank order* list the six countries from which most migrant workers went to West Germany in 1970. Put the country sending the largest number at the top of your list.

(ii) What is the largest number of migrants from any one country?

(b)   (i) Give **two** reasons why migrant workers leave their own country to work in another country.

(ii) State **two** problems which migrant workers and their families may face when they reach the new country.

(c)   Since 1970, West Germany has required fewer migrant workers.

State **two** problems migrant workers in West Germany face if they are no longer required.   (*LEAG*)

3 LANDSCAPE PROCESSES

(a)   The section shows the main features of a typical waterfall.

Fig C

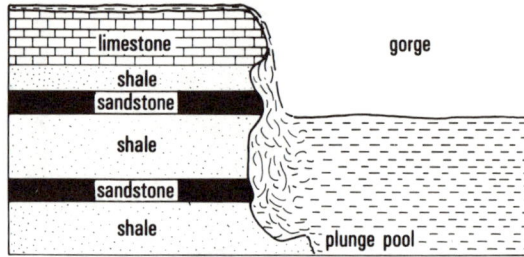

(i) Name a waterfall.

(ii) Which of the rocks on the diagram is most easily eroded?

(ii) How is a 'plunge pool' formed?

(iv) Why is there often a gorge downstream of a waterfall?

(v) Describe how one waterfall may hinder development, whiler another waterfall may be put to good use in the development of an area. Mention named examples.

(b)   Show, by means of a simple sketch map and labelled diagrams only, the distinctive physical features found in the middle course of a named river and its valley.

(c)   River terraces sometimes occur in the lower course of a river valley. They are shown in the section below:

Fig D

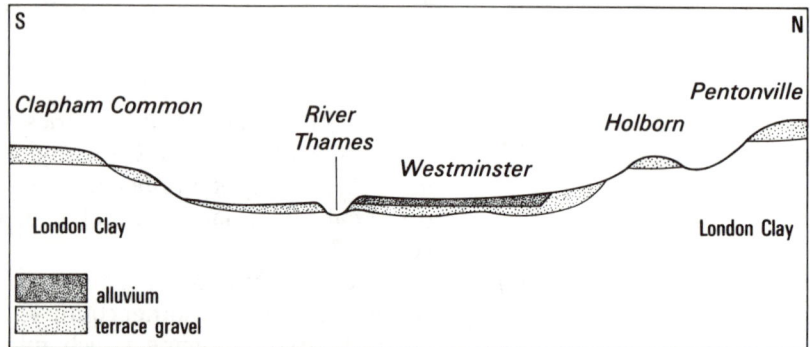

(i) How are such terraces formed?

(ii) Describe how river terraces may be of use to the local people.

(SEG)

Fig E The world's water cycle

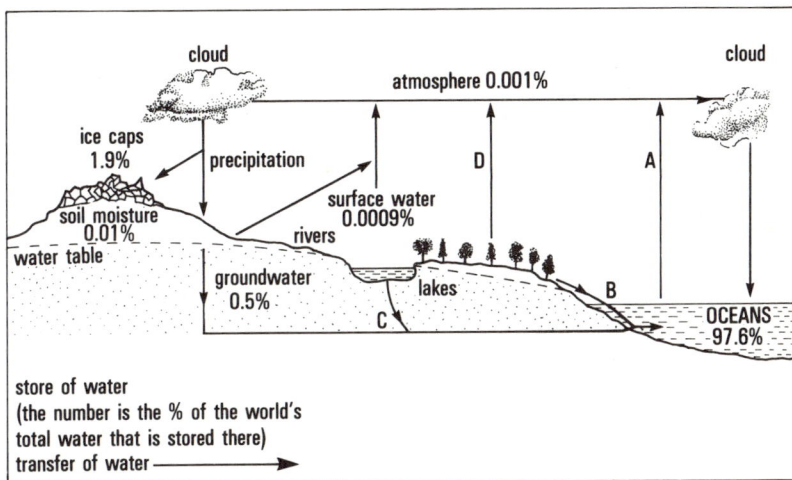

Some processes of water transfer

Condensation
Evaporation
Groundwater flow
Meltwater flow
Run-off
Spring flow
Throughflow
Transpiration

Study the figure labelled 'The world's water cycle'.

(a) (i) Which store contains the smallest percentage of the world's water?

(ii) Which store contains most of the world's freshwater?

(b) (i) Give **one** example of precipitation.

(ii) Explain what the water table is.

(c) Study Figure E above. Four processes of water transfer are labelled A, B, C and D. From the list of names in the above table choose the correct name for:

(i) process A
(ii) process B
(iii) process C
(iv) process D

(d) (i) What source of energy 'drives' the water cycle?

(ii) Why is the world's water cycle described as a 'closed system'?

(*LEAG*)

5 ENERGY

(a)   Study the map below.

Fig F

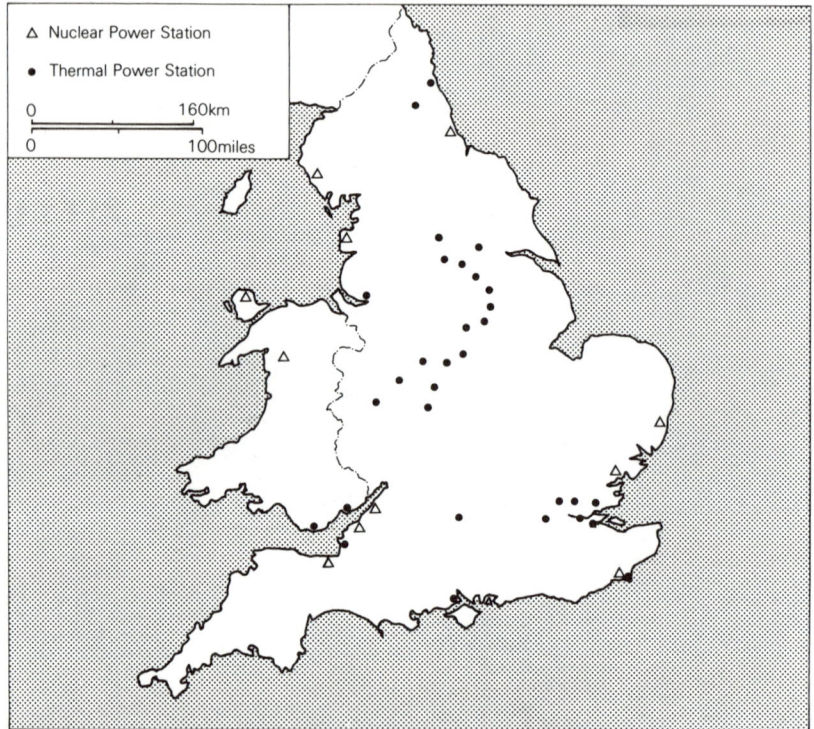

(i) Briefly describe the location of the nuclear power stations.

(ii) Give **one** reason for the location you have described.

(iii) Name the **two** main fuels used in the thermal power stations.

(iv) Give **two** arguments for, and **two** against, an increase in the number of nuclear power stations.

(b)   Study the table below.

Year	Production of coal in millions of tonnes	Manpower (in thousands)	Collieries	Output per man-shift (in tonnes)
1952	211	705	880	1.2
1957	207	708	822	1.3
1962	188	536	616	1.6
1967	164	410	443	1.8
1971	142	286	292	2.2
1975	124	246	246	2.2

(i) Give **three** reasons for the trend in coal production.

(ii) State **one** problems caused by the decline in manpower.

(iii) Give **two** reasons for the increase in output per man shift.

(iv) There has been much debate about plans to develop new coalfields, for example in the Vale of Belvoir, an area of attractive farmland in the Midlands. Discuss the argument for and against the development of such a coalfield.   (NEA)

6 POPULATION AND MIGRATION

Study the graphs below (A–D) which show four types of migration change as a country develops economically.

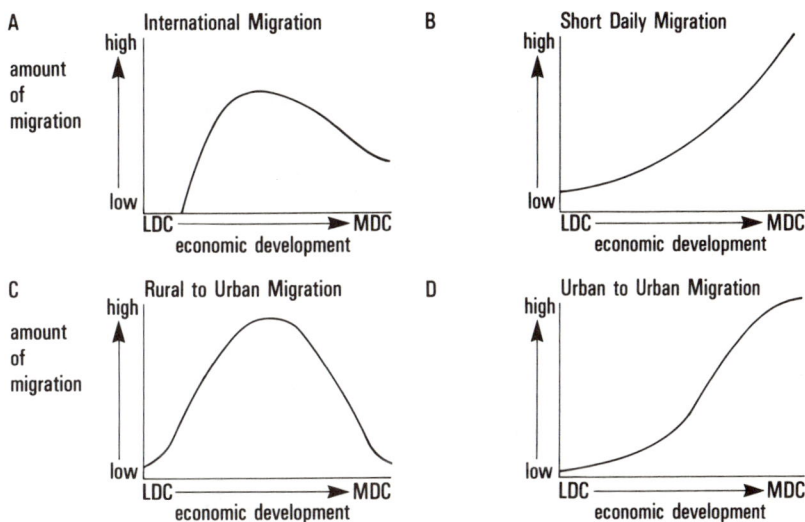

(a)   (i) Complete the table below to show the contrasts between Less Developed Countries (LDC) and More Developed Countries (MDC).

Type of migration	Less developed countries	More developed countries
International	No international migration at beginning builds up to a peak as country develops	
Short daily migrations		Very widespread and common for work and leisure etc.
Rural to urban		Declines to a very low volume in advanced countries
Urban to urban	At a very low level but steadily increases with development	

(ii) For any two types of migration shown (A–D) explain why the migration rate changes with economic development.

(*b*)   Study the diagram below which shows the migration process from rural to urban areas in Less Developed Countries.

Fig K

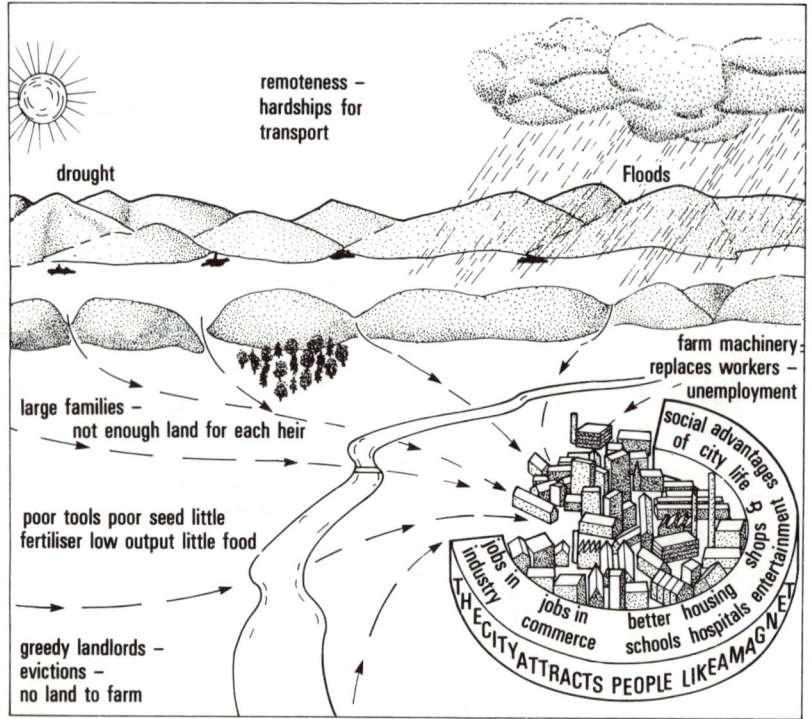

drought

remoteness – hardships for transport

Floods

farm machinery – replaces workers – unemployment

large families – not enough land for each heir

poor tools poor seed little fertiliser low output little food

greedy landlords – evictions – no land to farm

social advantages of city life

jobs in industry

jobs in commerce

better housing

schools hospitals

shops entertainment

THE CITY ATTRACTS PEOPLE LIKE A MAGNET

Imagine you were a member of a peasant farming family living in the countryside. Explain what factors would encourage you to migrate to the town.

(c)   Study the population 'pyramid' below which shows the structure of the migrating population.

Fig K1

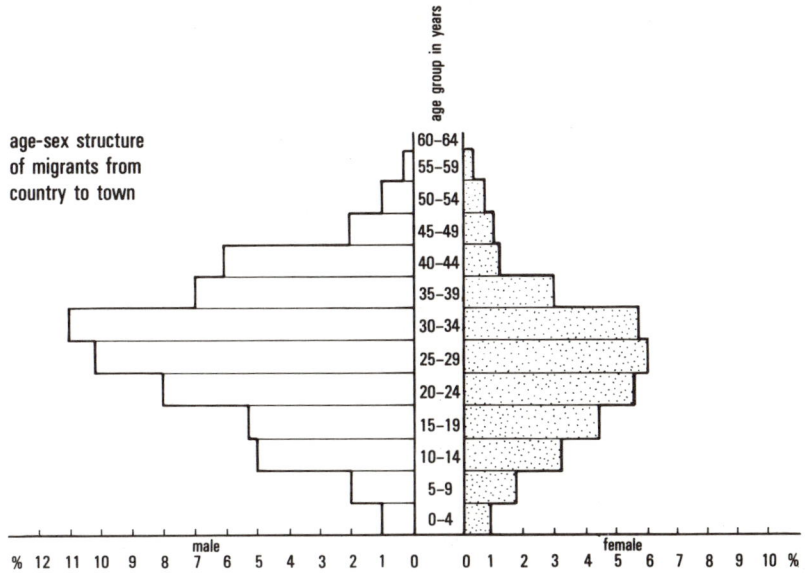

age-sex structure
of migrants from
country to town

(i) Describe and explain the pattern shown by the pyramid.
(ii) Explain what effect the migrations will have on the population *structure* of the countryside and towns.   (*NEA*)

SUGGESTED ANSWERS TO SPECIMEN QUESTIONS

1 INDUSTRY

(*a*)   Lack of capital, lack of prosperous home market, weak infrasructure (roads, railways, power supplies), workforce lacking necessary experience/skills/education.

(*b*)   (i) USA – nineteenth-century coalfields provided steam power, electrical power generated by oil, nuclear, coal, HEP readily transported throughout country via electrical grids, abundant/varied raw materials (coal – Appalachians, oil – interior and Gulf Coast, iron ore – superior etc.); large home market providing large demand; strong trading connections within Western Europe; well developed communications (road, rail, water – Great Lakes); well-educated and skilled workforce, high degree of technology; large capital etc.

(ii) USA – smaller number employed in manufacturing industry, greater use of robots, advanced technology, concentration on service industry.

(*c*)   (i) Northern England, West Midlands, Wales.

(ii) South-East England/Home Counties, East Anglia.

(*d*)   Greatest job losses in Northern Britain (north of a line linking Severn estuary with Humber estuary). Fewest job losses in South-East England (southeast of line from Wash to Test-Itchen estuary). East Midlands and South Western England form medium area.

(*e*)   Yorkshire and Humberside

Decline of certain heavy industries – coal mining, steel, engineering, textiles – due to smaller demand for products, foreign competition, lack of competitiveness. Drive for greater productivity with mechanization, automation, greater use of technology.

(**NB** The answers above are the responsibility of the authors and have not been provided or approved by the MEG.)

2 MIGRATION

(*a*)   (i) Yugoslavia, Italy, Turkey, Greece, Spain, Austria;
(ii) 200 000.

(*b*)   (i) Overpopulation, poverty, hunger and expectation of higher wages, better social facilities.
(ii) overcrowding, language/cultural problems, prejudice.

(*c*)   Resentment from local workers with reference to available jobs.

Not necessarily able to obtain full state benefits – increased for families etc.

Difficult to get another job if made redundant.

Reduction in living standard if forced to return to home country.

3 LANDSCAPE PROCESSES

(*a*)   (i) High Force, Tees, Niagara Falls, USA.
(ii) Shale.
(iii) Any one from: falling water scours hollow, explosive effect of trapped air in falling water (cavitation), collapsed rock whirled around hollow by water pressure (corrosion).
(iv) Waterfall retreats as falling water undercuts the fall, rest of valley unaffected by river.
(v) obstruction to navigation systems – e.g. Niagara Falls overcome by Welland Canal. Use for HEP development – Niagara Falls HEP station.

(*b*)   Points should include: meanders extending from one side of the valley to another, river cliffs, alluvial plain, bluffs, slip-off slope, quite wide valley etc.

(*c*)   (i) Flood plain created at the level of Pentonville and Clapham Common, river rejuvenated, active downcutting, new valley cut into flood plain, remnants of old plain remain as terraces, new plain created at lower level (Holborn) process repeated.
(ii) Sites for settlement above flood level, possible defensive sites, well drained (gravel) sites for market gardening, form building sites above fertile flood plain.

(**NB** The answers above are the responsibility of the authors and have not been provided or approved by the SEG.)

4 PHYSICAL

(*a*)   (i) atmosphere.
(ii) ice-caps.

(*b*)   (i) rain, snow or hail.
(ii) upper surface of the groundwater zone.

(*c*)   (i) evaporation.
(ii) run-off.

          (iii) groundwater flow.

          (iv) transpiration.

(*d*)   (i) sun.

          (ii) the total quantity of water circulating is finite – water is neither gained nor lost from the cycle.

5 ENERGY

(*a*)   (i) largely coastal.

          (ii) large quantities of water for cooling, disposal of low active waste.

          (iii) oil, coal.

          (iv) Arguments for:

               (*a*) cheaper running costs than thermal power stations.

               (*b*) need for alternative fuel sources than oil, coal and gas.

               (*c*) may lead to exports of British designed nuclear power stations.

          Arguments against:

               (*a*) fears over radiation leukemia.

               (*b*) problems over disposal of radioactive waste.

               (*c*) high initial construction costs.

(*b*)   (i) Fall in production owing to rivalry with cheaper fuels (natural gas) difficult/bulky to transport/store, dirty fuel/ smoke pollution. Therefore loss of markets (domestic, trains).

          (ii) Unemployment, few alternative jobs in coalmining areas.

          (iii) Mechanization/automation, closure of uneconomic pits.

          (iv) Arguments for:

               (*a*) large reserves for economic coal production, natural benefit.

               (*b*) employment prospects/reduce unemployment.

               (*c*) help develop the region by providing growth point for other industries.

          Arguments against:

               (*a*) destruction of attractive scenery.

               (*b*) disruption of rural way of life.

               (*c*) subsidence of land leading to housing/road problems.

6 POPULATION AND MIGRATION

(*a*)   (i) A. Declines to a low level as the country develops. B. Initially very low level of short daily migration which gradually increases. C. Initially low but rising to a peak on development. D. Very high level in all advanced countries.

          (ii) E.g. international – reaches a peak as country develops as migrants go abroad to seek work – frequently cannot find work on lands or towns – desire for wealth. As the country becomes more wealthy, jobs and wealth available at home and international migration becomes more selective, e.g. brain drain type.

(b)   *Push factors* – essentially rural poverty, too many people trying to farm land – subdivision of plots, famines, lack of potential farm employment, population explosion – overpopulation. Hardships of low technology farming, lack of food, easily ruined by natural disasters. Possible dispossession by land reforms – loss of jobs as agricultural mechanization begins.

Push factors – advanatges of 'softer' life with perceived better facilities for schooling, medical care etc. Much greater chance of employment in either factories or services as cities are zones of expansion. Perceived advantages of greater wealth/opportunity. Bright lights syndrome.

(c)   (i) Age selective – above all 15–40 (75%) as these are the young productive jobseekers. Sex selective – above all male dominated – presumably to seek work and send money home.

(ii) Removal of dynamic productive element (young child producing) – decline in BR in country – ageing population. Arrival of young productive element in towns – increase in BR very rapidly expanding population.

(d)   In the country the main problem is the neglect of agriculture because the work is left to the aged/female/child population. In town – rapid growth leads to all the problems of overrapid urbanization – growth of squatter settlements, shanty towns, lack of real employment – development of alternative economy, problems of overloading of urban resources such as sewers – health problems etc.

INDEX